BASEMENT & FOUNDATION

Other Publications:

AMERICAN COUNTRY

VOYAGE THROUGH THE UNIVERSE

THE THIRD REICH

THE TIME-LIFE GARDENER'S GUIDE

MYSTERIES OF THE UNKNOWN

TIME FRAME

FIX IT YOURSELF

FITNESS, HEALTH & NUTRITION

SUCCESSFUL PARENTING

HEALTHY HOME COOKING

UNDERSTANDING COMPUTERS

LIBRARY OF NATIONS

THE ENCHANTED WORLD

THE KODAK LIBRARY OF CREATIVE PHOTOGRAPHY

GREAT MEALS IN MINUTES

THE CIVIL WAR

PLANET EARTH

COLLECTOR'S LIBRARY OF THE CIVIL WAR

THE EPIC OF FLIGHT

THE GOOD COOK

WORLD WAR II

HOME REPAIR AND IMPROVEMENT

THE OLD WEST

BASEMENT & FOUNDATION

TIME-LIFE BOOKS
ALEXANDRIA, VIRGINIA

Fix It Yourself was produced by

ST. REMY PRESS

MANAGING EDITOR	Kenneth Winchester
MANAGING ART DIRECTOR	Pierre Léveillé

Staff for *Basement & Foundation*

Series Editor	Brian Parsons
Series Assistant Editor	Kent J. Farrell
Editor	Heather L. Mills
Series Art Director	Diane Denoncourt
Art Director	Normand Boudreault
Research Editor	Bryan Zuraw
Designers	Luc Germain, Julie Léger
Editorial Assistant	Dawn Upfold
Contributing Writers	Sarah Anderson, Karen Haughian, Linda Jarosiewicz, Cynthia Jervis, Christopher Little, Heather Marinos, Patricia Ryffranck
Contributing Illustrators	Gérard Mariscalchi, Jacques Proulx
Cover	Robert Monté
Index	Christine M. Jacobs
Administrator	Denise Rainville
Accounting Manager	Natalie Watanabe
Production Manager	Michelle Turbide
Systems Coordinator	Jean-Luc Roy
Studio Director	Maryo Proulx

Time-Life Books Inc. is a wholly owned subsidiary of

THE TIME INC. BOOK COMPANY

President and Chief Executive Officer	Kelso F. Sutton
President, Time Inc. Books Direct	Christopher T. Linen

TIME-LIFE BOOKS INC.

EDITOR	George Constable
Executive Editor	Ellen Phillips
Director of Design	Louis Klein
Director of Editorial Resources	Phyllis K. Wise
Editorial Board	Russell B. Adams Jr., Dale M. Brown, Roberta Conlan, Thomas H. Flaherty, Lee Hassig, Jim Hicks, Donia Ann Steele, Rosalind Stubenberg
Director of Photography and Research	John Conrad Weiser
PRESIDENT	John M. Fahey Jr.
Senior Vice Presidents	Robert M. DeSena, James L. Mercer, Paul R. Stewart, Curtis G. Viebranz, Joseph J. Ward
Vice Presidents	Stephen L. Bair, Stephen L. Goldstein, Juanita T. James, Andrew P. Kaplan, Susan J. Maruyama, Robert H. Smith
Supervisor of Quality Control	James King
Publisher	Joseph J. Ward

Editorial Operations

Copy Chief	Diane Ullius
Production	Celia Beattie
Library	Louise D. Forstall
Correspondents	Elisabeth Kraemer-Singh (Bonn); Christina Lieberman (New York); Maria Vincenza Aloisi (Paris); Ann Natanson (Rome).

THE CONSULTANTS

Consulting editor **David L. Harrison** served as an editor for several Time-Life Books do-it-yourself series, including *Home Repair and Improvement, The Encyclopedia of Gardening* and *The Art of Sewing*.

Richard Day, a do-it-yourself writer for nearly a quarter of a century, is a founder of the National Association of Home and Workshop Writers and is the author of several home repair books.

Jay Hedden, a former editor of Popular Mechanics and Workbench magazines, has written several books on home repair.

Don McCoy, a consultant and lecturer on foundations, founded McCoy Contractors in Milwaukee, Wisconsin, a concrete and masonry restoration company that has repaired over 18,000 structures since 1956. He is also the recipient of numerous professional and civic awards for his contributions to the industry and his community.

Ron Reierson, with over 35 years experience in the construction field, is Sales Manager at Property Doctors in Solana Beach, California, a referral service that coordinates a network of 163 contractors covering every aspect of home repair and construction.

Library of Congress Cataloging-in-Publication Data
Basement & foundation
      p. cm. – (Fix it yourself)
    Includes index.
    ISBN 0-8094-6232-X.
    ISBN 0-8094-6233-8 (lib. bdg.)
    1. Basements--Maintenance and repair--Amateurs' manuals.
    2. Foundations--Maintenance and repair--Amateurs' manuals.
    I Time-Life Books. II. Title: Basement and foundation. III. Series.
    TH4813.3.B37   1990
    643'.5—dc20   89-20650
                                      CIP

For information about any Time-Life book, please write:
Reader Information
Time-Life Customer Service
P.O. Box C-32068
Richmond, Virginia
23261-2068

CONTENTS

HOW TO USE THIS BOOK

Basement & Foundation is divided into three sections. The Emergency Guide on pages 8 to 13 provides information that can be indispensable, even lifesaving, in the event of a household emergency. Take the time to study this section *before* you need the important advice it contains.

The Repairs section—the heart of the book—is a comprehensive approach to troubleshooting and repairing basements and foundations. Shown below are four sample pages from the chapter on concrete foundations with captions describing the various features of the book and how they work.

For example, if the concrete foundation wall of your home is wet, the Troubleshooting Guide on page 16 will suggest a number of possible causes; if the problem is a leaking crack in the foundation wall, you will be directed to page 22 for instructions on how to plug the crack and to page 78 to troubleshoot any faulty drainage system. Or, if there are white, powdery deposits (efflorescence) on the foundation wall, the Troubleshooting Guide will refer you to page 17; there, you will be given information on cleaning the wall and referred to the cleaning chart on page 112 which lists cleaning agents for tougher stains.

Introductory text
Describes the construction of concrete, masonry or slab-on-grade foundations and any basement or crawlspace they enclose, as well as the most common problems and basic repair approaches.

Anatomy diagram
Locate and describe the various components of a concrete, masonry, slab-on-grade foundation; of a basement or crawlspace; or of the structural wood or drainage systems.

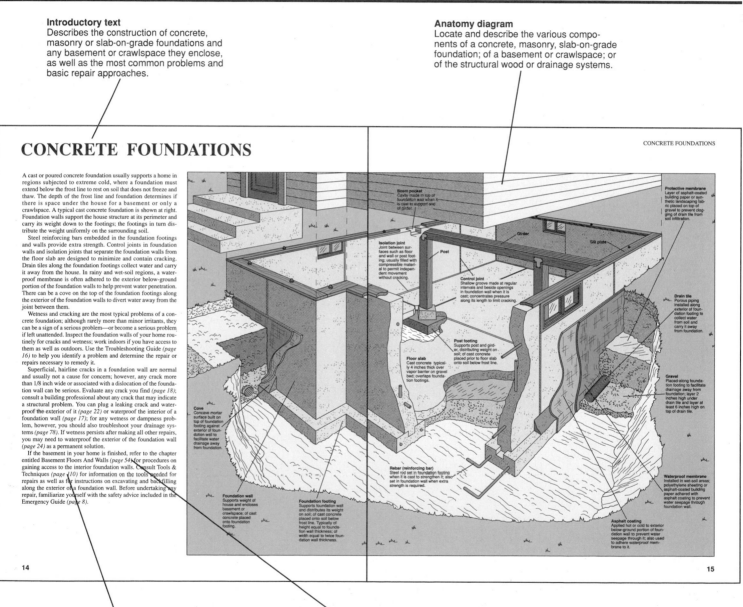

CONCRETE FOUNDATIONS

A cast or poured concrete foundation usually supports a home in regions subjected to extreme cold, where a foundation must extend below the frost line to rest on soil that does not freeze and thaw. The depth of the frost line and foundation determines if there is space under the house for a basement or only a crawlspace. A typical cast concrete foundation is shown at right. Foundation walls support the house structure at its perimeter and carry its weight down to the footings; the footings in turn distribute the weight uniformly on the surrounding soil.

Steel reinforcing bars embedded in the foundation footings and walls provide extra strength. Control joints in foundation walls and isolation joints that separate the foundation walls from the floor slab are designed to minimize and contain cracking. Drain tiles along the foundation footings collect water and carry it away from the house. In rainy and wet-soil regions, a waterproof membrane is often adhered to the exterior below-ground portion of the foundation walls to help prevent water penetration. There can be a cove on the top of the foundation footings along the exterior of the foundation walls to divert water away from the joint between them.

Wetness and cracking are the most typical problems of a concrete foundation; although rarely more than minor irritants, they can be a sign of a serious problem—or become a serious problem if left unattended. Inspect the foundation walls of your home routinely for cracks and wetness; work indoors if you have access to them as well as outdoors. Use the Troubleshooting Guide *(page 16)* to help you identify a problem and determine the repair or repairs necessary to remedy it.

Superficial, hairline cracks in a foundation wall are normal and usually not a cause for concern; however, any crack more than 1/8 inch wide or associated with a dislocation of the foundation wall can be serious. Evaluate any crack you find *(page 18)*; consult a building professional about any crack that may indicate a structural problem. You can plug a leaking crack and waterproof the exterior of it *(page 22)* or waterproof the interior of a foundation wall *(page 17)*; for any wetness or dampness problem, however, you should also troubleshoot your drainage systems *(page 78)*. If wetness persists after making all other repairs, you may need to waterproof the exterior of the foundation wall *(page 24)* as a permanent solution.

If the basement in your home is finished, refer to the chapter entitled Basement Floors And Walls *(page 54)* for procedures on gaining access to the interior foundation walls. Consult Tools & Techniques *(page 110)* for information on the tools needed for repairs as well as for instructions on excavating and backfilling along the exterior of a foundation wall. Before undertaking any repair, familiarize yourself with the safety advice included in the Emergency Guide *(page 8)*.

14

15

Tools and techniques
General information on techniques for repairs to concrete or masonry foundations and the basement or crawlspace within them is covered in the Tools & Techniques section *(page 110)*. When a specific tool or method is required for a job, it is described within the step-by-step repair.

Cross-references
Direct you to important information elsewhere in the book, including accessing steps and alternative techniques.

Each repair job has been rated by degree of difficulty and by the average time it will take for a do-it-yourselfer to complete. Keep in mind that this rating is only a suggestion and does not include any digging that may be necessary. Before deciding whether you should attempt a repair, first read all the instructions carefully. Then, be guided by your own confidence, as well as the tools and time available to you. For more complex or time-consuming repairs, such as waterproofing an exterior foundation wall, you may wish to call for professional help. You will still have saved time and money by diagnosing the problem yourself.

Most of the repairs in *Basement & Foundation* can be made with basic masonry tools such as hammers, chisels and trowels. Any special tool required is indicated in the Troubleshooting Guide. Information on basic tools—and the proper way to use them—as well as on digging and protecting excavations from cave-ins is presented in the Tools & Techniques section starting on page 110. If you are a novice at home repair, read this chapter first in preparation for a job. Repairing a basement or foundation can be simple and worry-free if you work logically and systematically, and follow all the safety tips and precautions.

Troubleshooting Guide
To use this chart, locate the symptom that most closely resembles your basement or foundation problem, review the possible causes in column 2, then follow the recommended procedures in column 3. Simple fixes may be explained on the chart; in most cases you will be directed to an illustrated, step-by-step repair sequence.

Name of repair
You will be referred by the Troubleshooting Guide to the first page of a specific repair.

Insets
Provide close-up views of specific steps and illustrate variations in techniques.

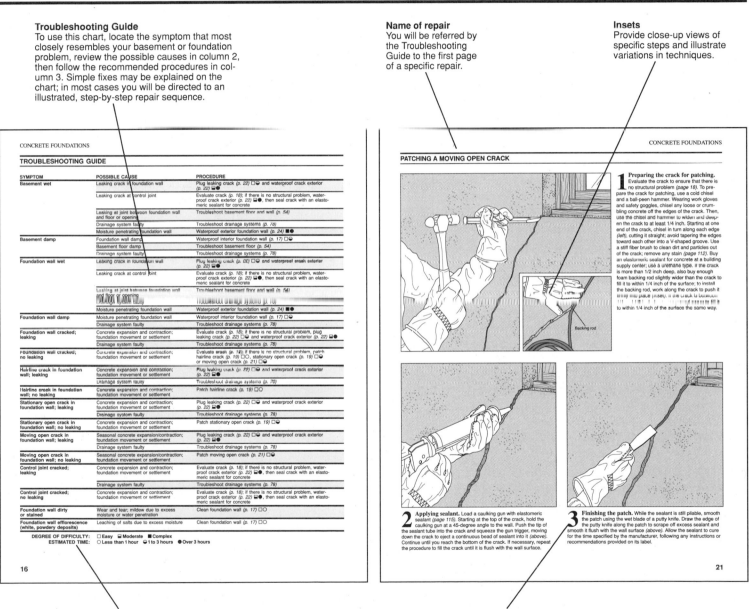

Degree of difficulty and time
Rate the complexity of each repair and how much time the job should take for a home-owner with average do-it-yourself skills.

Step-by-step procedure
Bold lead-ins summarize each step or highlight the key action pictured. Follow the numbered repair sequence carefully. Depending on the result of each step, you may be directed to a later step or to another part of the book to complete the repair.

EMERGENCY GUIDE

Preventing problems in basement and foundation repair.
When undertaking repairs to your basement or foundation, prevent an emergency from occurring by being safety-conscious at all times. Keep children and pets safe from harm away from the work area. If you stop partway through a repair, alert others to a potential hazard by setting up a temporary barrier; ensure that any danger is well lit at night. Most work mishaps arise from carelessness: the misuse of tools or the mishandling of materials. The list of safety tips at right covers basic guidelines for the repair of any basement or foundation; consult the particular chapter for more specific advice.

Accidents can befall even the most careful worker. Prepare yourself for an emergency before one happens by reviewing the Troubleshooting Guide on page 9; it puts emergency procedures at your fingertips, listing quick-action steps to take and referring you to pages 10 to 13 for detailed information. Have a well-stocked first-aid kit on hand. Install a smoke detector in the basement and keep a fire extinguisher rated ABC nearby; in the event of a fire, have the fire department check the house—even if the fire is out. Label or tag the main shutoff for each utility in your home; in an emergency, you will want anyone to be able to find them quickly.

During a repair, wear proper clothing as well as the safety gear recommended; remove your jewelry and tie back long hair. Fresh concrete and mortar are caustic and pressure-treated wood can be toxic; avoid skin contact by wearing long pants and a shirt with snug-fitting long sleeves. Fast action to treat chemical exposure *(page 13)* can prevent serious harm. Exercise caution when using any power tool, plugging it only into an outlet that is protected by a ground-fault circuit interrupter (GFCI); never use a power tool in wet or damp conditions. If you must rescue someone from an electrical current, do not touch him or the source; knock him free of the source using a wooden implement *(page 10)*.

A wet or damp basement, a common complaint of homeowners, usually does not constitute an emergency; flooding, however, can cause serious damage. If a leaky or broken pipe is the source of a flooding problem, shut off the main water supply *(page 11)*. Store a sandbag in your basement to place over the floor drain in the event the sewer backs up; or, install a backflow-prevention valve. Protect your possessions from floodwater, elevating any appliance onto a platform *(page 11)*. If seasonal or flash flooding is common in your region, have a sump pump installed in your basement and keep sandbags on hand to divert water away from the foundation of your house.

Whenever you are in doubt about your ability to handle an emergency, call for help. Post the emergency telephone numbers for your local medical, fire and utility services by the telephone and do not hesitate to use them; in most areas, dial 911 in the event you confront any life-threatening emergency. Also seek technical help whenever you need it. If you are ever concerned about the nature or safety of a repair, obtain an evaluation by a building professional *(page 119)*; even in non-emergency situations, a building professional can answer questions regarding the condition of your basement and foundation.

SAFETY TIPS

1. Before beginning any repair in this book, read the entire procedure. Familiarize yourself with the specific safety information presented in each chapter.

2. Always use the proper tool for the job. Refer to Tools & Techniques *(page 110)* for information on the correct use and maintenance of tools. When tools are not in use, store them in a dry location well out of the reach of children.

3. Wear the proper safety gear for the job: work gloves when handling cement, mortar or pressure-treated wood; safety goggles when chiseling, hammering or cutting; respiratory protection with tools that create dust or chemicals that emit hazardous vapors; a safety helmet in any area with limited headroom; steel-toed work boots when working with heavy materials.

4. If you are working in a basement or crawlspace where poisonous snakes, spiders or insects may be present, wear protective clothing and boots; watch where you step and where you reach with your hands.

5. For any work with concrete or mortar, wear protective clothing: long pants and a shirt with snug-fitting long sleeves. Wet concrete or mortar is caustic and can burn the skin if contact is prolonged; rinse off any splash immediately with clean water *(page 13)* and change any splashed clothes. Also change clothes after leaving the work area. Always launder your work clothes separately.

6. When using acids, solvents or other chemicals, keep away from sources of heat and make sure the work area is well ventilated. At the first sign of faintness, dizziness or nausea, leave the work area immediately and get fresh air *(page 13)*; continue your job only when the ventilation of the work area is improved.

7. Never undertake repairs when you are tired. To prevent heat exhaustion, wear a hat when working outdoors in hot, sunny weather; avoid working at the hottest part of the day.

8. Keep children and pets away from the work area. When you take a break or finish work for the day, put all tools and materials safely away. If any pit or trench is to be left open, set up a temporary barrier to block access to it. Ensure any dangerous area is well lit at night.

9. Follow basic safety rules when working on a ladder; read the safety instruction label on the siderail. Work with a helper or within earshot of someone else.

10. Never use a power tool in wet or damp conditions. To guard against electrical shock, plug a power tool only into an outlet protected by a ground-fault circuit interrupter (GFCI). If you are working outdoors, use only heavy-duty extension cords rated for outdoor use.

11. Keep a first-aid kit on hand; stock it with mild antiseptic, sterile gauze dressings and bandages, adhesive tape, scissors, tweezers and a packet of needles.

12. Post the telephone numbers of your local emergency medical service, poison control center, physician, fire department and utility companies near the telephone.

TROUBLESHOOTING GUIDE

SYMPTOM	PROCEDURE
Fire	Call fire department immediately
	If fire small and contained, use fire extinguisher rated ABC
	Have fire department inspect house—even if fire out
Flooding due to environmental causes	Tune in emergency broadcast station on radio or television and follow instructions of emergency management authorities
	Protect possessions from floodwater (p. 11)—if there is time
	Lay sandbags along exterior of foundation to divert floodwater
Flooding due to sewer backup	Call municipal sewage authorities
	Lay sandbag on floor drain of basement to contain sewage backup
	Protect possessions from floodwater (p. 11)
Flooding due to burst pipe	Shut off water supply (p. 11)
	Protect possessions from floodwater (p. 11)
Animal trapped in basement or crawlspace	For known, domestic animal, try to coax it out; otherwise, call animal control professional
Poisonous snake, insect or spider trapped in basement or crawlspace	Call animal control professional or exterminator
Electrical shock	Shut off electricity (p. 10) or knock victim free of source using wooden implement (p. 10)
	Call for medical help immediately
	If victim is not breathing, administer artificial respiration; if victim has no pulse, administer cardiopulmonary resuscitation (CPR) only if you are qualified
	If victim is breathing and has pulse and has no back or neck injury, place him in the recovery position (p. 10)
Head injury	If victim loses consciousness—even for only one second—call for medical help immediately
	If victim is not breathing, administer artificial respiration; if victim has no pulse, administer cardiopulmonary resuscitation (CPR) only if you are qualified
	If victim is breathing and has pulse and has no back or neck injury, place him in the recovery position (p. 10)
Cut or scratch	Treat cut or scratch (p. 12); if cut or scratch caused by rusty or dirty object, seek medical attention about need for tetanus treatment
Bruise	Apply ice pack to ease pain and reduce swelling; if pain or swelling persists, seek medical attention
Sprain or strain	Treat sprain or strain (p. 12)
Splinter	Pull out splinter using sterilized needle and tweezers; if splinter lodged deeply or wound becomes infected, seek medical attention
Foreign particle in eye	Do not rub eye
	Remove foreign particle from eye using moistened end of tissue (p. 12)
Chemical splashed in eye	Do not rub eye
	Flush chemical from eye (p. 13) and seek medical attention immediately
Chemical spilled on skin	Immediately brush off dry product or wipe off liquid product
	Flush chemical from skin (p. 13)
Chemical fumes exposure: faintness, dizziness, nausea or blurred vision	Escape toxic vapors (p. 13); if any symptom persists, seek medical attention immediately
Chemical product ingested	Do not give victim anything to eat or drink or induce vomiting unless advised by medical professional
	Immediately call local poison control center, hospital emergency room or physician for instructions; provide information on victim's age and weight, and type and amount of poison ingested
	If professional medical treatment necessary, bring product container with you
Snakebite	Treat snakebite victim (p. 12)
Spider bite or insect sting	Treat spider bite or insect sting (p. 13)

SHUTTING OFF THE ELECTRICITY

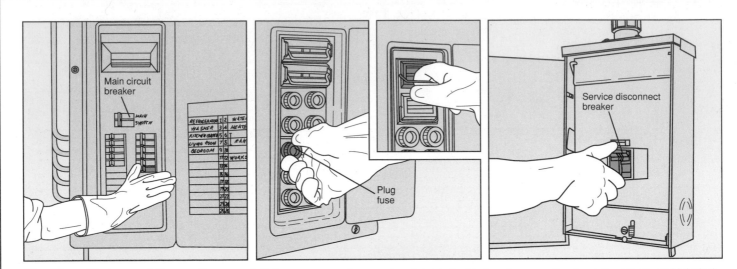

Shutting off power at the service panel. If the area around the service panel is flooded, call the electricity utility to shut off the power. If the area around the service panel is wet or damp, stand on a dry board or wear rubber boots. Wear heavy rubber gloves and use only one hand; keep the other hand behind your back, away from anything metal. At a circuit breaker panel, flip the circuit breaker for the circuit to OFF (above, left). If the circuit is not labeled, flip the main circuit breaker to OFF; the main circuit break-er is a linked, double breaker, usually above the others and labeled MAIN. At a fuse panel, grasp the plug fuse for the circuit by its insulated rim and unscrew it (above, center). If the circuit is not labeled, grip the main fuse block by its handle and pull it straight out (inset); if there is more than one main fuse block, pull out each one the same way. If there is no main circuit breaker or main fuse block, locate the service disconnect breaker in a separate box nearby or outdoors by the electricity meter and flip it to OFF (above, right).

RESCUING A VICTIM OF ELECTRICAL SHOCK

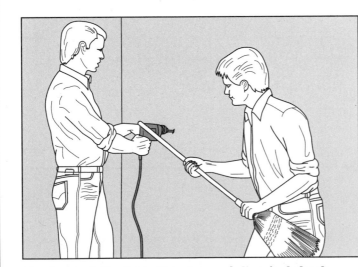

Freeing a victim from the source of electrical shock. A person who contacts live current is usually thrown back from the source; sometimes, however, muscles contract involuntarily around the source. Do not touch the victim or the source. Immediately shut off the power (step above). If the power cannot be shut off immediately, protect your hand with a thick, dry towel or heavy work glove and unplug the source. Or, use a wooden broom handle or other wooden implement to knock the victim free (above).

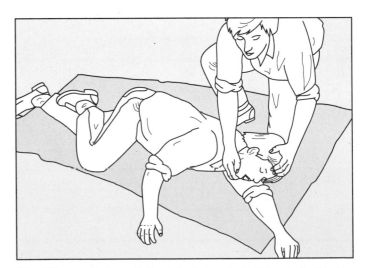

Handling a victim of electrical shock. Call for medical help immediately. Check the victim's breathing and pulse. If there is no breathing, administer artificial respiration; if there is no pulse, administer cardiopulmonary resuscitation (CPR) if you are qualified. If the victim is breathing and has no back or neck injury, place him in the recovery position (above), tilting the head back with the face to one side and the tongue forward to maintain an open airway. Keep the victim calm until medical help arrives.

SHUTTING OFF THE WATER SUPPLY

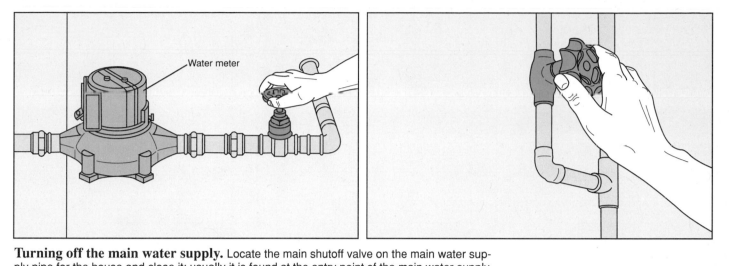

Turning off the main water supply. Locate the main shutoff valve on the main water supply pipe for the house and close it; usually it is found at the entry point of the main water supply pipe, indoors near the water meter *(above, left)* or elsewhere in the basement, utility room or crawlspace *(above, right)*. If your water supply is provided by a well, look for the main shutoff valve on the main water supply pipe near the pressure gauge or water pump. Turn the handle fully clockwise to close the valve, shutting off the water supply. If the water meter has two valves, close the valve on the supply side (before the water meter). To drain the water supply pipes in the house, open all the faucets.

PROTECTING POSSESSIONS FROM FLOODWATER

Elevating a major appliance onto a platform. Take easily-moved possessions upstairs to help safeguard them from floodwater. For a major appliance, elevate it onto a platform of plywood and concrete blocks. Turn off and unplug the appliance. With a clothes washer, also shut off the water supply to it or the main water supply *(step above)* and remove the water supply hoses from the faucets. With a clothes dryer, take off the exhaust hose. Place concrete blocks on the floor near the appliance, stacking them to the height you need; avoid stacking more than three blocks together. Then, cover the blocks with a plywood panel thick enough to support the weight of the appliance; if necessary, stack plywood panels. Working with a helper, lift the appliance and set it down on the platform *(left)*. **Caution:** To avoid back strain while lifting and lowering the appliance, bend at your knees, keeping your back straight.

PROVIDING MINOR FIRST AID

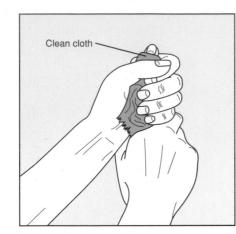

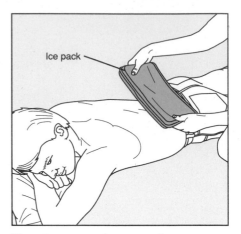

Treating a cut or scratch. To stop any bleeding, apply direct pressure to the wound with a gauze dressing or clean cloth, elevating the injury *(above)*. If the dressing or cloth becomes blood-soaked, add another one over the first one. If the wound is minor, wash it with soap and water, then bandage it; if bleeding persists or the wound is deep or gaping or becomes infected, seek medical help immediately.

Removing a foreign particle from the eye. Hold the eye open with the thumb and forefinger of one hand. **Caution:** Do not try to wipe away any particle that is on the cornea, is embedded or adhered, or cannot be seen. Otherwise, gently wipe away the particle using the twisted end of a tissue moistened with water *(above)*. If the particle cannot be removed, cover both eyes with gauze dressings and seek medical help immediately.

Treating a sprain or strain. Lie down and remove any clothing or footwear from the injury. Apply an ice pack or a plastic bag of ice cubes wrapped in a towel to soothe the injury and reduce any swelling *(above)*. After 48 hours, use a heating pad or hot water bottle to ease any pain and speed up the healing. If there is any doubt about the severity of the injury or if pain does not subside after several days, seek medical attention.

HANDLING A SNAKEBITE

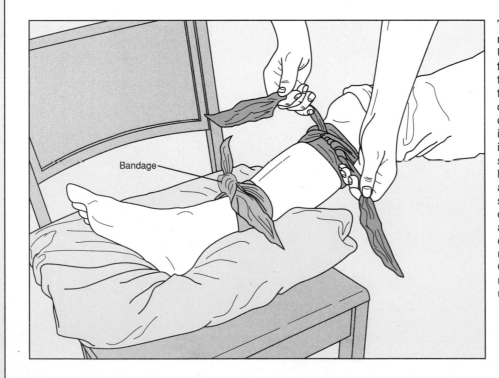

Treating a snakebite victim. Call for medical help immediately. Most snakes in the U.S. and Canada are not poisonous; the victim of a snakebite may experience no more than its initial pinch. A snakebite from a rattlesnake or a copperhead, water-moccasin or coral snake, however, can constitute a serious medical emergency if venom has been injected; although a lethal amount of venom is seldom injected, treat any potentially poisonous snakebite as serious. Have the victim lie down and keep still, placing the injury on a pillow and keeping it level. To limit the poisoning effects of any venom, restrict the flow of blood to the snakebite by tying a bandage about 4 inches from each side of it *(left)*; tie each bandage tight enough for a finger to fit under it and loosen it if any swelling occurs. **Caution:** Do not tie a bandage around the neck, head or torso. Keep the victim calm until medical help arrives.

HANDLING A SPIDER BITE OR INSECT STING

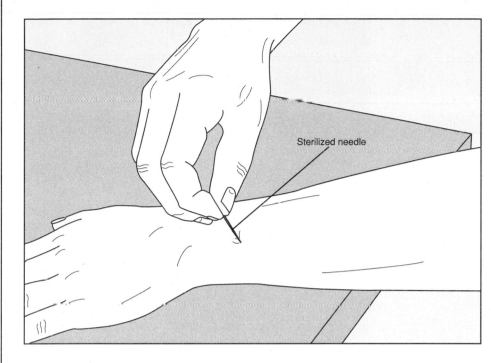

Sterilized needle

Treating a spider bite or insect sting. For a bite from a black widow or brown recluse (fiddleback) spider or a sting from a scorpion, call for medical help immediately; lie down and apply an ice pack to the injury until medical help arrives. For a bee sting, remove any stinger and sac immediately. Sterilize a needle by holding it over a flame, then wipe it clean with a sterile piece of gauze. Use the needle tip to work out the stinger and sac *(left)*. Do not use tweezers; they can squeeze additional venom out of the sac. Wash the injury with soap and water, then apply an ice pack to help relieve any pain or swelling. To reduce itchiness, use a cotton ball to dab the skin with hydrocortizone cream or calamine lotion. Seek medical help immediately if any chest or abdominal pain, breathing difficulty, or weakness or dizziness is experienced; also seek medical attention if any swelling, rash or itchiness does not subside within 2 to 3 days

TREATING CHEMICAL EXPOSURE

Escaping toxic vapors. Leave the work area immediately; go outdoors for fresh air. Remove any clothing splashed by chemicals or other caustic substances; loosen clothing at the waist, chest and neck. If you feel faint, sit with your head lowered between your knees *(above)*. Have someone ventilate the work area and close all containers. Call your local poison control center for medical help.

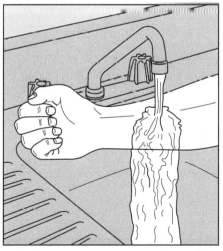

Flushing caustic substances from the skin. Gently remove any clothing from the injury—unless it is adhered to the skin. If the injury is severe, cover it with a gauze dressing and seek medical help immediately. Otherwise, flush the skin with a gentle flow of cold water *(above)* for at least 5 minutes, then bandage it with a gauze dressing. Launder any affected clothing before rewearing it.

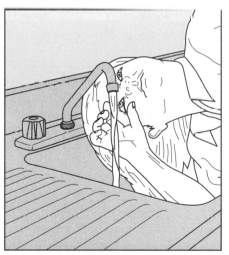

Flushing chemicals from the eye. Holding the eyelids of the injured eye apart, position the eye under a gentle flow of cool water from a faucet *(above)* or pitcher; tilt the head to one side to prevent the chemical from washing into the uninjured eye. Flush the eye for 15 to 30 minutes, then cover both eyes with gauze dressings to prevent eye movement and seek medical help immediately.

CONCRETE FOUNDATIONS

A cast or poured concrete foundation usually supports a home in regions subjected to extreme cold, where a foundation must extend below the frost line to rest on soil that does not freeze and thaw. The depth of the frost line and foundation determines if there is space under the house for a basement or only a crawlspace. A typical cast concrete foundation is shown at right. Foundation walls support the house structure at its perimeter and carry its weight down to the footings; the footings in turn distribute the weight uniformly on the surrounding soil.

Steel reinforcing bars embedded in the foundation footings and walls provide extra strength. Control joints in foundation walls and isolation joints that separate the foundation walls from the floor slab are designed to minimize and contain cracking. Drain tiles along the foundation footings collect water and carry it away from the house. In rainy and wet-soil regions, a waterproof membrane is often adhered to the exterior below-ground portion of the foundation walls to help prevent water penetration. There can be a cove on the top of the foundation footings along the exterior of the foundation walls to divert water away from the joint between them.

Wetness and cracking are the most typical problems of a concrete foundation; although rarely more than minor irritants, they can be a sign of a serious problem—or become a serious problem if left unattended. Inspect the foundation walls of your home routinely for cracks and wetness; work indoors if you have access to them as well as outdoors. Use the Troubleshooting Guide *(page 16)* to help you identify a problem and determine the repair or repairs necessary to remedy it.

Superficial, hairline cracks in a foundation wall are normal and usually not a cause for concern; however, any crack more than 1/8 inch wide or associated with a dislocation of the foundation wall can be serious. Evaluate any crack you find *(page 18)*; consult a building professional about any crack that may indicate a structural problem. You can plug a leaking crack and waterproof the exterior of it *(page 22)* or waterproof the interior of a foundation wall *(page 17)*; for any wetness or dampness problem, however, you should also troubleshoot your drainage systems *(page 78)*. If wetness persists after making all other repairs, you may need to waterproof the exterior of the foundation wall *(page 24)* as a permanent solution.

If the basement in your home is finished, refer to the chapter entitled Basement Floors And Walls *(page 54)* for procedures on gaining access to the interior foundation walls. Consult Tools & Techniques *(page 110)* for information on the tools needed for repairs as well as for instructions on excavating and backfilling along the exterior of a foundation wall. Before undertaking any repair, familiarize yourself with the safety advice included in the Emergency Guide *(page 8)*.

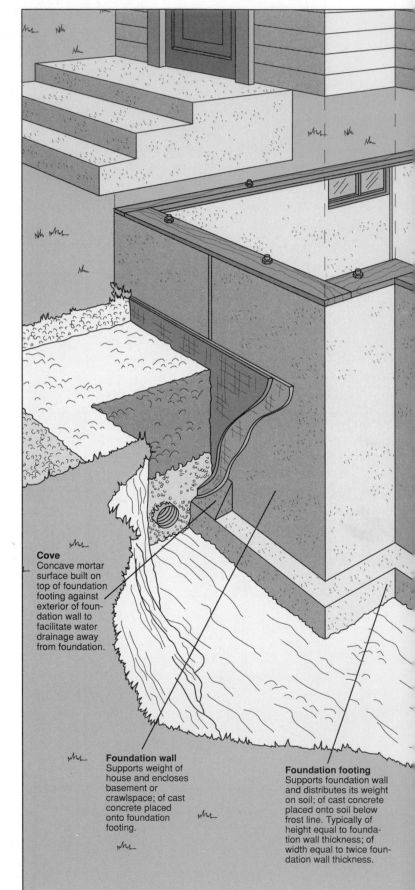

Cove
Concave mortar surface built on top of foundation footing against exterior of foundation wall to facilitate water drainage away from foundation.

Foundation wall
Supports weight of house and encloses basement or crawlspace; of cast concrete placed onto foundation footing.

Foundation footing
Supports foundation wall and distributes its weight on soil; of cast concrete placed onto soil below frost line. Typically of height equal to foundation wall thickness; of width equal to twice foundation wall thickness.

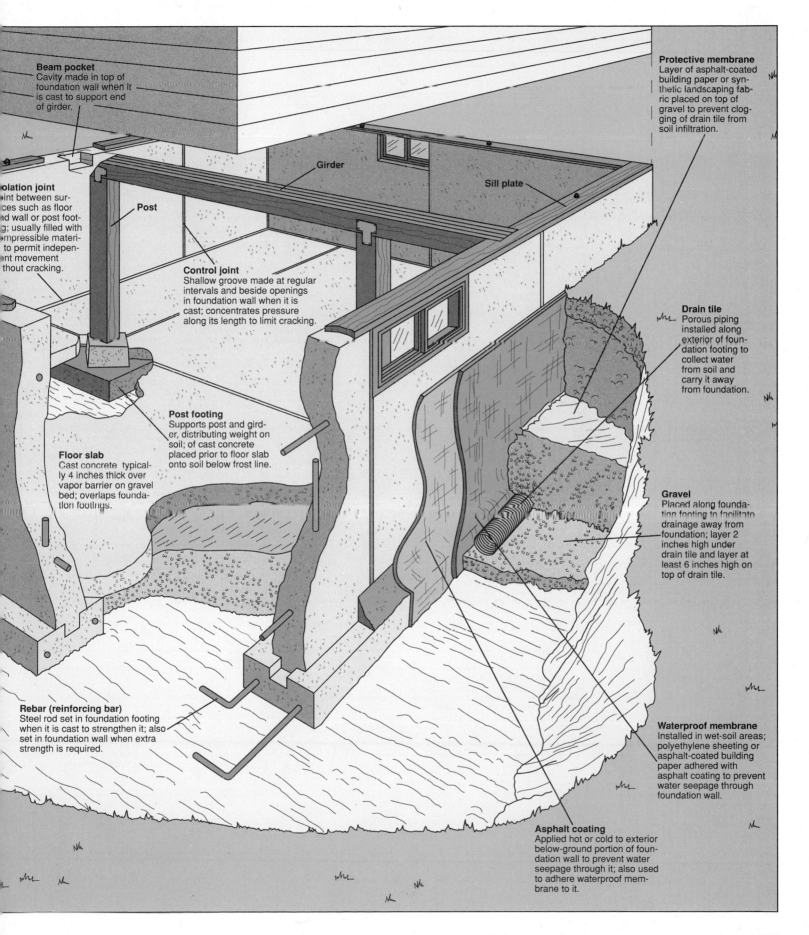

Beam pocket
Cavity made in top of foundation wall when It is cast to support end of girder.

Girder

Sill plate

Protective membrane
Layer of asphalt-coated building paper or synthetic landscaping fabric placed on top of gravel to prevent clogging of drain tile from soil infiltration.

Isolation joint
Joint between surfaces such as floor and wall or post footing; usually filled with compressible material to permit independent movement without cracking.

Post

Control joint
Shallow groove made at regular intervals and beside openings in foundation wall when it is cast; concentrates pressure along its length to limit cracking.

Drain tile
Porous piping installed along exterior of foundation footing to collect water from soil and carry it away from foundation.

Post footing
Supports post and girder, distributing weight on soil; of cast concrete placed prior to floor slab onto soil below frost line.

Floor slab
Cast concrete typically 4 inches thick over vapor barrier on gravel bed; overlaps foundation footings.

Gravel
Placed along foundation footing to facilitate drainage away from foundation; layer 2 inches high under drain tile and layer at least 6 inches high on top of drain tile.

Rebar (reinforcing bar)
Steel rod set in foundation footing when it is cast to strengthen it; also set in foundation wall when extra strength is required.

Waterproof membrane
Installed in wet-soil areas; polyethylene sheeting or asphalt-coated building paper adhered with asphalt coating to prevent water seepage through foundation wall.

Asphalt coating
Applied hot or cold to exterior below-ground portion of foundation wall to prevent water seepage through it; also used to adhere waterproof membrane to it.

TROUBLESHOOTING GUIDE

SYMPTOM	POSSIBLE CAUSE	PROCEDURE
Basement wet	Leaking crack in foundation wall	Plug leaking crack (p. 22) □◕ and waterproof crack exterior (p. 22) ◼●
	Leaking crack at control joint	Evaluate crack (p. 18); if there is no structural problem, waterproof crack exterior (p. 22) ◼●, then seal crack with an elastomeric sealant for concrete
	Leaking at joint between foundation wall and floor or opening	Troubleshoot basement floor and wall (p. 54)
	Drainage system faulty	Troubleshoot drainage systems (p. 78)
	Moisture penetrating foundation wall	Waterproof exterior foundation wall (p. 24) ◼●
Basement damp	Foundation wall damp	Waterproof interior foundation wall (p. 17) □◕
	Basement floor damp	Troubleshoot basement floor (p. 54)
	Drainage system faulty	Troubleshoot drainage systems (p. 78)
Foundation wall wet	Leaking crack in foundation wall	Plug leaking crack (p. 22) □◕ and waterproof crack exterior (p. 22) ◼●
	Leaking crack at control joint	Evaluate crack (p. 18); if there is no structural problem, waterproof crack exterior (p. 22) ◼●, then seal crack with an elastomeric sealant for concrete
	Leaking at joint between foundation wall and floor or opening	Troubleshoot basement floor and wall (p. 54)
	Drainage system faulty	Troubleshoot drainage systems (p. 78)
	Moisture penetrating foundation wall	Waterproof exterior foundation wall (p. 24) ◼●
Foundation wall damp	Moisture penetrating foundation wall	Waterproof interior foundation wall (p. 17) □◕
	Drainage system faulty	Troubleshoot drainage systems (p. 78)
Foundation wall cracked; leaking	Concrete expansion and contraction; foundation movement or settlement	Evaluate crack (p. 18); if there is no structural problem, plug leaking crack (p. 22) □◕ and waterproof crack exterior (p. 22) ◼●
	Drainage system faulty	Troubleshoot drainage systems (p. 78)
Foundation wall cracked; no leaking	Concrete expansion and contraction; foundation movement or settlement	Evaluate crack (p. 18); if there is no structural problem, patch hairline crack (p. 19) □○, stationary open crack (p. 19) □◕ or moving open crack (p. 21) □◕
Hairline crack in foundation wall; leaking	Concrete expansion and contraction; foundation movement or settlement	Plug leaking crack (p. 22) □◕ and waterproof crack exterior (p. 22) ◼●
	Drainage system faulty	Troubleshoot drainage systems (p. 78)
Hairline crack in foundation wall; no leaking	Concrete expansion and contraction; foundation movement or settlement	Patch hairline crack (p. 19) □○
Stationary open crack in foundation wall; leaking	Concrete expansion and contraction; foundation movement or settlement	Plug leaking crack (p. 22) □◕ and waterproof crack exterior (p. 22) ◼●
	Drainage system faulty	Troubleshoot drainage systems (p. 78)
Stationary open crack in foundation wall; no leaking	Concrete expansion and contraction; foundation movement or settlement	Patch stationary open crack (p. 19) □◕
Moving open crack in foundation wall; leaking	Seasonal concrete expansion/contraction; foundation movement or settlement	Plug leaking crack (p. 22) □◕ and waterproof crack exterior (p. 22) ◼●
	Drainage system faulty	Troubleshoot drainage systems (p. 78)
Moving open crack in foundation wall; no leaking	Seasonal concrete expansion/contraction; foundation movement or settlement	Patch moving open crack (p. 21) □◕
Control joint cracked; leaking	Concrete expansion and contraction; foundation movement or settlement	Evaluate crack (p. 18); if there is no structural problem, waterproof crack exterior (p. 22) ◼●, then seal crack with an elastomeric sealant for concrete
	Drainage system faulty	Troubleshoot drainage systems (p. 78)
Control joint cracked; no leaking	Concrete expansion and contraction; foundation movement or settlement	Evaluate crack (p. 18); if there is no structural problem, waterproof crack exterior (p. 22) ◼●, then seal crack with an elastomeric sealant for concrete
Foundation wall dirty or stained	Wear and tear; mildew due to excess moisture or water penetration	Clean foundation wall (p. 17) □○
Foundation wall efflorescence (white, powdery deposits)	Leaching of salts due to excess moisture	Clean foundation wall (p. 17) □○

DEGREE OF DIFFICULTY: □ Easy ◼ Moderate ◼ Complex
ESTIMATED TIME: ○ Less than 1 hour ◕ 1 to 3 hours ● Over 3 hours

CLEANING A FOUNDATION WALL

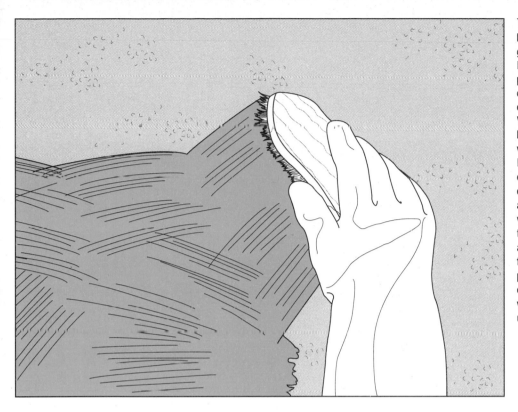

Washing off dirt and stains. Wearing rubber gloves and safety goggles, mix as many gallons of cleaner as needed in a bucket. For light dirt, mix a little household detergent per gallon of water; for tough grime, mix 1/2 cup of TSP (trisodium phosphate) and 1/2 cup of household detergent per gallon of water. Working section by section, use a stiff nylon brush to scrub the solution onto the wall *(left)*; when the wall is clean, rinse it with clean water. For any remaining stain, choose an appropriate cleaning agent *(page 112)*. For example, to clean stubborn efflorescence off the wall, mix a solution of 1 part muriatic acid to 12 parts water. **Caution:** Wear a respirator and pour the acid into the water; never pour water into acid. Working on a small section at a time, wet the wall with water to keep the solution from penetrating too deeply, then scrub the solution onto it using the brush and rinse it with clean water. Neutralize any leftover solution with sodium bicarbonate (baking soda).

WATERPROOFING AN INTERIOR FOUNDATION WALL

Waterproofing an interior wall. To waterproof an interior wall, remove any paint from it; otherwise, waterproof the exterior wall *(page 24)*. After removing any paint from the wall, clean it *(step above)*. Buy a cement-based waterproof coating at a building supply center; if recommended by the manufacturer, also buy a bonding agent for it. Wearing work gloves and safety goggles, mix a small test batch of the coating and apply it on a small section of the wall following the manufacturer's instructions. Apply a brushable coating using a tampico fiber brush, first working it into the concrete pores with a semi-circular motion, then smoothing it evenly on the surface *(left)*. Allow the coating to cure for the time specified by the manufacturer, misting it periodically. Then, use a cold chisel and a ball-peen hammer to try shearing the coating off the wall. If the coating shears off cleanly, clean the wall again and repeat the test. If the coating still does not adhere to the wall, waterproof the exterior wall. Otherwise, mix enough of the coating to cover the wall and apply it, working on one small section at a time. Allow the coating to cure, then mix and apply a second coat of it.

EVALUATING AND MONITORING A CRACK

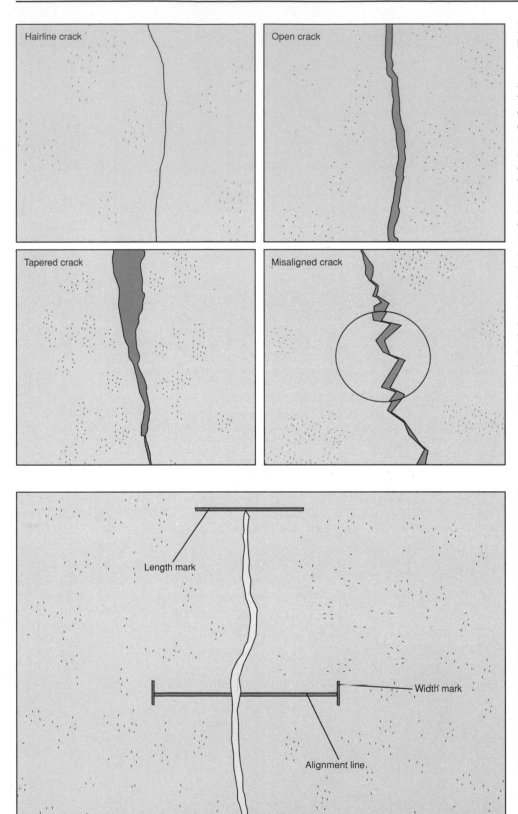

Hairline crack

Open crack

Tapered crack

Misaligned crack

Length mark

Width mark

Alignment line

Evaluating a crack. A crack in a wall can be evidence of a serious structural problem and must be evaluated carefully. A crack in a wall is a sign of movement, usually from foundation settlement or concrete expansion and contraction with temperature fluctuations. Uniform foundation settlement typically produces superficial cracks at stress points in a wall such as the corners of windows. However, uneven foundation settlement can cause a serious crack in a wall: continuous vertically near a corner or horizontally or diagonally across the center, for example. Closely inspect the edges of any crack in a wall. A hairline crack *(far left, top)* or an open crack *(near left, top)* is usually not serious if its edges are up to 1/8 inch apart, parallel and aligned. However, a crack can be serious if its edges are more than 1/8 inch apart, tapered *(far left, bottom)* or misaligned (not matched in shape or position) *(near left, bottom)*. Consult a building professional *(page 119)* for any serious or questionable crack; also for any crack that appears suddenly—after an earthquake or nearby excavation, for example. When you determine that a crack is not serious, plug it if it is leaking *(page 22)* or patch it if it is dry and hairline *(page 19)*; otherwise, monitor it *(step below)*.

Monitoring a crack. Monitor a dry, open crack in a wall to determine if it should be repaired as a stationary or moving crack. To monitor a crack in a wall, mark it using a felt-tipped pen: a length mark at each end of the crack; a width mark at the center on each side of the crack; and an alignment line between the width marks at a 90-degree angle across the crack *(left)*. Measure and record the distance between the width marks, then monitor the crack monthly over a 6- to 12-month period; brush out any particles that collect in it and keep it open. Consult a building professional *(page 119)* if: the distance between the width lines increases by more than 1/8 inch; points of the alignment line shift or deflect; or a crack 3 feet or longer extends in length by more than 1/4 of the distance between the length marks. Otherwise, patch the crack as a stationary crack *(page 19)* if it is stable; as a moving crack *(page 21)* if it widens and narrows.

PATCHING A HAIRLINE CRACK

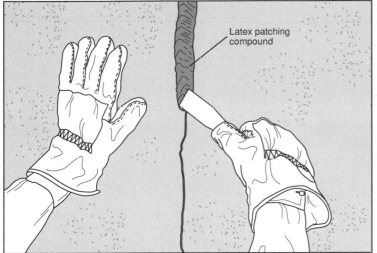

Latex patching compound

Applying patching compound. Evaluate the crack to ensure that there is no structural problem *(page 18)*. To prepare the crack for patching, use a stiff fiber brush to clean out dirt and particles; remove any stain *(page 112)*. Buy a latex concrete patching compound at a building supply center; if recommended by the manufacturer, also a bonding agent. Follow the manufacturer's instructions to apply any bonding agent to the crack. Prepare a sufficient quantity of the patching compound for the job, mixing it to a thin consistency that can be worked to a featheredge. Wearing work gloves, start at one end of the crack and use a putty knife to patch a section of it at a time with the patching compound. Draw the putty knife across the crack, using the tip of it to press in the patching compound; overfill the crack slightly. Continue the same way along the crack *(above, left)* to the other end of it. Then, draw the putty knife along the patch *(above, right)* to scrape off excess patching compound and smooth it flush with the wall. Allow the patching compound to cure for the time specified by the manufacturer; mist it with water when it lightens at the edges and keep plastic taped over it until it cures.

PATCHING A STATIONARY OPEN CRACK

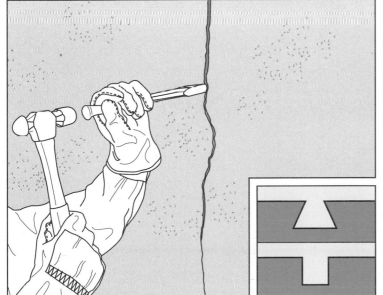

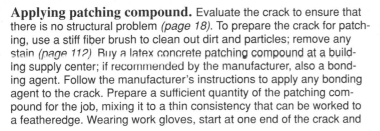

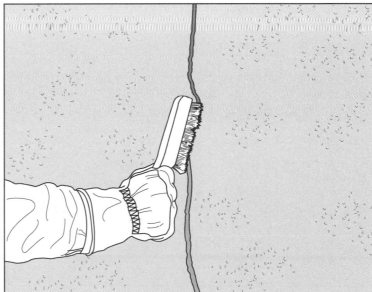

1 **Preparing the crack for patching.** Evaluate the crack to ensure that there is no structural problem *(page 18)*. To prepare the crack for patching, use a cold chisel and a ball-peen hammer. Wearing work gloves and safety goggles, chisel any loose or crumbling concrete off the edges of the crack; if a rebar (reinforcing bar) is visible in the crack, chisel out about 1 inch of the concrete behind it. Then, use the chisel and hammer to widen the crack to 1/4 inch and deepen it to 1/2 inch. Starting at one end of the crack, chisel in turn along each edge *(above, left)*, undercutting it, if possible *(inset, top)*, or cutting it straight *(inset, bottom)*; avoid tapering the edges toward each other into a V-shaped groove. Use a stiff fiber brush to clean dirt and particles out of the crack *(above, right)*; remove any stain *(page 112)*. Buy a latex concrete patching compound at a building supply center; if recommended by the manufacturer, also a bonding agent.

PATCHING A STATIONARY OPEN CRACK (continued)

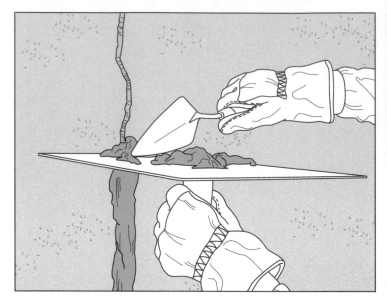

2 **Applying a bonding agent.** If a wet surface is recommended by the patching compound manufacturer, soak the crack with water, then apply the patching compound *(step 3)*. If a bonding agent is recommended by the patching compound manufacturer, prepare a sufficient quantity of it for the job. Wearing rubber gloves, use an old paintbrush to apply an even coat of the bonding agent into the crack, working from one end to the other end of it *(above)*. Allow the bonding agent to set until it becomes tacky—usually about 15 minutes is specified by the manufacturer.

3 **Applying patching compound.** Prepare a sufficient quantity of the patching compound following the manufacturer's instructions, mixing it on a mason's hawk to a thick consistency that does not run. Wearing work gloves, start at the bottom of the crack and use a pointing trowel to patch a section of it at a time. Hold the mason's hawk below the section and pack in the patching compound, pressing it into the crack with the tip of the trowel; overfill the crack slightly. If a rebar is exposed, pack in enough patching compound to fill the cavity behind it. Continue the same way up the crack *(above)* to the top of it.

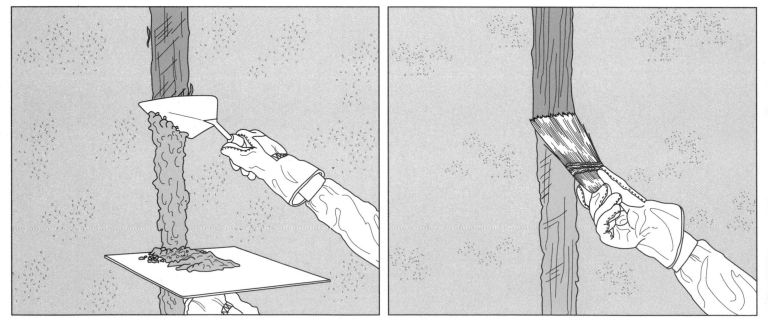

4 **Finishing the patch.** Working from the top to the bottom of the patch, draw the edge of the pointing trowel along it, scraping off excess patching compound onto the mason's hawk *(above, left)*. Then, draw the back of the trowel along the patch to smooth it flush with the wall; work from the top to the bottom of it using a slight curving motion. If desired, texture the patch to match any wall texture; working from the top to the bottom of it, draw the bristle tips of a whisk broom lightly over it *(above, right)*. Allow the patching compound to cure for the time specified by the manufacturer; mist it with water when it lightens at the edges and keep plastic taped over it until it cures.

PATCHING A MOVING OPEN CRACK

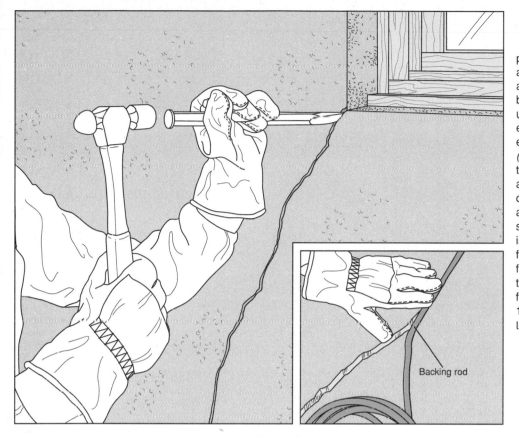

1 **Preparing the crack for patching.**
Evaluate the crack to ensure that there is no structural problem *(page 18)*. To prepare the crack for patching, use a cold chisel and a ball-peen hammer. Wearing work gloves and safety goggles, chisel any loose or crumbling concrete off the edges of the crack. Then, use the chisel and hammer to widen and deepen the crack to at least 1/4 inch. Starting at one end of the crack, chisel in turn along each edge *(left)*, cutting it straight; avoid tapering the edges toward each other into a V-shaped groove. Use a stiff fiber brush to clean dirt and particles out of the crack; remove any stain *(page 112)*. Buy an elastomeric sealant for concrete at a building supply center; use a urethane type. If the crack is more than 1/2 inch deep, also buy enough foam backing rod slightly wider than the crack to fill it to within 1/4 inch of the surface; to install the backing rod, work along the crack to push it firmly into place *(inset)*. If the crack is between 1/4 and 1/2 inch deep, use waxed paper to fill it to within 1/4 inch of the surface the same way.

Backing rod

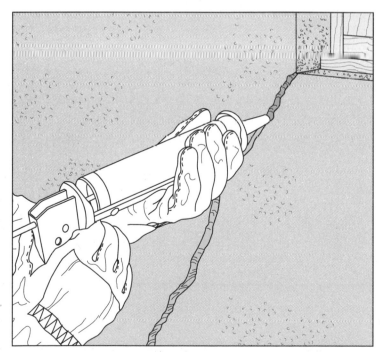

2 **Applying sealant.** Load a caulking gun with elastomeric sealant *(page 115)*. Starting at the top of the crack, hold the caulking gun at a 45-degree angle to the wall. Push the tip of the sealant tube into the crack and squeeze the gun trigger, moving down the crack to eject a continuous bead of sealant into it *(above)*. Continue until you reach the bottom of the crack. If necessary, repeat the procedure to fill the crack until it is flush with the wall surface.

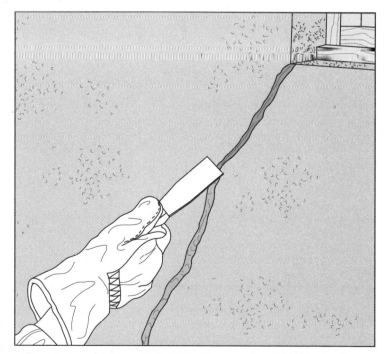

3 **Finishing the patch.** While the sealant is still pliable, smooth the patch using the wet blade of a putty knife. Draw the edge of the putty knife along the patch to scrape off excess sealant and smooth it flush with the wall surface *(above)*. Allow the sealant to cure for the time specified by the manufacturer, following any instructions or recommendations provided on its label.

PLUGGING A LEAKING CRACK

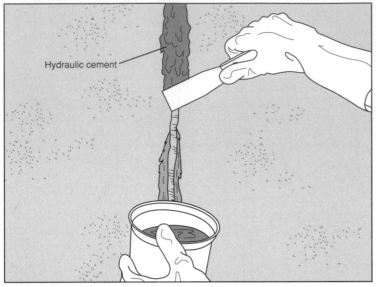

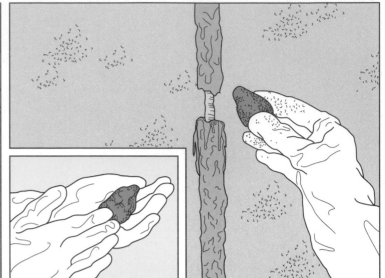

Applying hydraulic cement. Evaluate the crack to ensure that there is no structural problem *(page 18)*. Prepare the crack for patching as you would a stationary open crack *(page 19)*, widening and deepening it to at least 3/4 inch. Buy hydraulic cement at a building supply center; wearing rubber gloves, follow the manufacturer's instructions to mix a sufficient quantity of it for the job. Starting at the driest end of the crack, use a putty knife or your gloved hand to pack the cement into a section of it at a time; hold the cement in place for a moment to ensure it sets. Continue the same way along the crack to the point of heaviest

leakage *(above, left)*, leaving it unfilled; work back to it from the other end of the crack the same way. Then, mix a small quantity of cement and use your gloved hands to mold it into a cone-shaped plug *(inset)*. Press the plug into the crack at the unfilled point *(above, right)* and hold it in place until it sets—usually about three minutes. Working from one end to the other end of the patch, use the putty knife to scrape off excess cement and smooth the packed cement flush with the wall. Locate the exterior of the crack and waterproof it *(steps below)*.

WATERPROOFING AN EXTERIOR CRACK

Posthole digger

1 Excavating around the crack.
Evaluate the crack to ensure that there is no structural problem *(page 18)*. Patch an above-ground exterior crack as you would any interior hairline crack *(page 19)*, stationary open crack *(page 19)* or moving open crack *(page 21)*. Otherwise, waterproof the below-ground portion of an exterior crack by excavating around it and building a dam of bentonite—an absorbent clay-like mineral that swells on contact with water. To waterproof the exterior of a crack in an interior wall, estimate the below-ground location of it using a reference point such as a window or wall edge. Before excavating around the crack, identify any utility entering the house near it and notify the utility company; the utility may need to be shut off. To excavate around the crack, first remove any sod or vegetation *(page 120)* adjacent to it or its estimated location. Lay a plastic sheet on the ground to hold the soil excavated, then dig down along the foundation to the top of its footing. For a crack that runs perpendicular to the ground, use a posthole digger to dig a hole slightly wider than the crack *(left)*; for a crack that runs at an angle to the ground, use a spade to dig a trench *(page 121)* long enough to expose it.

WATERPROOFING AN EXTERIOR CRACK (continued)

2 **Preparing and installing a form.** Measure the depth of the hole or trench and prepare a form for the bentonite dam; buy the materials needed at a building supply center. For a vertical crack, use half of a cylindrical cardboard form; cut it slightly longer than the depth of the hole and then in half with a compass saw *(above, left)*. For a crack at an angle to the ground, use a sheet of heavy cardboard as a form; folded into a V shape along its center, it should be large enough to span the crack with a gap of 2 to 3 inches between its fold and the wall. Before installing the form, bail any standing water out of the hole or trench. Then, insert the form into the hole *(above, right)* or trench, pushing it down until it rests on the foundation footing. Center the form around the crack with its edges flush against the wall; if necessary, remove it to trim any edge to fit.

3 **Backfilling and filling the form with bentonite.** Keeping the form centered around the crack with its edges flush against the wall, use a spade to backfill around it with the soil you removed *(above, left)*; compact the soil using the end of a 2-by-4 as you backfill to hold the form in position. Continue backfilling and compacting soil around the form until you reach the top of it, then fill it with granular bentonite. Using a bucket or the spade, pour the bentonite into the form *(above, right)*; tap on the top of the form to help settle the bentonite as you go. When the form is filled with bentonite, use the spade to cover the top of it with a layer of soil; patch any above-ground portion of the crack as you would any interior hairline crack *(page 19)*, stationary open crack *(page 19)* or moving open crack *(page 21)*. Allow the bentonite to expand and contract through a few rainstorms for 2 to 3 months. Then, remove any outcropping soil and bentonite with the spade, level the ground and put back any sod or vegetation you removed.

WATERPROOFING AN EXTERIOR FOUNDATION WALL

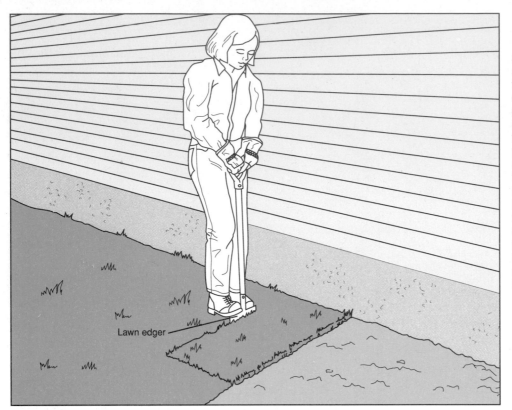

1 **Excavating along the wall.**
Waterproof an exterior foundation wall if wetness in the basement persists after all other repairs have been made. Plan to dig a trench 3 feet wide along the wall and a few feet along the wall at each end of it to the depth of the foundation footing; wait for a dry period. Identify any utility entering the house along the wall and notify the utility company; the utility may need to be shut off. Also consult your municipal authorities about the need for any building permit. To excavate along the wall, first remove any sod or vegetation *(page 120)* adjacent to it, using a lawn edger to cut any sod into strips *(left)*. Lay plastic sheets on the ground to hold the soil excavated. Hire a backhoe operator *(page 122)* for the digging or use a spade to dig the trench yourself *(page 121)*, protecting it as necessary *(page 123)*. If you reach a layer of gravel at the foundation footing, work carefully to avoid damaging any drain tile under it.

Lawn edger

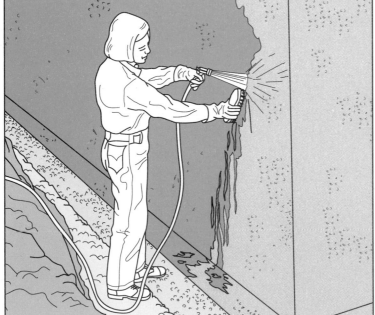

Cove

Mortar

2 **Preparing the wall for waterproofing.** Starting at one end of the wall and working from the top of it to the footing, use a garden hose fitted with a pressure nozzle and a wire brush to clean off any dirt and particles. Continue to the other end of the wall the same way *(above, left)*; remove any stain *(page 112)*. Wearing safety goggles, use a cold chisel and a hand drilling hammer to chip any projections off the wall. Evaluate and repair any crack in the wall *(page 18)*. If there is no cove along the top of the footing to divert water away from it, prepare a sufficient quantity of mortar *(page 114)* to construct a cove. Working from end to end of the wall, use a mason's trowel to pack the mortar onto the footing, banking it up the wall to a height equal to the footing width *(above, right)*; smooth and slope the mortar, making the cove slightly concave in shape. If the wall leaks heavily, also parge it as you would a masonry wall *(page 40)*. Allow the mortar to cure for at least 2 days, covering it with plastic until it cures to keep it moist. If necessary, replace any damaged drain tiles or install drain tiles to improve water drainage *(page 78)*. To waterproof the wall, install polyethylene sheeting *(step 3)* or bentonite sheets *(step 5)*.

3 **Installing polyethylene sheeting.** Buy enough 6-mil polyethylene sheeting and cold-applied asphalt foundation coating for the job at a building supply center; plan to cover from ground level to the outside edge of the footing along the wall and 2 feet along the wall at each end of it. Wearing work gloves, use a mason's trowel to apply the asphalt coating *(above, left)*. Then, install the sheeting vertically, cutting continuous sections of it to length. Starting around the corner at one end of the wall, align a section of the sheeting at the top of the asphalt coating and press it into place, wrapping it snugly around the corner; smooth It down to the bottom of the wall and across

the footing. If necessary, slit the sheeting to fit at a wall obstruction, then seal it with asphalt coating. Continue along the wall and around the corner at the other end of it the same way, overlapping sections of the sheeting by 6 inches *(above, right)*; lift the overlap and apply a band of asphalt coating to the sheeting under it to seal the joint. After installing the sheeting, apply a band of asphalt coating along the top of it to seal the joint between it and the wall. If desired, protect the sheeting with rigid foam panels *(step 4)*. Otherwise, backfill the trench *(page 122)*, working carefully to avoid tearing the sheeting; then, put back any sod or vegetation you removed.

4 **Installing rigid foam panels.** Buy enough rigid foam panels at a building supply center to cover the sheeting on the walls; also an adhesive recommended for adhering them. Also buy aluminum or vinyl J-channel to hold the panels at the top of the sheeting. Wearing work gloves, work from one end to the other end along the top of the sheeting to position the J-channel and nail it *(page 117)* to the wall *(inset)*; if necessary, cut it to length using tin snips. Then, work from one end to the other end of the sheeting to install the panels one at a time between the J-channel and the footing. Trim each panel in turn to size with a utility knife, cutting it to fit around any wall obstruction. Apply adhesive along the edges on the back of the panel, then fit it between the J-channel and the footing, butting it against any adjacent panel and pressing it into place against the sheeting *(left)*. After installing the panels, apply a sealant *(page 115)* along the joint between the J-channel and the wall. Backfill the trench *(page 122)*, then put back any sod or vegetation you removed.

WATERPROOFING AN EXTERIOR FOUNDATION WALL (continued)

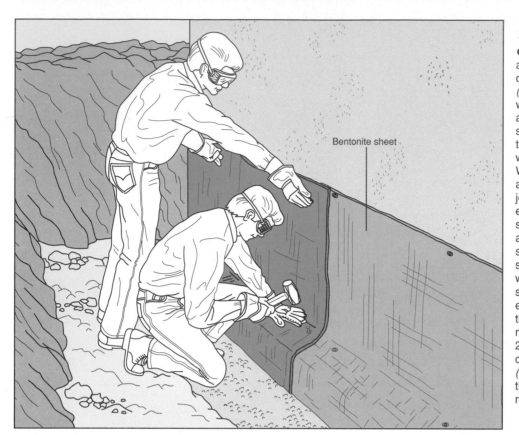

Bentonite sheet

5 **Installing a starter row of bentonite sheets.** Dig a narrow trench along the footing down to the bottom of it using a spade; work carefully to avoid damaging any drain tiles, removing them only if necessary *(page 78)*. Clean dirt and particles off the footing with a wire brush. Buy enough bentonite sheets and sealing compound for the job at a building supply center; plan to cover from ground level to the bottom edge of the footing along the wall and 2 feet along the wall at each end of it. Wearing work gloves, use a putty knife to apply a wide band of sealing compound along the joint between the footing and the wall and any expansion or control joint. Then, install the sheets one at a time with the open-weave side against the wall; work with a helper and wear safety goggles. Install the first sheet of the starter row around the corner at one end of the wall *(step 6)*. To install the second sheet of the starter row, overlap the first sheet by a few inches and cut it to fit at any obstruction *(step 7)*, then use a hand drilling hammer to drive a masonry nail fitted with a washer into it every 2 feet along the top and side edges. Install the other sheets of the starter row the same way *(left)*, fitting the last sheet around the corner at the other end of the wall; then, install the upper rows of sheets *(step 8)*.

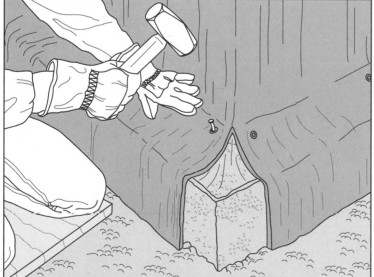

6 **Fitting a sheet of the starter row around a corner.** Position a sheet at one end of the wall with its long side aligned along the bottom of the footing and extended enough to lap 2 feet around the corner; if necessary, cut it to fit at an obstruction *(step 7)*. Smooth the sheet up and across the footing and up the wall, then fasten it *(page 117)*. Using a hand drilling hammer, drive a masonry nail fitted with a washer into the sheet every 2 feet along the top edge and the side edge away from the corner as well as along the top of the footing. To fold the sheet around the corner, make a slit from its point at the bottom of the wall to its bottom corner using a utility knife. Fold the sheet around the corner and fasten it to the wall and the footing the

same way *(above, left)*. To cover the exposed footing, cut a section of a sheet large enough to overlap the edge of the sheet on each side of it by 6 inches. Fold the section around the exposed footing and make a slit from its point at the top of the footing to its top edge; fold the section on each side of the slit onto the top of the footing and up the wall, making slits as necessary for it to lie flat *(above, right)*. Use a putty knife to apply a band of sealing compound along the edges and each slit of the section *(inset)*, then fasten it to the top of the footing on each side of the corner. Install the other sheets of the starter row *(step 5)*, then fit a sheet around the corner at the other end of the wall the same way.

7 **Fitting a bentonite sheet at an obstruction.** Use a utility knife to cut a sheet to fit around an obstruction such as a pipe. Calculate the point on the sheet where the obstruction will intersect it, then cut to the point from the nearest edge of it. Position the sheet on the wall around the obstruction *(above, left)*, then trim it to fit snugly around the obstruction and lie flat against the wall. Using a hand drilling hammer, drive a masonry nail fitted with a washer into the sheet every 2 feet along the top and side edges of it. Use a putty knife to

apply a thick band of sealing compound along the cut in the sheet and around the obstruction *(above, center)*. Then, cut a section of a sheet large enough to fit around the obstruction and cover the cut in the sheet around it. Calculate the point on the section where the obstruction will intersect it, then cut to the point from the nearest edge of it and position it; offset the cut in it from the cut in the sheet under it. Trim the section to fit snugly around the obstruction and lie flat on the wall, then fasten it to the wall at each corner *(above, right)*.

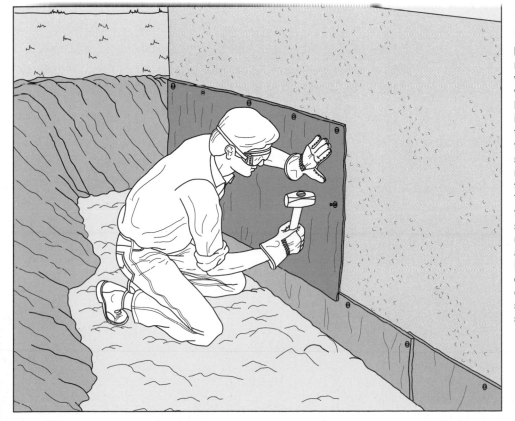

8 **Installing upper rows of bentonite sheets.** Backfill the trench *(page 122)* against the starter row to a level 6 inches below the top of it, then install an upper row; if necessary, trim each sheet of the row to align it with ground level. Starting at one end of the wall, position a sheet with its bottom edge overlapping the row below it by a few inches and fold it around the corner with its side edges offset from the side edges of any sheet below it; cut it to fit at any obstruction *(step 7)*. To fasten the sheet, use a hand drilling hammer to drive a masonry nail fitted with a washer through it into the wall every 2 feet along each edge of it *(left)*. To install the second sheet of the row, overlap the first sheet by a few inches and fasten it the same way. Install the other sheets of the row using the same procedure, fitting the last sheet around the corner at the other end of the wall. Backfill against the row and install another row, continuing until you reach ground level; fasten every 12 inches along the top edge of the sheets of the last row. Then, put back any sod or vegetation you removed.

MASONRY FOUNDATIONS

A masonry foundation may support a home in a cold region, where a foundation must extend below the frost line to rest on soil that does not freeze and thaw. Blocks of concrete are the most common masonry units used, although the foundation of an old home may be of bricks or stones; if the foundation of your home is of stones, consult a professional stone mason for any repairs. The depth of the frost line and foundation determines if there is space under the house for a basement or only a crawlspace. A typical block foundation is shown at right. Foundation walls support the house structure at its perimeter and carry its weight down to the footings; the footings in turn distribute the weight uniformly on the surrounding soil.

A block foundation wall is a single tier of blocks laid in staggered rows on top of one another; joints between adjacent blocks and between adjacent rows are filled with mortar. For added strength, the cores of blocks may be filled with mortar; the cores of a column of blocks may also contain steel reinforcing bars. Isolation joints that separate the foundation walls from the floor slab minimize cracking. Drain tiles along the foundation footings collect water and carry it away from the house. In rainy and wet-soil regions, a waterproof membrane is often adhered to the exterior below-ground portion of the foundation walls to help prevent water penetration. There can be a cove on the top of the foundation footings along the exterior of the foundation walls to divert water away from the joint between them.

Wetness and cracking are the most typical problems of a masonry foundation; although rarely more than minor irritants, they can be a sign of a serious problem—or become a serious problem if left unattended. Inspect the foundation walls of your home routinely for cracks and wetness; work indoors if you have access to them as well as outdoors. Use the Troubleshooting Guide *(page 30)* to help you identify a problem and determine the necessary repair.

Superficial, hairline cracks in the blocks or bricks and mortar joints of a foundation wall are normal and usually not a cause for concern; however, any crack more than 1/8 inch wide or associated with a dislocation of the foundation can be serious. Evaluate any crack you find *(page 35)*; consult a building professional about any crack that may indicate a structural problem. You can plug a leaking crack in a block or brick *(page 38)* and waterproof the exterior of it *(page 22)* or waterproof the interior of a foundation wall *(page 31)*; for any wetness or dampness problem, however, you should also troubleshoot your drainage systems *(page 78)*. If wetness persists after making all other repairs, you may need to waterproof the exterior of the foundation wall *(page 40)* as a permanent solution.

If the basement of your home is finished, refer to the chapter entitled Basement Floors And Walls *(page 54)* for procedures on gaining access to the interior foundation walls. Consult Tools & Techniques *(page 110)* for information on the tools needed for repairs as well as for instructions on excavating and backfilling along the exterior of a foundation wall. Before undertaking any repair, familiarize yourself with the safety advice included in the Emergency Guide *(page 8)*.

Mortar joint
Layer of mortar 3/8 inch thick bonds adjacent blocks or bricks together, creating a watertight barrier that permits slight movement of blocks or bricks without cracking. May be struck flush with wall or in concave or V shape.

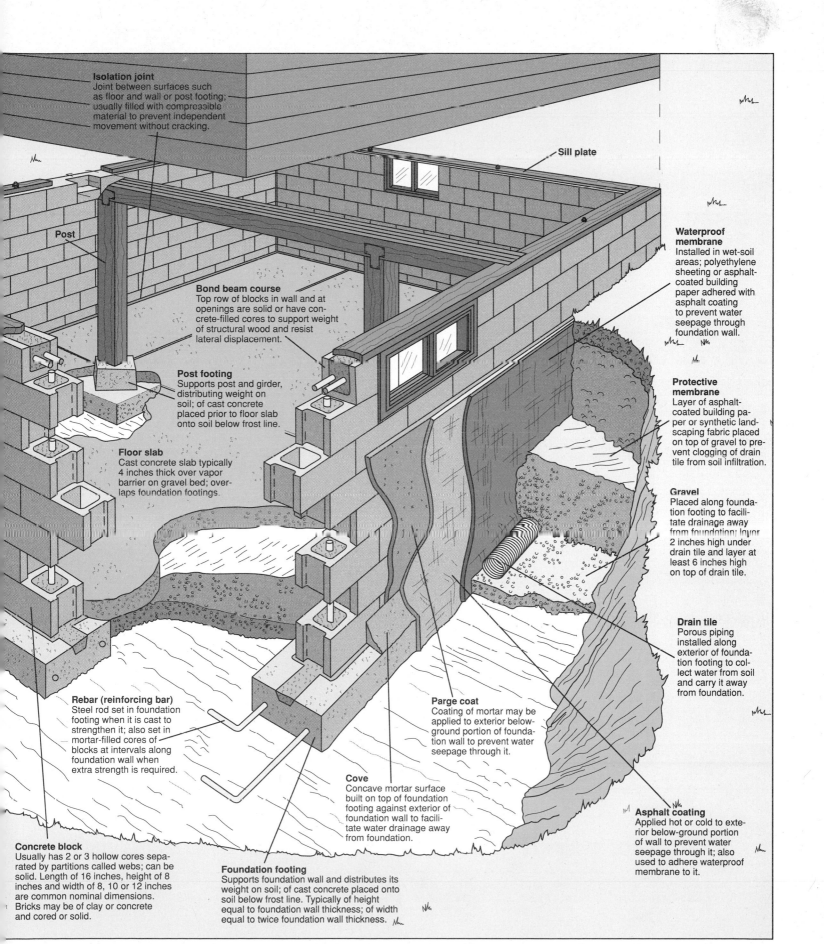

Isolation joint
Joint between surfaces such as floor and wall or post footing; usually filled with compressible material to prevent independent movement without cracking.

Post

Sill plate

Bond beam course
Top row of blocks in wall and at openings are solid or have concrete-filled cores to support weight of structural wood and resist lateral displacement.

Post footing
Supports post and girder, distributing weight on soil; of cast concrete placed prior to floor slab onto soil below frost line.

Floor slab
Cast concrete slab typically 4 inches thick over vapor barrier on gravel bed; overlaps foundation footings.

Waterproof membrane
Installed in wet-soil areas; polyethylene sheeting or asphalt-coated building paper adhered with asphalt coating to prevent water seepage through foundation wall.

Protective membrane
Layer of asphalt-coated building paper or synthetic landscaping fabric placed on top of gravel to prevent clogging of drain tile from soil infiltration.

Gravel
Placed along foundation footing to facilitate drainage away from foundation; layer 2 inches high under drain tile and layer at least 6 inches high on top of drain tile.

Drain tile
Porous piping installed along exterior of foundation footing to collect water from soil and carry it away from foundation.

Rebar (reinforcing bar)
Steel rod set in foundation footing when it is cast to strengthen it; also set in mortar-filled cores of blocks at intervals along foundation wall when extra strength is required.

Parge coat
Coating of mortar may be applied to exterior below-ground portion of foundation wall to prevent water seepage through it.

Cove
Concave mortar surface built on top of foundation footing against exterior of foundation wall to facilitate water drainage away from foundation.

Asphalt coating
Applied hot or cold to exterior below-ground portion of wall to prevent water seepage through it; also used to adhere waterproof membrane to it.

Concrete block
Usually has 2 or 3 hollow cores separated by partitions called webs; can be solid. Length of 16 inches, height of 8 inches and width of 8, 10 or 12 inches are common nominal dimensions. Bricks may be of clay or concrete and cored or solid.

Foundation footing
Supports foundation wall and distributes its weight on soil; of cast concrete placed onto soil below frost line. Typically of height equal to foundation wall thickness; of width equal to twice foundation wall thickness.

TROUBLESHOOTING GUIDE

SYMPTOM	POSSIBLE CAUSE	PROCEDURE
Basement wet	Leaking crack in block or brick	Plug leaking crack *(p. 38)* □◒ and waterproof crack exterior *(p. 22)* ◼●; if desired, replace brick *(p. 38)* ◼◒
	Leaking crack in mortar joint	Evaluate crack *(p. 35)*; if there is no structural problem, waterproof crack exterior *(p. 22)* ◼●, then repoint mortar joint *(p. 33)* ◼◒
	Leaking at joint of foundation wall and floor	Troubleshoot basement floor and wall *(p. 54)*
	Drainage system faulty	Troubleshoot drainage systems *(p. 78)*
	Moisture penetrating foundation wall	Waterproof exterior foundation wall *(p. 40)* ◼●
Basement damp	Foundation wall damp	Waterproof interior foundation wall *(p. 31)* □◒
	Basement floor damp	Troubleshoot basement floor *(p. 54)*
	Drainage system faulty	Troubleshoot drainage systems *(p. 78)*
Foundation wall wet	Leaking crack in block or brick	Plug leaking crack *(p. 38)* □◒ and waterproof crack exterior *(p. 22)* ◼●; if desired, replace brick *(p. 38)* ◼◒
	Leaking crack in mortar joint	Evaluate crack *(p. 35)*; if there is no structural problem, waterproof crack exterior *(p. 22)* ◼●, then repoint mortar joint *(p. 33)* ◼◒
	Leaking at joint of foundation wall and floor	Troubleshoot basement floor and wall *(p. 54)*
	Drainage system faulty	Troubleshoot drainage systems *(p. 78)*
	Moisture penetrating foundation wall	Waterproof exterior foundation wall *(p. 40)* ◼●
Foundation wall damp	Moisture penetrating foundation wall	Waterproof interior foundation wall *(p. 31)* □◒
	Drainage system faulty	Troubleshoot drainage systems *(p. 78)*
Foundation wall cracked; leaking	Masonry expansion and contraction; foundation movement or settlement	Evaluate crack *(p. 35)*; if there is no structural problem, plug leaking crack *(p. 38)* □◒ and waterproof crack exterior *(p. 22)* ◼●; if desired, replace brick *(p. 38)* ◼◒ or repoint mortar joint *(p. 33)* ◼◒
	Drainage system faulty	Troubleshoot drainage systems *(p. 78)*
Foundation wall cracked; no leaking	Masonry expansion and contraction; foundation movement or settlement	Evaluate crack *(p. 35)*; if there is no structural problem, patch hairline crack *(p. 36)* □○, stationary open crack *(p. 36)* □◒ or moving open crack *(p. 37)* □◒; if desired, replace brick *(p. 38)* ◼◒ or repoint mortar joint *(p. 33)* ◼◒
Hairline crack in block or brick; leaking	Masonry expansion and contraction; foundation movement or settlement	Plug leaking crack *(p. 38)* □◒ and waterproof crack exterior *(p. 22)* ◼●; if desired, replace brick *(p. 38)* ◼◒
	Drainage system faulty	Troubleshoot drainage systems *(p. 78)*
Hairline crack in mortar; leaking	Masonry expansion and contraction; foundation movement or settlement	Waterproof crack exterior *(p. 22)* ◼●, then repoint mortar joint *(p. 33)* ◼◒
	Drainage system faulty	Troubleshoot drainage systems *(p. 78)*
Hairline crack in block, brick or mortar; no leaking	Masonry expansion and contraction; foundation movement or settlement	Patch hairline crack *(p. 36)* □○; if desired, replace brick *(p. 38)* ◼◒ or repoint mortar joint *(p. 33)* ◼◒
Stationary open crack in block or brick; leaking	Masonry expansion and contraction; foundation movement or settlement	Plug leaking crack *(p. 38)* ◼◒ and waterproof crack exterior *(p. 22)* ◼●; if desired, replace brick *(p. 38)* ◼◒
	Drainage system faulty	Troubleshoot drainage systems *(p. 78)*
Stationary open crack in mortar; leaking	Masonry expansion and contraction; foundation movement or settlement	Waterproof crack exterior *(p. 22)* ◼●, then repoint mortar joint *(p. 33)* ◼◒
	Drainage system faulty	Troubleshoot drainage systems *(p. 78)*
Stationary open crack in block, brick or mortar; no leaking	Masonry expansion and contraction; foundation movement or settlement	Patch stationary open crack *(p. 36)* □◒; if desired, replace brick *(p. 38)* ◼◒ or repoint mortar joint *(p. 33)* ◼◒
Moving open crack in block or brick; leaking	Seasonal masonry expansion/contraction; foundation movement or settlement	Plug leaking crack *(p. 38)* ◼◒ and waterproof crack exterior *(p. 22)* ◼●; if desired, replace brick *(p. 38)* ◼◒
	Drainage system faulty	Troubleshoot drainage systems *(p. 78)*
Moving open crack in mortar; leaking	Seasonal masonry expansion/contraction; foundation movement or settlement	Waterproof crack exterior *(p. 22)* ◼●, then repoint mortar joint *(p. 33)* ◼◒ or seal crack with an elastomeric sealant
	Drainage system faulty	Troubleshoot drainage systems *(p. 78)*
Moving open crack in block, brick or mortar; no leaking	Seasonal masonry expansion/contraction; foundation movement or settlement	Patch moving open crack *(p. 37)* □◒; if desired, replace brick *(p. 38)* ◼◒ or repoint mortar joint *(p. 33)* ◼◒
Foundation wall dirty or stained	Wear and tear; mildew due to excess moisture or water penetration	Clean foundation wall *(p. 31)* □●
Foundation wall efflorescence (white powdery deposits)	Leaching of salts due to excess moisture	Clean foundation wall *(p. 31)* □●

DEGREE OF DIFFICULTY: □ Easy ◼ Moderate ◼ Complex
ESTIMATED TIME: ○ Less than 1 hour ◒ 1 to 3 hours ● Over 3 hours

CLEANING A FOUNDATION WALL

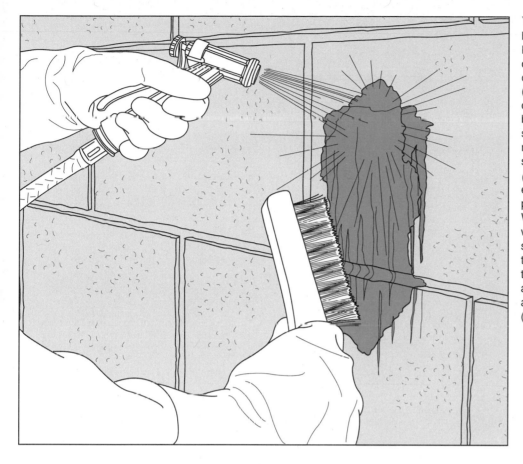

Washing off dirt and stains. Wearing rubber gloves and safety goggles, mix as many gallons of cleaner as needed in a bucket. For light dirt, mix a little household detergent per gallon of water; for tough grime, mix 1/2 cup of TSP (trisodium phosphate) and 1/2 cup of household detergent per gallon of water. Working section by section, using a stiff nylon brush to scrub the solution onto the wall; when the wall is clean, rinse it with clean water. For any remaining stain, choose an appropriate cleaning agent *(page 112)*. For example, to clean stubborn efflorescence off the wall, mix a solution of 1 part muriatic acid to 12 parts water. **Caution:** Wear a respirator and pour the acid into the water; never pour water into acid. Working on a small section at a time, wet the wall with water to keep the solution from penetrating too deeply, then scrub the solution onto it using the brush and rinse it with clean water *(left)*. Neutralize any leftover solution with sodium bicarbonate (baking soda).

WATERPROOFING AN INTERIOR FOUNDATION WALL

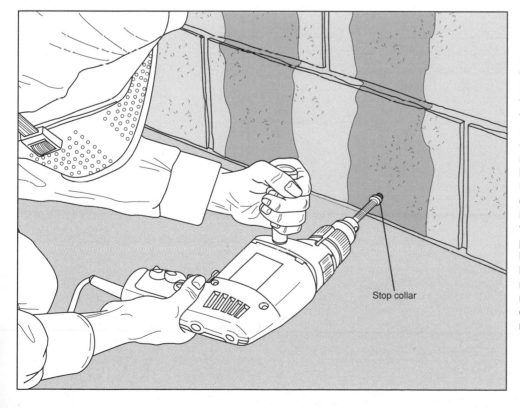

Stop collar

1 Draining a block wall. To waterproof a brick wall, apply a waterproof coating *(step 2)*. To waterproof a block wall, check each block in the bottom row for wetness—indicating water in its core; drain any wet core of a block before applying a waterproof coating. To drain the core of a block, make a weep hole through the face of the block 4 inches from one side near the bottom of it. To start the hole, use an electric drill fitted with a masonry bit; install a stop collar on the bit 1/2 inch from the tip to keep from drilling into the wet core. Plug the drill into an outlet protected by a GFCI (ground-fault circuit interrupter). Wearing safety goggles, drill into the face of the block *(left)* until you reach the drilling depth, then withdraw the bit. To complete the hole, use a star drill and a hand drilling hammer; holding the star drill with its tip in the hole, strike the end of it sharply with the hammer. Alternately, use a cordless drill fitted with a masonry bit to drill all the way into the core. Let each weep hole drain until seepage is minimal, mopping up the water as necessary.

WATERPROOFING AN INTERIOR FOUNDATION WALL (continued)

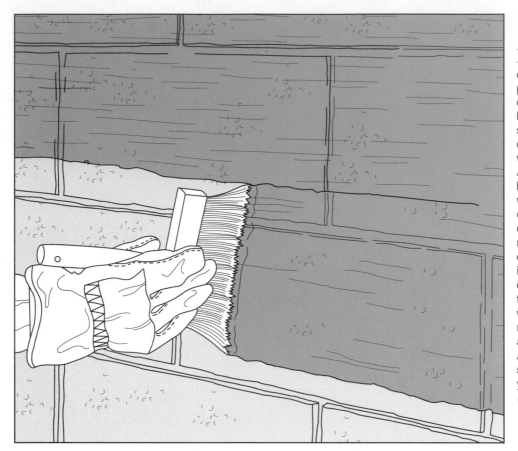

2 **Applying a waterproof coating.**
Remove any paint from the wall; otherwise, waterproof the exterior wall *(page 40)*. After removing any paint from the wall, clean it *(page 31)*. Buy a cement-based waterproof coating at a building supply center; if recommended by the manufacturer, also buy a bonding agent for it. Wearing work gloves and safety goggles, mix a small test batch of the coating and apply it on a small section of the wall following the manufacturer's instructions. Apply a brushable coating using a tampico fiber brush, first working it into the concrete pores with a semi-circular motion, then smoothing it evenly on the surface *(left)*. Allow the coating to cure for the time specified by the manufacturer, misting it periodically with water. Then, use a cold chisel and a ball-peen hammer to try shearing the coating off the wall. If the coating shears off cleanly, clean the wall again and repeat the test. If the coating still does not adhere to the wall, waterproof the exterior wall. Otherwise, mix enough of the coating to cover the wall and apply it, working on one small section at a time. Allow the coating to cure, then mix and apply a second coat of it, first plugging any weep hole you drilled *(step 1)* as you would a leaking crack *(page 38)*.

PREPARING MORTAR

MORTAR	USES	DRY INGREDIENTS
TYPE M	• For repointing exterior mortar joints below ground • For replacing a brick on an exterior wall below ground • For parging an exterior wall below ground • For building a cove on the footing of an exterior wall below ground	1 part portland cement, 1/4 part hydrated lime and 3 parts sand 1 part portland cement, 1 part type II masonry cement and 6 parts sand
TYPE N	• For repointing exterior mortar joints above ground • For repointing interior mortar joints • For replacing a brick on an exterior wall above ground • For replacing a brick on an interior wall	1 part portland cement, 1 part hydrated lime and 6 parts sand 1 part type II masonry cement and 3 parts sand

1 **Choosing a mortar recipe.** Mortar is the bedding and bonding material that holds bricks and blocks together; it must be properly mixed in the right proportions for a sound repair. For small repairs, premixed mortar is available; simply add water. For large jobs, you can produce workable mortar using one of the recipes above. Different proportions may be required, especially in colder climates; check your local building code or consult a masonry distributor or a restoration specialist. Also consult a building professional for a repair to an older brick foundation; older mortar recipes contained more lime than today's mortar recipes and should be duplicated as closely as possible. Use one of two types of cement: portland cement, a bonding agent, must be mixed with hydrated lime which gives the mixture workability; masonry cement is a portland cement and lime mixture. All mortar recipes call for clean, fine building sand and clean water; never use salty beach sand and avoid using water with a high mineral content to help prevent efflorescence. Because the exact amount of water required for mortar depends on the humidity, the temperature and the moisture in the sand, there is no recommended water ratio. Follow the guidelines in step 3 to judge the correct amount of water to add; for repointing work, consider replacing 10 to 15 percent of the water with a liquid bonding agent to ensure adherence between the masonry units and the mortar. Mix only as much mortar as you can use in a 2-hour period; if it dries, retemper it by adding a small amount of water. Retemper a batch of mortar only once; if it dries again, dispose of it and mix a new batch.

PREPARING MORTAR (continued)

Sand

Mortar box

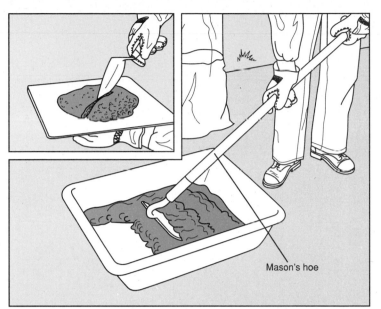

Mason's hoe

2 **Measuring and adding the dry ingredients.** Wearing work gloves, follow one of the mortar recipes *(step 1)*, measuring the dry ingredients in a clean, dry container; for most home repairs, a mortar box is a convenient size for mixing. First, measure and pour the sand into the mortar box *(above)*, then measure and add the cement. Use a mason's hoe or trowel to mix the sand and cement together thoroughly. Then, measure and add any hydrated lime if the recipe you are using calls for it. Mix the dry ingredients together until they are well blended.

3 **Mixing in water and testing the mortar.** Wearing work gloves, use a mason's hoe to make a well in the center of the dry ingredients. If you are using a liquid bonding agent, mix it with water according to the manufacturer's instructions. Add water to the dry ingredients a bit at a time, mixing it in with the hoe *(above)* until the mortar is thick and buttery and holds its shape. To test the consistency of the mortar, place a small mound on a mason's hawk and slice down the center of it with a trowel *(inset)*; it should hold its shape. If the mortar collapses, it is too wet; add dry ingredients in the correct proportions. If the mortar crumbles or is stiff, add water a little at a time.

REPOINTING MORTAR JOINTS

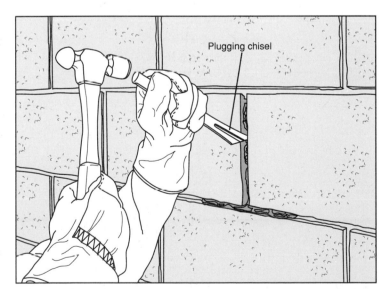

Plugging chisel

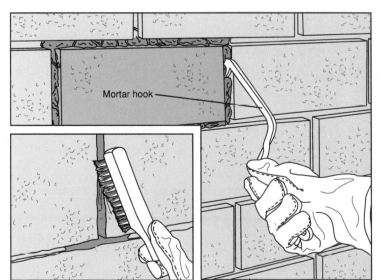

Mortar hook

1 **Cutting back the joint.** Repair a cracked or crumbling mortar joint the moment you notice it to prevent a major problem. Wearing work gloves and safety goggles, use a plugging chisel or a cold chisel and a ball-peen hammer or hand drilling hammer to cut back the joint to a maximum of 1/2 to 3/4 inch *(above)*—far enough to break up the damaged surface mortar and reach the solid mortar behind it. Work carefully to avoid damaging the adjacent blocks or bricks.

2 **Cleaning the joint.** Use a mortar hook to rake large pieces of broken mortar out of the cut-back joint *(above)*, then use a stiff fiber brush or a vacuum cleaner to clean dust and small mortar particles out of it *(inset)*. To prevent the adjacent blocks or bricks from leaching moisture out of fresh mortar, soak the joint and the adjacent blocks or bricks with water, using the fine spray of a garden hose or brushing on water with a large paintbrush.

REPOINTING MORTAR JOINTS (continued)

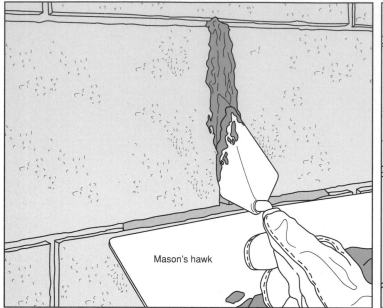

Mason's hawk

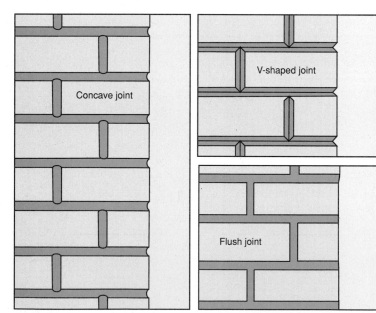

Joint filler

3 **Repointing the joint.** Wearing work gloves, mix a batch of mortar *(page 32)* on a mason's hawk; avoid working in direct sunlight which can dry the mortar too quickly. To repoint more than one mortar joint, first repoint any vertical joint, then repoint any horizontal joint. To repoint a vertical joint, hold the mason's hawk just below it to catch any falling mortar and use a pointing trowel to pack mortar into it. Press the mortar into the joint with the tip of the trowel *(above, left)*,

overfilling it slightly, then draw the edge of the trowel along it to scrape off excess mortar. To repoint a horizontal joint, hold the mason's hawk just below it and use a joint filler to slice off a batch of mortar and pack it into the joint *(above, right)*. Press the mortar into the joint with the back of the joint filler, overfilling it slightly, then draw the edge of the joint filler along it to scrape off excess mortar.

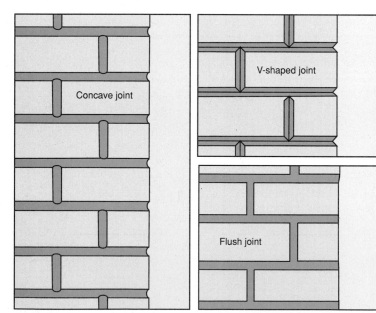

Concave joint

V-shaped joint

Flush joint

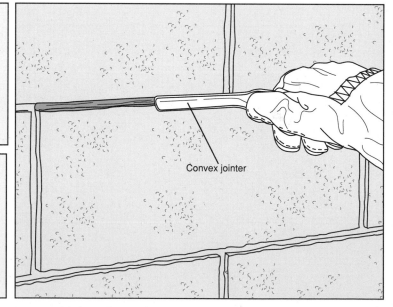

Convex jointer

4 **Striking the joint.** Allow the mortar to set until it is just hard enough to hold a thumbprint—usually about 30 minutes. To strike a repointed joint, examine the other joints *(above, left)* to determine the tool to use. For a concave joint, use a convex jointer or the back of an old spoon. For a V-shaped joint, use a V-shaped jointer or the tip of a pointing trowel. For a flush joint, use the edge of a pointing trowel. Check that each joint is filled to the surface with mortar; if necessary, add more mortar *(step 3)*. To strike more than one mortar joint, first strike any vertical joint, then strike any horizontal joint. To strike a

concave joint, as shown, wet a convex jointer with clean water and drag it smoothly along the joint *(above, right)*, then use the edge of a pointing trowel to scrape off excess mortar forced out of the joint by the pressure of the jointer. Allow the mortar to set for 24 hours, then use a stiff fiber brush to scrub any dried mortar particles off the adjacent blocks or bricks. Allow the mortar to cure, keeping it damp for at least 3 days. Mist the surface occasionally with the fine spray of water from a garden hose; or, in hot weather, hang a wet cloth on the surface using duct tape and moisten it periodically.

EVALUATING AND MONITORING A CRACK

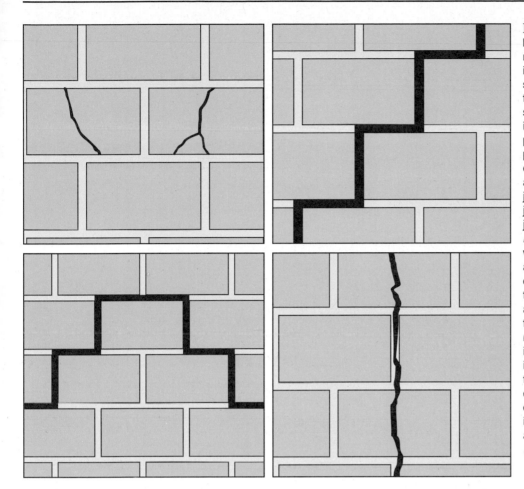

Evaluating a crack. A crack in a wall can be evidence of a serious structural problem and must be evaluated carefully. A crack in a wall is a sign of movement, usually from foundation settlement or expansion and contraction with temperature fluctuations. Uniform foundation settlement typically produces superficial cracks in single blocks or bricks *(far left, top)* or stepped along mortar joints *(near left, top)* at stress points such as the corners of windows. However, uneven foundation settlement can cause a serious crack in a wall: stepped along mortar joints near a corner, pyramidal along mortar joints *(far left, bottom)*, vertically along mortar joints and across blocks or bricks *(near left, bottom)* or horizontally across the center of the wall, for example. Closely inspect the edges of any crack in a wall. A hairline crack or an open crack is usually not serious if its edges are up to 1/8 inch apart, parallel and aligned. However, a crack can be serious if its edges are more than 1/8 inch apart, tapered or misaligned (not matched in shape or position). Consult a building professional *(page 119)* for any crack that is serious or questionable; also for any crack that appears suddenly—after an earthquake or nearby excavation, for example. When you determine that a crack is not serious, plug it if it is leaking *(page 38)* or patch it if it is dry and hairline *(page 36)*; otherwise, monitor it *(step below)*.

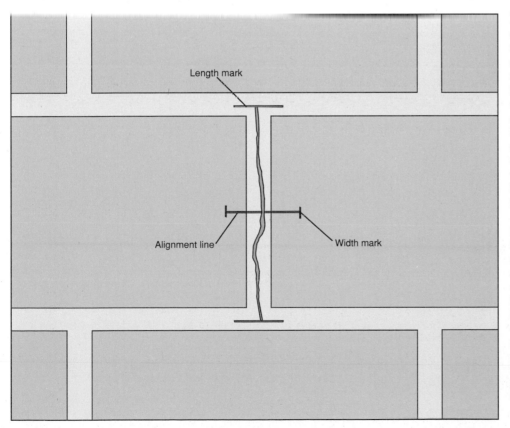

Length mark

Alignment line

Width mark

Monitoring a crack. Monitor a dry, open crack in a wall to determine if it should be repaired as a stationary crack or as a moving crack that goes through cycles of widening and narrowing. To monitor a crack in a wall, mark it using a felt-tipped pen: a length mark at each end of the crack; a width mark at the center on each side of the crack; and an alignment line between the width marks at a 90-degree angle across the crack *(left)*. Measure and record the distance between the width marks, then monitor the crack monthly over a 6- to 12-month period; brush out any particles that collect in it and keep it open. Consult a building professional *(page 119)* if: the distance between the width marks increases by more than 1/8 inch; points of the alignment line shift out of position or deflect; a crack extends in length along mortar joints and across bricks or blocks; or a crack 3 feet or longer in a mortar joint extends in length by more than 1/4 of the distance between the length marks or extends in a pyramidal pattern. Otherwise, if the crack remains stable, repoint the mortar joint *(page 33)*, patch the stationary crack in the block or brick *(page 36)* or replace the brick *(page 38)*; if it widens and narrows, patch the moving crack in the mortar joint, block or brick *(page 37)*, or repoint the mortar joint or replace the brick.

PATCHING A HAIRLINE CRACK

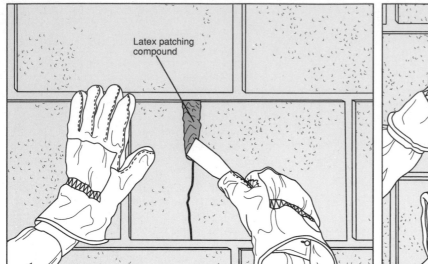

Applying patching compound. Evaluate the crack to ensure that there is no structural problem *(page 35)*. To prepare the crack for patching, use a stiff fiber brush to clean out dirt and particles; remove any stain *(page 112)*. Buy a latex concrete patching compound at a building supply center; if recommended by the manufacturer, also a bonding agent. Following the manufacturer's instructions, apply any bonding agent to the crack. Prepare a sufficient quantity of the patching compound for the job, mixing it to a thin consistency that can be worked to a featheredge. Wearing work gloves, start at one end of the crack and use a putty knife to patch a section of it at a time with the patching compound. Draw the putty knife across the crack, using the tip of it to press in the patching compound. Continue the same way along the crack *(above, left)* to the other end of it. Then, draw the putty knife along the patch *(above, right)* to scrape off excess patching compound and smooth it flush with the wall. Allow the patching compound to cure for the time specified by the manufacturer; mist it with water when it lightens at the edges and keep plastic taped over it until it cures.

PATCHING A STATIONARY OPEN CRACK

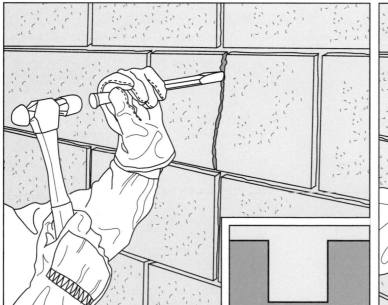

1 **Preparing the crack for patching.** Evaluate the crack to ensure that there is no structural problem *(page 35)*. To prepare the crack for patching, use a cold chisel and ball-peen hammer. Wearing work gloves and safety goggles, chisel any loose or crumbling particles off the edges of the crack. Then, use the chisel and hammer to widen the crack to 1/4 inch and deepen it to 1/2 inch. Starting at one end of the crack, chisel in turn along each edge *(above, left)*, cutting it straight *(inset)*; avoid tapering the edges toward each other into a V-shaped groove. Use a stiff fiber brush to clean dirt and particles out of the crack *(above, right)*; remove any stain *(page 112)*. Buy a latex concrete patching compound at a building supply center; if recommended by the manufacturer, also a bonding agent.

PATCHING A STATIONARY OPEN CRACK (continued)

2 **Applying patching compound.** If a wet surface is recommended by the patching compound manufacturer, soak the crack with water; If a bonding agent is recommended, follow the manufacturer's instructions to apply it into the crack and wait for it to set. Prepare a sufficient quantity of patching compound following the manufacturer's instructions, mixing it to a thick consistency that does not run. Wearing work gloves, start at the bottom of the crack and use a pointing trowel to patch a section of it at a time. Pack the patching compound into the crack *(above, left)*, pressing it in with the tip of the trowel; overfill the crack slightly. Continue the same way up the crack to the top of it. Working from the top to the bottom of the patch, draw the edge of the pointing trowel along it, scraping off excess patching compound *(above, right)*. Then, draw the back of the trowel along the patch to smooth it flush with the wall; work from the top to the bottom of it using a slight curving motion. If desired, texture the patch to match any wall texture; working from the top to the bottom of it, draw the bristle tips of a whisk broom over it. Let the patching compound cure for the time specified by the manufacturer; mist it with water when it lightens at the edges and keep plastic taped over it until it cures.

PATCHING A MOVING OPEN CRACK

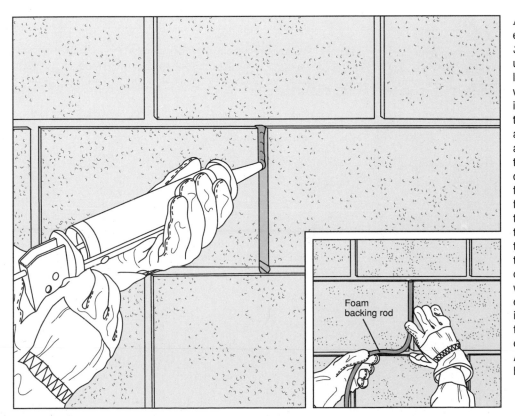

Foam backing rod

Applying sealant. Evaluate the crack to ensure that there is no structural problem *(page 35)*. Wearing work gloves and safety goggles, use a cold chisel and ball-peen hammer to chip loose particles off the edges of the crack, then widen and deepen it to at least 1/4 inch. Chisel in turn along each edge, cutting it straight; avoid tapering the edges into a V-shaped groove. Use a stiff fiber brush to clean out the crack; remove any stain *(page 112)*. Buy an elastomeric urethane sealant at a building supply center. For a crack more than 1/2 inch deep, also buy enough foam backing rod slightly wider than the crack to fill it to within 1/4 inch of the surface; work along the crack to push it in *(inset)*. For a crack between 1/4 and 1/2 inch deep, use waxed paper to fill it the same way. Load a caulking gun with the sealant *(page 115)*. Starting at the top of the crack, hold the gun at a 45-degree angle to the wall and squeeze the trigger, moving down the crack to eject a continuous bead of sealant into it *(left)*. If necessary, repeat the procedure to fill the crack level with the wall. Draw the wet edge of a putty knife along the patch to smooth it. Allow the sealant to cure for the time specified by the manufacturer.

PLUGGING A LEAKING CRACK

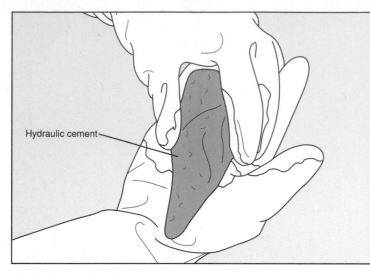

Applying hydraulic cement. Evaluate the crack to ensure that there is no structural problem *(page 35)*. Prepare the crack for patching as you would a stationary open crack *(page 36)*, widening it to 3/4 inch and deepening it to 1/2 inch. Buy hydraulic cement at a building supply center; wearing rubber gloves, follow the manufacturer's instructions to mix a sufficient quantity of it for the job. Starting at the driest end of the crack, use a putty knife or your gloved hand to pack the cement into a section of it at a time; hold the cement in place for a moment to ensure it sets. Continue the same way along the crack to the point of heaviest leakage, leaving it unfilled; work back to it from the other end of the crack the same way. Then, mix a small quantity of cement and use your gloved hands to mold it into a cone-shaped plug *(above, left)*. Press the plug into the crack at the unfilled point and hold it in place until it sets *(above, right)*—usually about three minutes. Working from one end to the other end of the patch, use the putty knife to scrape off excess cement and smooth the packed cement flush with the wall. Locate the exterior of the crack and waterproof it *(page 22)*.

REPLACING A BRICK

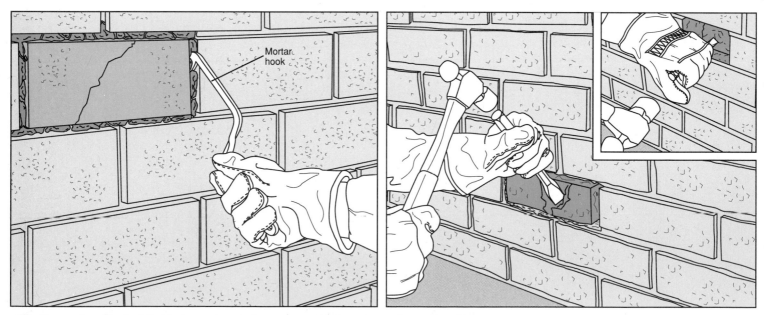

1 Removing the brick. Evaluate any crack to ensure that there is no structural problem *(page 35)*. Wearing work gloves and safety goggles, try to pry the brick out of the wall. Use a mortar hook to rake as much mortar as possible out of the joints around the brick *(above, left)*, then work the end of a pry bar or a cold chisel behind it to gently pry it out. If the brick cannot be pried out of the wall, break it out in pieces using a cold chisel and ball-peen hammer: chipping it out completely if it is a stretcher (a long face is exposed) *(above, right)*; cutting it back about 4 inches if it is a header (a short face is exposed) *(inset)*. Buy a replacement brick at a building supply center; if necessary, take a piece of the old brick to match it.

REPLACING A BRICK (continued)

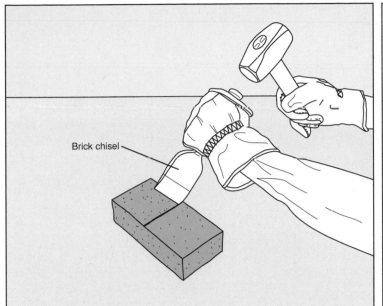

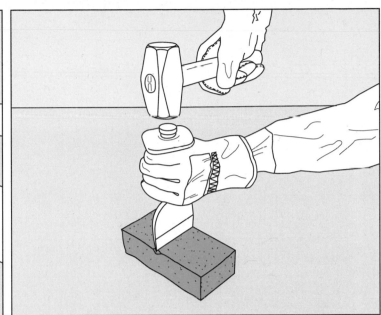

2 **Cutting a replacement brick.** To cut a replacement brick to fit, have extra bricks on hand; a clean cut may take more than one try. Measure and mark a cutting line on the top and the bottom of the brick. Wearing safety goggles and work gloves, start at one end of the cutting line on the top of the brick to score along it. Holding a brick chisel at a 45-degree angle to the surface, align a corner of its cutting edge with the cutting line and tap the handle with a hand drilling hammer, scoring to a depth of at least 1/8 inch *(above, left)*. Work to the other end of the cutting line the same way, then turn over the brick and repeat the procedure along the cutting line on the bottom of it. To cut the scored brick, hold the chisel perpendicular to the surface and align the cutting edge with the scored line; then, strike the handle once sharply with the hammer *(above, right)*. If the brick does not cut cleanly, repeat the procedure with another brick.

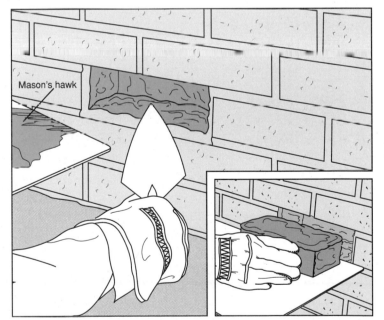

3 **Preparing the wall cavity.** To prevent the replacement brick from leaching moisture out of fresh mortar, soak it in a bucket of clean water. Wearing work gloves and safety goggles, use a cold chisel and ball-peen hammer or hand drilling hammer to chip any remaining old mortar out of the wall cavity *(above)*; work carefully to avoid damaging the adjacent bricks. Clean dust and loose particles out of the wall cavity using a stiff fiber brush, then wet the wall cavity thoroughly with clean water, applying it with a paintbrush or using the fine spray of a garden hose.

4 **Installing the replacement brick.** Wearing work gloves, mix a batch of mortar *(page 32)*. Use a pointing trowel to spread a 3/4-inch layer of the mortar on the back, sides and bottom of the wall cavity *(above)*, then on the top, sides and back of the brick. Holding the brick on a mason's hawk, align it with the wall cavity and slide it in *(inset)* until it is flush with the adjacent bricks; if necessary, tap it into place. If mortar does not squeeze out around the brick, the joint is too thin; remove the brick, add mortar to the wall cavity and the brick, then reinsert the brick. Repoint and strike the joints *(page 34)*.

WATERPROOFING AN EXTERIOR FOUNDATION WALL

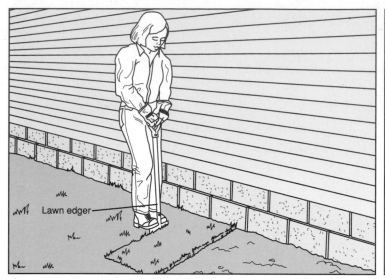

1 Excavating along the wall. Waterproof an exterior foundation wall if wetness in the basement persists after all other repairs have been made. Plan to dig a trench 3 feet wide along the wall and a few feet along the wall at each end of it to the depth of the foundation footing; wait for a dry period. Identify any utility entering the house along the wall and notify the utility company; the utility may need to be shut off. Also consult your municipal authorities about the need for any building permit. To excavate along the wall, first remove any sod or vegetation *(page 120)* adjacent to it, using a lawn edger to cut any sod into strips *(above, left)*. Lay plastic sheets on the ground to hold the soil excavated. Hire a backhoe operator *(page 122)* for the digging or use a spade to dig the trench yourself *(page 121)*, protecting it as necessary *(page 123)*. If you reach a layer of gravel at the foundation footing, work carefully to avoid damaging any drain tile under it. Starting at one end of the wall and working from the top of it to the footing, use a garden hose fitted with a pressure nozzle and a wire brush to clean off any dirt and particles. Continue to the other end of the wall the same way *(above, right)*; remove any stain *(page 112)*. Wearing safety goggles, use a cold chisel and a hand drilling hammer to chip any projections off the wall. Evaluate and repair any crack in the wall *(page 35)* and repoint any damaged mortar joint *(page 33)*. If necessary, replace any damaged drain tiles or install drain tiles to improve water drainage *(page 78)*.

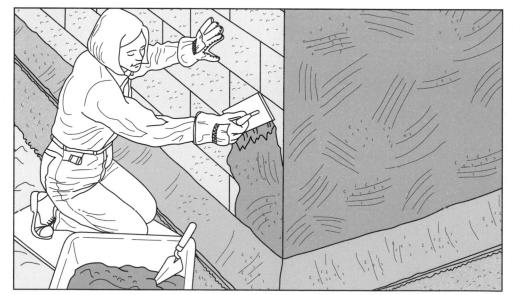

2 Building a cove. If there is a cove along the top of the footing to divert water away, parge the wall *(step 3)*. Otherwise, mix enough mortar *(page 32)* for a cove. Working along the wall, use a mason's trowel to pack mortar onto the footing, banking it up the wall to a height equal to the footing width *(above)*; smooth and slope it, making the cove slightly concave in shape. Allow the mortar to cure for at least 2 days, covering it with plastic until it cures to keep it moist.

3 Parging the wall. If the wall is protected by a waterproof coating or membrane, install polyethylene sheeting *(step 4)* or bentonite sheets *(step 6)*. Otherwise, first mix enough mortar *(page 32)* to parge the wall—covering it with a 1/4-inch layer of mortar. Use a garden hose to wet the wall, then work from one end to the other end of the wall from ground level to the footing using a rectangular trowel to spread the mortar *(above)*. Let the mortar harden enough to hold a thumbprint, then use chicken wire to scratch the surface, providing a base for a second coat. Let the mortar set for 24 hours, spraying it several times with a garden hose; then, apply the second coat of mortar the same way. Allow the mortar to cure for at least 2 days, covering it with plastic to keep it moist. To waterproof the wall, install polyethylene sheeting or bentonite sheets.

4 **Installing polyethylene sheeting.** Buy enough 6-mil polyethylene sheeting and cold-applied asphalt foundation coating for the job at a building supply center; plan to cover from ground level to the outside edge of the footing along the wall and 2 feet along the wall at each end of it. Wearing work gloves, use a mason's trowel to apply the asphalt coating *(above, left)*. Then, install the sheeting vertically, cutting continuous sections of it to length. Starting around the corner at one end of the wall, align a section of the sheeting at the top of the asphalt coating and press it into place, wrapping it snugly around the corner; smooth it down to the bottom of the wall and across the

footing. If necessary, slit the sheeting to fit at a wall obstruction, then seal it with asphalt coating. Continue along the wall and around the corner at the other end of it the same way, overlapping sections of the sheeting by 6 inches *(above, right)*; lift the overlap and apply a band of asphalt coating to the sheeting under it *(inset)* to seal the joint. After installing the sheeting, apply a band of asphalt coating along the top of it to seal the joint between it and the wall. If desired, protect the sheeting with rigid foam panels *(step 5)*. Otherwise, backfill the trench *(page 122)*, working carefully to avoid tearing the sheeting; then, put back any sod or vegetation you removed.

5 **Installing rigid foam panels.** Buy enough rigid foam panels at a building supply center to cover the sheeting on the walls; also an adhesive recommended for adhering them. Also buy aluminum or vinyl J-channel to hold the panels at the top of the sheeting. Wearing work gloves, work from one end to the other end along the top of the sheeting to position the J-channel and nail it *(page 117)* to the wall *(inset)*; if necessary, cut it to length using tin snips. Then, work from one end to the other end of the sheeting to install the panels one at a time between the J-channel and the footing. Trim each panel in turn to size with a utility knife, cutting it to fit around any wall obstruction. Apply adhesive along the edges on the back of the panel, then fit it between the J-channel and the footing, butting it against any adjacent panel and pressing it into place against the sheeting *(left)*. After installing the panels, apply a sealant *(page 115)* along the joint between the J-channel and the wall. Backfill the trench *(page 122)*, then put back any sod or vegetation you removed.

WATERPROOFING AN EXTERIOR FOUNDATION WALL (continued)

Bentonite sheet

6 **Installing a starter row of bentonite sheets.** Dig a narrow trench along the footing down to the bottom of it using a spade; work carefully to avoid damaging any drain tiles, removing them only if necessary *(page 78)*. Clean dirt and particles off the footing with a wire brush. Buy enough bentonite sheets and sealing compound for the job at a building supply center; plan to cover from ground level to the bottom edge of the footing along the wall and 2 feet along the wall at each end of it. Wearing work gloves, use a putty knife to apply a wide band of sealing compound along the joint between the footing and the wall. Then, install the sheets one at a time with the open-weave side against the wall; work with a helper and wear safety goggles. Install the first sheet of the starter row around the corner at one end of the wall *(step 7)*. To install the second sheet of the starter row, overlap the first sheet by a few inches and cut it to fit at any obstruction *(step 8)*, then use a hand drilling hammer to drive a masonry nail fitted with a washer through it into a mortar joint every 2 feet along the top edge and along the cove. Install the other sheets of the starter row the same way *(left)*, fitting the last sheet around the corner at the other end of the wall; then, install the upper rows of sheets *(step 9)*.

7 **Fitting a sheet of the starter row around a corner.** Position a sheet at one end of the wall with its long side aligned along the bottom of the footing and extended enough to lap 2 feet around the corner; if necessary, cut it to fit at an obstruction *(step 8)*. Smooth the sheet up and across the footing and up the wall, then fasten it *(page 117)*. Using a hand drilling hammer, drive a masonry nail fitted with a washer through the sheet into a mortar joint every 2 feet along the top edge and the side edge away from the corner as well as along the top of the footing. To fold the sheet around the corner, make a slit from its point at the bottom of the wall to its bottom corner using a utility knife. Fold the sheet around the corner and fasten it to the wall

and the footing the same way *(above, left)*. To cover the exposed footing, cut a section of a sheet large enough to overlap the edge of the sheet on each side of it by 6 inches. Fold the section around the exposed footing and make a slit from its point at the top of the footing to its top edge; fold the section on each side of the slit onto the top of the footing and up the wall, making slits as necessary for it to lie flat *(above, right)*. Use a putty knife to apply a band of sealing compound along the edges and each slit of the section *(inset)*, then fasten it to the top of the footing on each side of the corner. Install the other sheets of the starter row *(step 6)*, then fit a sheet around the corner at the other end of the wall the same way.

8 **Fitting a bentonite sheet at an obstruction.** Use a utility knife to cut a sheet to fit around an obstruction such as a pipe. Calculate the point on the sheet where the obstruction will intersect it, then cut to the point from the nearest edge of it. Position the sheet on the wall around the obstruction *(above, left)*, then trim it to fit snugly around the obstruction and lie flat against the wall. Using a hand drilling hammer, drive a masonry nail fitted with a washer through the sheet into a mortar joint every 2 feet along the top and side edges of it.

Use a putty knife to apply a thick band of sealing compound along the cut in the sheet and around the obstruction *(above, center)*. Then, cut a section of a sheet large enough to fit around the obstruction and cover the cut in the sheet around it. Calculate the point on the section where the obstruction will intersect it, then cut to the point from the nearest edge of it and position it; offset the cut in it from the cut in the sheet under it. Trim the section to fit snugly around the obstruction and lie flat on the wall, then fasten it to a mortar joint in the wall near each corner *(above, right)*.

9 **Installing upper rows of bentonite sheets.** Backfill the trench *(page 122)* against the starter row to a level 6 inches below the top of it, then install an upper row; if necessary, trim each sheet of the row to align it with ground level. Starting at one end of the wall, position a sheet with its bottom edge overlapping the row below it by a few inches and fold it around the corner with its side edges offset from the side edges of any sheet below it; cut it to fit at any obstruction *(step 8)*. To fasten the sheet, use a hand drilling hammer to drive a masonry nail fitted with a washer through it into a mortar joint every 2 feet along each edge of it *(left)*. To install the second sheet of the row, overlap the first sheet by a few inches and fasten it the same way. Install the other sheets of the row using the same procedure, fitting the last sheet around the corner at the other end of the wall. Backfill against the row and install another row, continuing until you reach ground level; fasten every 12 inches into a mortar joint along the top edge of the sheets of the last row. Then, put back any sod or vegetation you removed.

SLAB-ON-GRADE FOUNDATIONS

With a slab-on-grade foundation, a floor slab of cast concrete provides structural support for the house above it. A slab-on-grade foundation may support an entire house or it may support only a part of a house such as the garage. A slab-on-grade foundation has no basement or crawlspace under it since the floor slab rests directly on the soil near ground level. Although the floor slab typically is reinforced by steel mesh, the soil under it plays a vital role in supporting it; ideally, the soil is solidly packed and well drained. In regions where soil conditions are less than ideal, a slab-on-grade foundation is usually reinforced with steel reinforcing bars in its walls.

Two common types of slab-on-grade foundations are shown at right. The combined slab and wall type is used primarily in warm areas where there is little or no frost and no need for deep foundation footings; it supports all of the house framing that rests on it. The independent slab and wall type, commonly used in areas with a shallow frost line or wet soil, has walls and footings that are cast separately from the floor slab, permitting some independent movement of the walls and floor without cracking; the walls support the perimeter framing of the house and the slab supports the interior framing of the house.

Coldness, wetness and cracking are the most typical problems of a slab-on-grade foundation; although rarely more than minor irritants, they can be a sign of a serious problem—or become one if left unattended. Inspect the interior floor slab and the exterior walls of the slab routinely. Use the Troubleshooting Guide *(page 46)* to help you identify a problem and determine the repair or repairs necessary to remedy it. If there is a finished floor installed on top of the floor slab in your home, refer to the information presented in Basement Floors And Walls for gaining access to it *(page 67)*.

A cold floor slab is a common problem in cold regions; to reduce coldness, you can insulate the slab exterior *(page 51)*. If the slab surface is scaling or flaking or there are popouts in it, you can repair the surface damage *(page 47)*. However, a crack in the slab may be evidence of a serious structural problem, especially if it widens and narrows or is associated with any dislocation of the slab. Evaluate any crack in the slab you find *(page 48)*; consult a building professional about any crack that may indicate a structural problem. You can patch a hairline crack or a stationary open crack if it is dry *(page 49)*; if it is leaking, troubleshoot your drainage systems *(page 78)* and patch the crack only when it is dry.

Consult Tools & Techniques *(page 110)* for information on the tools needed for repairs to the slab-on-grade foundation of your home as well as for instructions on excavating and backfilling along the exterior of it. Homes in certain regions can be vulnerable to high levels of radon gas, a consequence of radium in the soil or groundwater under the floor slab; find out if you live in an area where radon gas is a problem and test for it *(page 119)*. Before undertaking any repair, familiarize yourself with the safety advice presented in the Emergency Guide *(page 8)*.

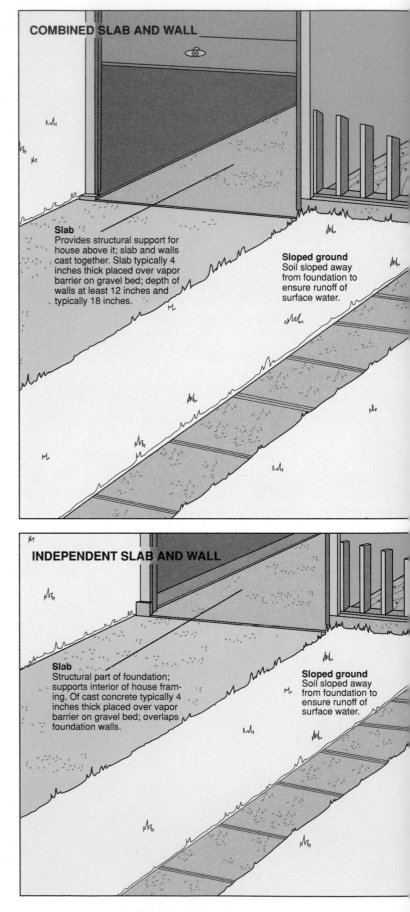

COMBINED SLAB AND WALL

Slab
Provides structural support for house above it; slab and walls cast together. Slab typically 4 inches thick placed over vapor barrier on gravel bed; depth of walls at least 12 inches and typically 18 inches.

Sloped ground
Soil sloped away from foundation to ensure runoff of surface water.

INDEPENDENT SLAB AND WALL

Slab
Structural part of foundation; supports interior of house framing. Of cast concrete typically 4 inches thick placed over vapor barrier on gravel bed; overlaps foundation walls.

Sloped ground
Soil sloped away from foundation to ensure runoff of surface water.

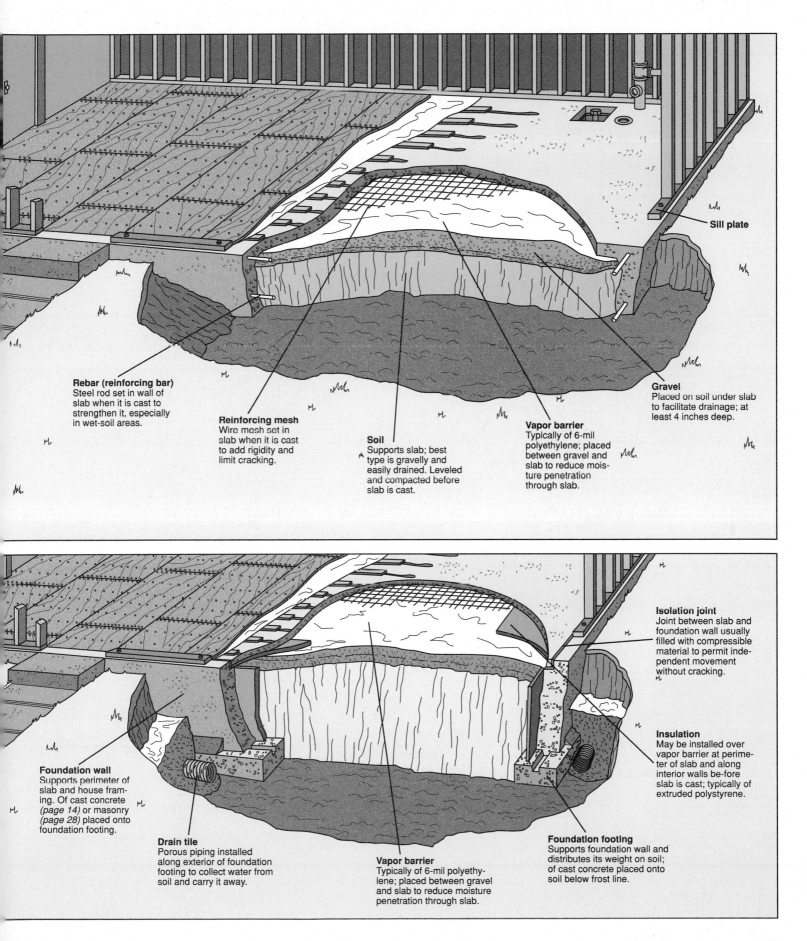

Rebar (reinforcing bar)
Steel rod set in wall of slab when it is cast to strengthen it, especially in wet-soil areas.

Reinforcing mesh
Wire mesh set in slab when it is cast to add rigidity and limit cracking.

Soil
Supports slab; best type is gravelly and easily drained. Leveled and compacted before slab is cast.

Vapor barrier
Typically of 6-mil polyethylene; placed between gravel and slab to reduce moisture penetration through slab.

Sill plate

Gravel
Placed on soil under slab to facilitate drainage; at least 4 inches deep.

Isolation joint
Joint between slab and foundation wall usually filled with compressible material to permit independent movement without cracking.

Insulation
May be installed over vapor barrier at perimeter of slab and along interior walls before slab is cast; typically of extruded polystyrene.

Foundation wall
Supports perimeter of slab and house framing. Of cast concrete (page 14) or masonry (page 28) placed onto foundation footing.

Drain tile
Porous piping installed along exterior of foundation footing to collect water from soil and carry it away.

Vapor barrier
Typically of 6-mil polyethylene; placed between gravel and slab to reduce moisture penetration through slab.

Foundation footing
Supports foundation wall and distributes its weight on soil; of cast concrete placed onto soil below frost line.

TROUBLESHOOTING GUIDE

SYMPTOM	POSSIBLE CAUSE	PROCEDURE
Slab floor flooded	Flood	Remove standing water using a submersible pump or a wet-dry vacuum
	Drainage system faulty	Troubleshoot drainage systems (p. 78)
Slab floor wet	Drainage system faulty	Troubleshoot drainage systems (p. 78)
	Leaking crack in slab	Evaluate crack (p. 48); if there is no structural problem, troubleshoot drainage systems (p. 78), then patch dry hairline crack (p. 49) □○ or stationary open crack (p. 49) □◗
	Leaking slab-wall joint (combined slab and wall type)	Evaluate crack (p. 48); if there is no structural problem, troubleshoot drainage systems (p. 78), then seal dry slab-wall joint (p. 50) □◗
Slab floor damp	Drainage system faulty	Troubleshoot drainage systems (p. 78)
	Moisture penetrating slab wall	Waterproof exterior concrete (p. 24) ■● or masonry (p. 40) ■● slab wall
	Moisture penetrating slab floor	Consult a building professional to damp-proof slab floor
Slab floor cold	Slab floor unfinished	If desired, install finished floor on slab floor
	Insulation inadequate	Insulate slab (p. 51) ■●
	Heating inadequate	Consult a building professional
Slab cracked; leaking	Drainage system faulty	Evaluate crack (p. 48); if there is no structural problem, troubleshoot drainage systems (p. 78), then patch dry hairline crack (p. 49) □○ or stationary open crack (p. 49) □◗ or seal dry slab-wall joint (p. 50) □◗
Slab cracked; no leaking	Concrete expansion and contraction; slab movement or settlement	Evaluate crack (p. 48); if there is no structural problem, patch hairline crack (p. 49) □○ or stationary open crack (p. 49) □◗ or seal slab-wall joint (p. 50) □◗
Hairline crack in slab; leaking	Drainage system faulty	Troubleshoot drainage systems (p. 78), then patch dry hairline crack (p. 49) □○
Hairline crack in slab; no leaking	Concrete expansion and contraction; slab movement or settlement	Patch hairline crack (p. 49) □○
Stationary open crack in slab; leaking	Drainage system faulty	Troubleshoot drainage systems (p. 78), then patch dry stationary open crack (p. 49) □◗
Stationary open crack in slab; no leaking	Concrete expansion and contraction; slab movement or settlement	Patch stationary open crack (p. 49) □◗
Moving open crack in slab; leaking or no leaking	Seasonal concrete expansion/contraction; slab movement or settlement	Consult a building professional
Control joint in slab cracked; leaking	Drainage system faulty	Evaluate crack (p. 48); if there is no structural problem, troubleshoot drainage systems (p. 78), then seal dry crack with an elastomeric sealant for concrete
Control joint in slab cracked; no leaking	Concrete expansion and contraction; slab movement or settlement	Evaluate crack (p. 48); if there is no structural problem, seal crack with an elastomeric sealant for concrete
Slab-wall joint (combined slab and wall type) open; leaking	Drainage system faulty	Troubleshoot drainage systems (p. 78), then seal dry slab-wall joint (p. 50) □◗
Slab-wall joint (combined slab and wall type) open; no leaking	Concrete expansion and contraction; slab movement or settlement	Seal slab-wall joint (p. 50) □◗
Slab scaling or flaking (surface peeling)	Normal concrete expansion and contraction; faulty concrete installation and curing	Repair slab surface (p. 47) □◗
Slab popouts (shallow surface holes)	Expansion of gravel near concrete surface due to freezing	Repair slab surface (p. 47) □◗
Slab dusting (fine, powdery dust)	Normal concrete aging; faulty concrete installation and curing	Treat dusting slab floor (p. 47) □◗
Slab dirty or stained	Wear and tear; mildew due to excess moisture or water penetration	Clean slab floor (p. 57) □○
Slab efflorescence (white, powdery deposits)	Leaching of salts due to excess moisture	Clean slab floor (p. 57) □○

DEGREE OF DIFFICULTY: □ Easy ■ Moderate ■ Complex
ESTIMATED TIME: ○ Less than 1 hour ◗ 1 to 3 hours ● Over 3 hours

TREATING A DUSTING FLOOR

Floor hardener

Applying a floor hardener. To treat a dusting slab floor, apply a commercial concrete floor hardener containing zinc or magnesium fluosilicate or sodium silicate (water glass); buy it at a building supply center. To prepare the floor, clean it *(page 57)* and remove any stain *(page 112)*. Wearing work gloves and safety goggles, use a cold chisel and a ball-peen hammer to chip off any protuberances. Evaluate and repair any crack *(page 48)*; repair any surface scaling, flaking or popouts *(steps below)*. Wearing rubber gloves, prepare the hardener following the manufacturer's instructions. Pour a small amount of the hardener into a container, then use a paintbrush to apply a wide band of it on the floor along the edge of each wall or post footing; avoid coating any isolation joint. To coat the rest of the floor, pour the hardener into a roller tray and use a long-nap roller fitted onto an extension pole. Applying firm pressure, roll the hardener in overlapping strips back and forth onto a section of the floor at a time, working it into the concrete pores. Continue the same way *(left)* until the floor is coated evenly. Allow the hardener to cure for the time specified by the manufacturer; follow any recommendations for additional coats and follow-up treatment.

REPAIRING THE FLOOR SURFACE

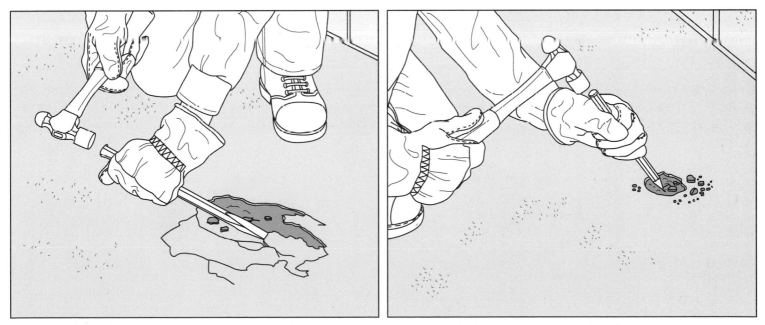

1 **Preparing the surface for patching.** To prepare a scaling or flaking floor surface for patching, use a cold chisel and a ball-peen hammer. Wearing work gloves and safety goggles, hold the chisel at a low angle to the surface to break up any loose or crumbling concrete *(above, left)* and chisel out a flat-bottomed depression; make it slightly larger than the damaged surface, cutting the sides straight to a depth of at least 1/4 inch. To prepare a popout in the floor surface for patching, follow the same procedure to chisel out a depression, first using a bull-point chisel and the hammer to chip out any exposed gravel at the bottom of it *(above, right)*. Use a stiff fiber brush to clean dirt and particles out of the depression, then vacuum it. Buy a latex concrete patching compound at a building supply center; if recommended by the manufacturer, also a bonding agent.

REPAIRING THE FLOOR SURFACE (continued)

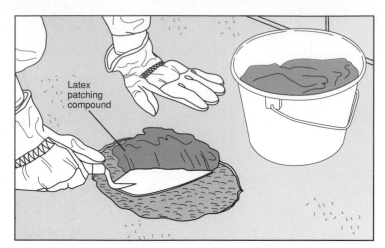

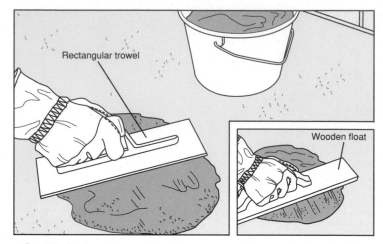

2 **Applying patching compound.** If recommended by the patching compound manufacturer, soak the depression with water. If a bonding agent is recommended by the patching compound manufacturer, wear rubber gloves and apply an even coat of it into the depression with an old paintbrush; allow it to set for the time specified. Prepare the patching compound following the manufacturer's instructions, mixing it to a thick consistency that does not run. Wearing work gloves, use a mason's trowel to patch the depression, packing the compound into it *(above)* and overfilling it slightly.

3 **Finishing the patch.** Use a rectangular trowel to level and smooth the patch. Keeping the trowel almost flat on the surface, pull it across the patch, lightly feathering the patching compound at the edges of the patch *(above)*. If desired, texture the patch to match any floor texture; working across the patch, draw a wooden float *(inset)* or the bristle tips of a whisk broom lightly over it. Allow the patching compound to cure for the time specified by the manufacturer; mist with water when it lightens at the edges and keep plastic taped over it until it cures.

EVALUATING AND MONITORING A SLAB CRACK

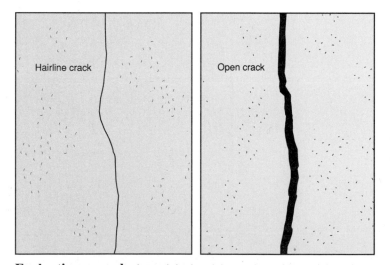

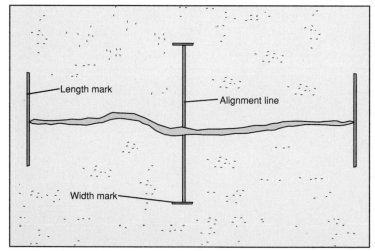

Evaluating a crack. A crack in the slab may be evidence of a structural problem and must be evaluated carefully. A crack is a sign of movement, usually from foundation settlement or concrete expansion and contraction with temperature fluctuations. Closely inspect the edges of any crack. A hairline crack *(above, left)* or an open crack *(above, right)* is usually not serious if its edges are up to 1/16 inch apart and level with each other. However, a crack can be serious if its edges are more than 1/16 inch apart or slope away or toward each other. Consult a building professional *(page 119)* for any serious or questionable crack; also for any crack that appears suddenly—after an earthquake or nearby excavation, for example. When you determine that a crack is not serious, troubleshoot the drainage systems if it is leaking *(page 78)* or patch it if it is dry and hairline *(page 49)*; otherwise, monitor it *(step right)*.

Monitoring a crack. Monitor a dry, open crack in the slab to determine if it can be repaired or should be examined by a building professional. To monitor a crack, mark it using a felt-tipped pen: a length mark at each end of it; a width mark at the center on each side of it; and an alignment line between the width marks at a 90-degree angle across it *(above)*. Measure and record the distance between the width marks, then monitor the crack monthly over a 6- to 12-month period; brush out particles that keep it open. Consult a building professional *(page 119)* if: the distance between the width lines increases by more than 1/16 inch; the crack alternately widens and narrows; points of the alignment line shift or deflect; or a crack 3 feet or longer extends in length by more than 1/4 of the distance between the length marks. Otherwise, patch the crack as a stationary crack *(page 49)*.

PATCHING A HAIRLINE CRACK

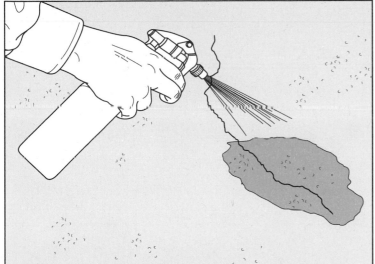

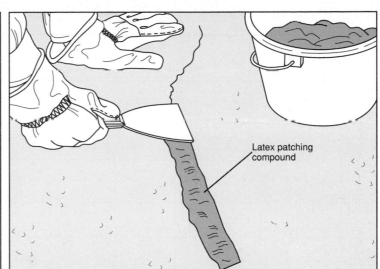

Latex patching compound

Applying patching compound. Evaluate the crack to ensure that there is no structural problem *(page 48)*. To prepare the crack for patching, use a stiff fiber brush to clean out dirt and particles; remove any stain *(page 112)*. Buy a latex concrete patching compound at a building supply center; if recommended by the manufacturer, also a bonding agent. If you are applying a bonding agent, wear rubber gloves and apply an even coat of it into the crack with an old paintbrush; allow it to set for the time specified. Prepare enough of the patching compound for the job, mixing it to a thin consistency that can be worked to a feather-edge; if recommended by the patching compound manufacturer, soak the crack with water *(above, left)*. Wearing work gloves, start at one end of the crack and use a putty knife to patch a section of it at a time with the patching compound. Draw the putty knife across the crack, using the tip of it to press in the patching compound; overfill the crack slightly. Continue the same way along the crack *(above, right)* to the other end of it. Then, draw the putty knife along the patch to scrape off excess compound and smooth it flush with the floor. Allow the patching compound to cure for the time specified by the manufacturer; mist it with water when it lightens at the edges and keep plastic taped over it until it cures.

PATCHING A STATIONARY OPEN CRACK

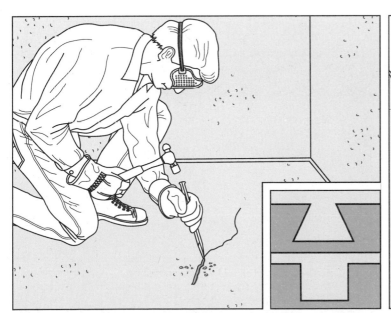

1 Preparing the crack for patching. Evaluate the crack to ensure that there is no structural problem *(page 48)*. To prepare the crack for patching, use a cold chisel and a ball-peen hammer. Wearing work gloves and safety goggles, chisel any loose or crumbling concrete off the edges of the crack. Then, use the chisel and hammer to widen the crack to 1/4 inch and deepen it to 1/2 inch. Starting at one end of the crack, chisel in turn along each edge *(above,* left*)*, undercutting it, if possible *(inset, top)*, or cutting it straight *(inset, bottom)*; avoid tapering the edges toward each other into a V-shaped groove. Use a stiff fiber brush to clean dirt and particles out of the crack *(above, right)*; remove any stain *(page 112)*. Buy a latex concrete patching compound at a building supply center; if recommended by the manufacturer, also a bonding agent.

PATCHING A STATIONARY OPEN CRACK (continued)

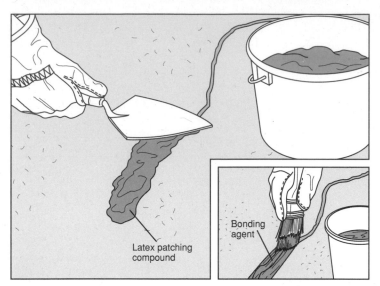

Latex patching compound

Bonding agent

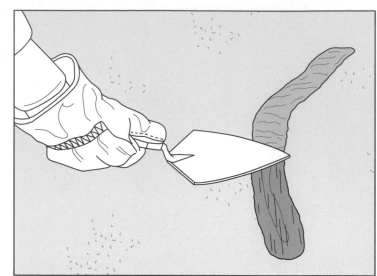

2 **Applying patching compound.** If a bonding agent is recommended by the patching compound manufacturer, wear rubber gloves and use an old paintbrush to spread an even coat of it into the crack *(inset)*; allow it to set for the time specified. If a wet surface is recommended by the patching compound manufacturer, soak the crack with water. Prepare enough of the patching compound for the job following the manufacturer's instructions, mixing it to a thick consistency that does not run. Wearing work gloves, use a pointing trowel to patch a section of the crack at a time, packing the patching compound into it *(above)* and overfilling it slightly.

3 **Finishing the patch.** Working from one end to the other end of the patch, draw the edge of the pointing trowel along it, scraping off excess patching compound. Then, draw the back of the trowel along the patch to smooth it flush with the floor *(above)*; use a slight curving motion. If desired, texture the patch to match any floor texture; working from one end to the other end of it, draw a wooden float or the bristle tips of a whisk broom lightly over it. Allow the patching compound to cure for the time specified by the manufacturer; mist it with water when it lightens at the edges and keep plastic taped over it until it cures.

SEALING A SLAB-WALL JOINT

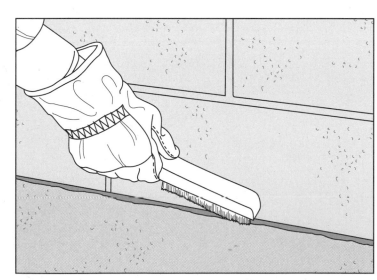

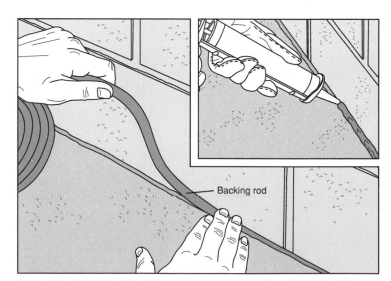

Backing rod

1 **Preparing the joint.** For any crack or gap more than 1/4 inch wide along the joint, consult a building professional *(page 119)*. If the joint is leaking, troubleshoot your drainage systems *(page 78)* and undertake any repair necessary; seal the joint only when it is dry. To prepare the joint for sealing, use a cold chisel and a ball-peen hammer. Wearing work gloves and safety goggles, chisel any loose or crumbling concrete off the edges of the joint; cut straight along the edges, avoiding tapering them into a V-shaped groove. Use a stiff fiber brush to clean dirt and particles out of the joint *(above)*; remove any stain *(page 112)*.

2 **Sealing the joint.** Buy an elastomeric sealant for concrete at a building supply center; use a urethane type. If the joint is more than 1/2 inch deep, fill it to within 1/4 inch of the surface with foam backing rod *(above)*; if it is between 1/4 and 1/2 inch deep, use waxed paper. Load a caulking gun with the sealant *(page 115)*. Starting at one end of the joint, hold the caulking gun at a 45-degree angle to the floor and squeeze the trigger, ejecting a continuous bead of sealant *(inset)*. Draw the wet edge of a putty knife along the patch, scraping off excess sealant and smoothing it flush with the floor surface. Allow the sealant to cure.

INSULATING THE SLAB

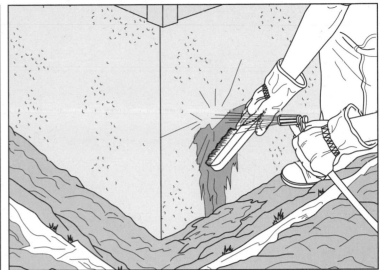

1 **Preparing to insulate the slab.** Insulate the exterior foundation walls around the perimeter of the slab to reduce coldness in the floor. Plan to dig a trench 1 foot wide along each wall down to the base of it; wait for a dry period. Identify any utility entering the house along a wall and notify the utility company; the utility may need to be shut off. To excavate along a wall, first remove any sod or vegetation *(page 120)* adjacent to it. Lay plastic sheets on the ground to hold the soil excavated. Hire a backhoe operator *(page 122)* for the digging or dig the trench yourself *(page 121)* using a spade *(above, left)*, protecting it as necessary *(page 123)*. If you reach a layer of gravel, work carefully to avoid damaging any drain tile under it. When the trench is

dug, work along each wall in turn from the top to the bottom of it using a garden hose fitted with a pressure nozzle and a wire brush to clean off any dirt and particles *(above, right)*. Wearing safety goggles, use a cold chisel and a hand drilling hammer to chip any protuberances off the wall. If the wall is of concrete, evaluate and repair any crack in it as you would a crack in the slab *(page 48)*. If the wall is of masonry, evaluate any crack *(page 35)* and repair only a stationary crack with edges up to 1/16 inch apart; otherwise, consult a building professional *(page 119)*. If necessary, replace any damaged drain tiles or install drain tiles to improve water drainage *(page 78)*.

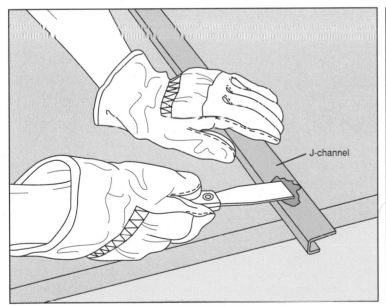

J-channel

Notch

2 **Installing the J-channel.** If a kit of finished rigid-foam insulation panels is available at your local building supply center, buy it and follow the manufacturer's instructions to install the panels. Or, buy enough extruded polystyrene-foam insulation panels for the job and an adhesive recommended for adhering them to the walls; plan to cover each wall from the base of it up to the bottom edge of any siding or masonry above it. Also buy aluminum or vinyl J-channel to hold the panels and an adhesive recommended for adhering it to the walls. Wearing work gloves, work in turn along the top of each wall from one

end to the other end of it to install the J-channel. Use a putty knife to coat the back of the J-channel with adhesive *(above, left)*, then press it into place at the top of the wall, butting it snugly against the bottom edge of the siding or masonry above it. At a corner, cut a J-channel section to fit flush with the edge of one wall using tin snips and press it into place. Notch the back of another J-channel section *(inset)* to fit flush with the first J-channel section and the edge of the other wall, then press it into place *(above, right)*.

INSULATING THE SLAB (continued)

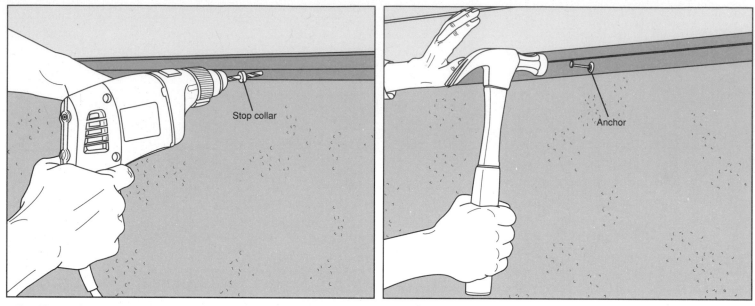

3 **Fastening the J-channel.** To fasten the J-channel to the wall, use plastic nail anchors *(page 117)*. To drill holes for the anchors, use an electric drill fitted with a masonry bit and a stop collar; work only in dry conditions and plug the drill into an outlet protected by a GFCI (ground-fault circuit interrupter). Wearing work gloves and safety goggles, work in turn along each wall from one end to the other end of it to drill a hole for an anchor every 2 feet through the J-channel *(above, left)*; if the wall is of masonry, avoid drilling at a mortar joint. Use a hammer to tap an anchor into each hole, then drive a nail into each anchor *(above, right)*.

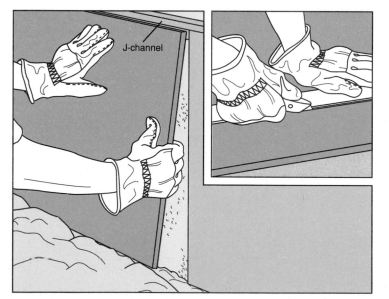

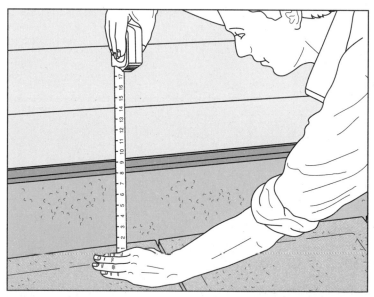

4 **Installing the insulation panels.** Working in turn along each wall from one end to the other end of it, install the insulation panels one at a time between the J-channel and the bottom of the wall. Trim each panel in turn to size, cutting it to fit around any wall obstruction; score it using a straightedge and a utility knife *(inset)*, then snap it along the scored line. Apply adhesive along the edges on the back of the panel (the side with writing), then fit it between the J-channel and the bottom of the wall, butting it against any adjacent panel *(above)* and pressing it against the wall. Where a surface such as a patio, walk or driveway butts the wall, fit panels above ground *(step 5)*; at each end of the wall, fit panels at the corner *(step 6)*.

5 **Fitting insulation panels above ground.** Where a surface such as a patio, walk or driveway butts the wall, install insulation panels above ground along it. Measure the distance from the surface to the J-channel *(above)* and subtract 1 inch, then cut as many panels as necessary to size; score each panel using a straightedge and a utility knife, then snap it along the scored line. To hold the bottom of the panels, use J-channel; install *(step 2)* and fasten *(step 3)* it along the wall 1/2 inch above the surface, then fill the gap between it and the ground with foam backing rod. Work along the wall to install each panel, applying adhesive along the edges on the back of it and fitting it between the J-channels, butted snugly against any adjacent panel.

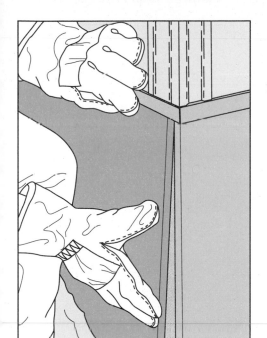

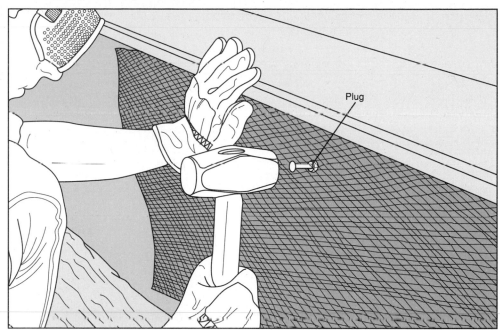

Plug

6 **Fitting insulation panels at a corner.** At a corner, cut an insulation panel to fit flush with the edge of one wall and install it *(step 4)*. Install another panel on the wall on the other side of the corner the same way, applying adhesive along the edges on the back of it and fitting it between the J-channels, then butting it snugly against the back of the first panel *(above)*.

7 **Installing lath.** Finish the above-ground portion of the panels. If a brushable coating is available at your local building supply center, buy it and follow the manufacturer's instructions to apply it. Or, install lath and parge it. Buy enough corrosion-resistant metal stucco lath for the job; also self-furring nails to fasten it *(page 117)*. Wearing work gloves and safety goggles, install the lath vertically, using tin snips to cut continuous sections of it to length. Working in turn along each wall from one end to the other end, fit the top of a section into the J-channel and overlap any adjacent section by 4 inches, then install a self-furring nail every 16 inches along it in rows 16 inches apart. To install a self-furring nail, position the plug behind the section and use a hand drilling hammer to drive the nail into it *(above)*.

Mason's hawk

8 **Parging the lath.** Work in turn along each wall from one end to the other end to parge the lath—covering it with mortar. Prepare a sufficient quantity of mortar *(page 114)* for parging, then wet the wall using a garden hose and work along it from the bottom to the top of the lath to apply the mortar with a rectangular trowel *(left)*. Let the mortar harden enough to hold a thumbprint, then use a scrap piece of lath to scratch the surface, providing a base for a second coat. Let the mortar set for 24 hours, spraying it several times with a garden hose. Then, apply a second coat of mortar 1/4 inch thick the same way. When the second coat of mortar hardens enough to hold a thumbprint, texture the surface: drawing a rectangular trowel across it for a smooth texture; a wooden float or the bristle tips of a whisk broom for a rough texture. Allow the mortar to cure for at least 2 days, covering it with plastic to keep it moist. Apply a sealant *(page 115)* along the joint between the J-channel and the wall at the top of the mortar *(inset)*, then backfill the trench *(page 122)* and put back any sod or vegetation you removed.

BASEMENT FLOORS AND WALLS

A foundation set in the soil below the frost line usually encloses a basement; in regions where the frost line is not far below ground level, there may be only a crawlspace *(page 68)*. A typical basement is shown at right; the floor, the interior of the foundation walls and the structural wood that supports the house are its bare bones. Although the floor can be of soil, it is usually a slab of cast concrete placed over a vapor barrier on a gravel bed with its perimeter resting on the foundation footings. The walls typically are of concrete or masonry. Joints isolating the floor from the walls and the post footings are designed to permit independent movement and settling of surfaces, minimizing cracking; control joints are designed to contain cracking. Openings in the walls for pipes, cables, vents and windows are sealed against the elements and pests.

Wetness and cracks are the most common problems of a basement; although in most instances they are not causes for strong concern, they can be a symptom of a serious problem—or become one if the needed repairs are not undertaken. Routinely check the basement of your home for cracks and wetness. To help you identify a problem and the steps to take to remedy it, use the Troubleshooting Guide in this chapter *(page 56)*; for the foundation walls, also the Troubleshooting Guide in Concrete Foundations *(page 14)* or Masonry Foundations *(page 28)*. If your basement is finished, refer to the information presented in this chapter on gaining access for basement repairs *(page 65)*.

Superficial cracking and pitting of a concrete floor is normal; if desired, you can resurface it *(page 64)*. However, a wide crack or a crack associated with a dislocation of the floor or foundation wall may be serious. Evaluate any crack in the floor you find *(page 61)*; consult a building professional about any crack that may indicate a structural problem. You can plug a leaking crack *(page 63)*, but for any wetness or dampness problem, you should troubleshoot your drainage systems *(page 78)*. Painting the basement floor and walls *(page 59)* can help ease humidity, but if moisture seepage from outdoors is the problem, the paint is likely to peel off.

Consult Tools & Techniques *(page 110)* for information on the tools needed for repairs to your basement, as well as for guidance on consulting a building professional when you require expert technical assistance *(page 119)*. The basements of homes in certain regions can be vulnerable to high levels of radon gas, a consequence of radium in the soil or groundwater under the floor and around the walls; find out if you live in an area where radon gas is a problem and test for it *(page 119)*. Before undertaking a basement repair, familiarize yourself with the safety advice presented in the Emergency Guide *(page 8)*.

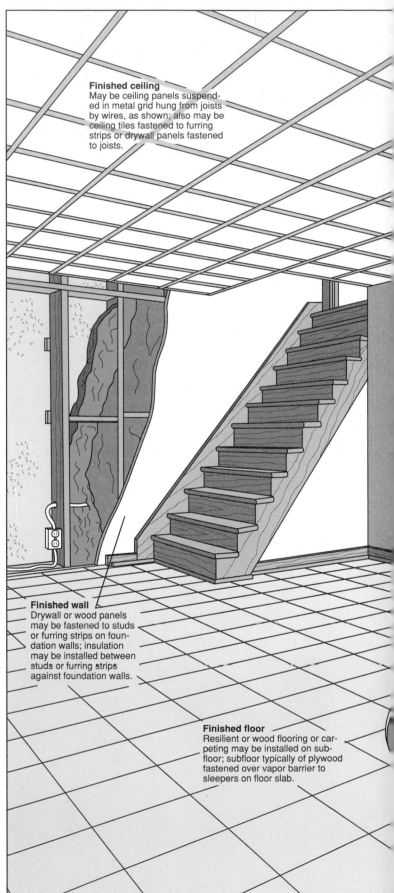

Finished ceiling
May be ceiling panels suspended in metal grid hung from joists by wires, as shown; also may be ceiling tiles fastened to furring strips or drywall panels fastened to joists.

Finished wall
Drywall or wood panels may be fastened to studs or furring strips on foundation walls; insulation may be installed between studs or furring strips against foundation walls.

Finished floor
Resilient or wood flooring or carpeting may be installed on subfloor; subfloor typically of plywood fastened over vapor barrier to sleepers on floor slab.

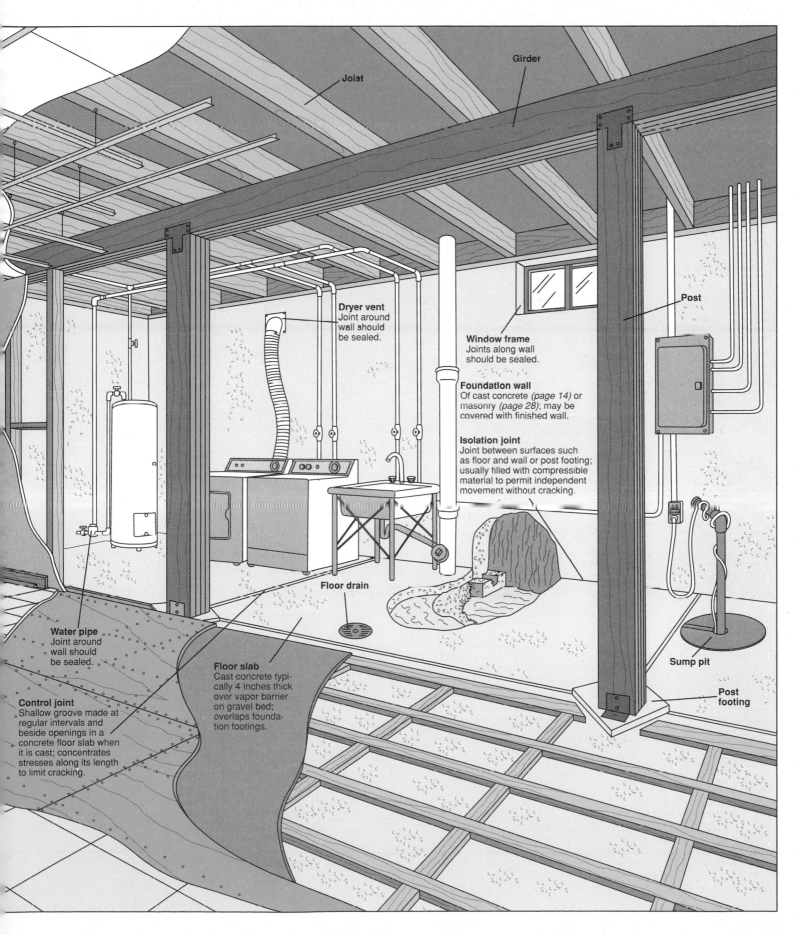

Joist

Girder

Post

Dryer vent
Joint around
wall should
be sealed.

Window frame
Joints along wall
should be sealed.

Foundation wall
Of cast concrete *(page 14)* or
masonry *(page 28)*; may be
covered with finished wall.

Isolation joint
Joint between surfaces such
as floor and wall or post footing;
usually filled with compressible
material to permit independent
movement without cracking.

Floor drain

Sump pit

**Post
footing**

Water pipe
Joint around
wall should
be sealed.

Control joint
Shallow groove made at
regular intervals and
beside openings in a
concrete floor slab when
it is cast; concentrates
stresses along its length
to limit cracking.

Floor slab
Cast concrete typi-
cally 4 inches thick
over vapor barrier
on gravel bed;
overlaps founda-
tion footings.

TROUBLESHOOTING GUIDE

SYMPTOM	POSSIBLE CAUSE	PROCEDURE
Basement flooded	Flood; drainage system faulty	Remove standing water (p. 58) □●▲ ; troubleshoot drainage systems (p. 78)
Basement wet	Leaking joint at window or dryer vent	Seal joint at wall opening (p. 60) □○
	Leaking wall-floor joint	Seal wall-floor joint (p. 64) □◖; if necessary, gain access (p. 65) ◨◖
	Leaking crack in floor slab	Plug leaking crack (p. 63) □◖; if necessary, gain access (p. 65) ◨◖
	Leaking crack in foundation wall	Troubleshoot concrete (p. 14) or masonry (p. 28) foundation; if necessary, gain access (p. 65) ◨◖
	Drainage system faulty	Troubleshoot drainage systems (p. 78)
Basement damp	Soil floor	Install vapor barrier (p. 57) □◖
	Floor slab damp	Paint floor (p. 59) □◖
	Foundation wall damp	Troubleshoot concrete (p. 14) or masonry (p. 28) foundation; if necessary, gain access (p. 65) ◨◖
	Drainage system faulty	Troubleshoot drainage systems (p. 78)
Foundation wall wet, damp or cracked	Foundation wall faulty	Troubleshoot concrete (p. 14) or masonry (p. 28) foundation; if necessary, gain access (p. 65) ◨◖
Floor slab cracked; leaking	Concrete expansion and contraction; foundation movement or settlement	Evaluate crack (p. 61); if there is no structural problem, plug leaking crack (p. 63) □◖
	Drainage system faulty	Troubleshoot drainage systems (p. 78)
Floor slab cracked; no leaking	Concrete expansion and contraction; foundation movement or settlement	Evaluate crack (p. 61); if there is no structural problem, patch stationary open crack (p. 62) □◖ or moving open crack (p. 63) □◖
Stationary open crack in floor slab; leaking	Concrete expansion and contraction; foundation movement or settlement	Plug leaking crack (p. 63) □◖
	Drainage system faulty	Troubleshoot drainage systems (p. 78)
Stationary open crack in floor slab; no leaking	Concrete expansion and contraction; foundation movement or settlement	Patch stationary open crack (p. 62) □◖
Moving open crack in floor slab; leaking	Seasonal concrete expansion/contraction; foundation movement or settlement	Plug leaking crack (p. 63) □◖
	Drainage system faulty	Troubleshoot drainage systems (p. 78)
Moving open crack in floor slab; no leaking	Seasonal concrete expansion/contraction; foundation movement or settlement	Patch moving open crack (p. 63) □◖
Control joint in floor cracked; leaking	Concrete expansion and contraction; foundation movement or settlement	Evaluate crack (p. 61); if there is no structural problem, plug leaking crack (p. 63) □◖
	Drainage system faulty	Troubleshoot drainage systems (p. 78)
Control joint in floor cracked; no leaking	Concrete expansion and contraction; foundation movement or settlement	Evaluate crack (p. 61); if there is no structural problem, seal crack with an elastomeric sealant for concrete
Wall-floor joint open	Concrete expansion and contraction; foundation movement or settlement	Seal wall-floor joint (p. 64) □◖
Floor slab pitted or flaking; superficial hairline cracks	Normal concrete expansion and contraction; faulty concrete installation and curing	Resurface concrete floor (p. 64) □◖
Foundation wall or floor slab dirty or stained	Wear and tear; mildew due to excess moisture or water penetration	Clean concrete (p. 17) □○ or masonry (p. 31) □○ wall; clean concrete floor (p. 57) □○
Foundation wall or floor slab efflorescence (white, powdery deposits)	Leaching of salts due to excess moisture	Clean concrete (p. 17) □○ or masonry (p. 31) □○ wall; clean concrete floor (p. 57) □○
Painted foundation wall or floor slab peeling, flaking or powdery	Moisture penetrating foundation wall or floor slab	Troubleshoot concrete (p. 14) or masonry (p. 28) foundation and drainage systems (p. 78)
	Failure of paint due to age	Scrape off old paint and paint walls and floor (p. 59) □◖
Unpainted floor slab dusting (fine, powdery dust)	Normal concrete aging; faulty concrete installation and curing	Treat dusting floor (p. 59) □◖

DEGREE OF DIFFICULTY: □ Easy ◨ Moderate ■ Complex
ESTIMATED TIME: ○ Less than 1 hour ◖ 1 to 3 hours ● Over 3 hours ▲ Special tool required

INSTALLING A VAPOR BARRIER

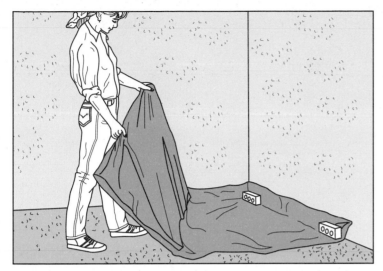

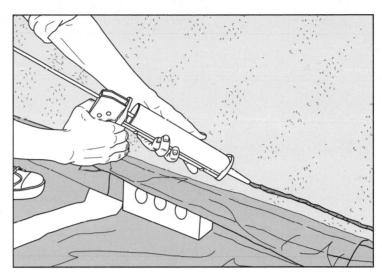

1 Installing polyethylene. Buy enough 6-mil polyethylene sheeting at a building supply center to cover the floor; if it is heavily trafficked, plan to install a double layer of sheeting. Level the soil of the floor using a spade and a garden rake. Use a utility knife to cut sections of sheeting long enough to lap 6 inches up the walls; trim any section to fit at an obstruction such as a post footing. Working one section of sheeting at a time, lay it flat on the floor and lapped up the walls, holding down the ends of it with bricks *(above)*. Continue the same way, overlapping sections of sheeting by 12 inches. Seal the seams between overlapping sections of sheeting and the edges of the sheeting at obstructions with duct tape.

2 Adhering the polyethylene. Adhere the sheeting to the walls using a construction-grade adhesive. Load a caulking gun with adhesive *(page 115)* and start at one end of a wall, folding back the sheeting to apply adhesive behind it. Holding the caulking gun at a 45-degree angle to the wall, squeeze the trigger to eject a continuous bead of adhesive along it *(above)*. Smooth the sheeting up the wall and press it evenly into the adhesive. Continue along the wall to the other end of it, then work in turn along the other walls the same way. If necessary, install a second layer of sheeting *(step 1)* and adhere it using the same procedure. Protect the sheeting by laying panels of exterior-grade plywood on it for walkways and to support heavy objects.

CLEANING THE FLOOR

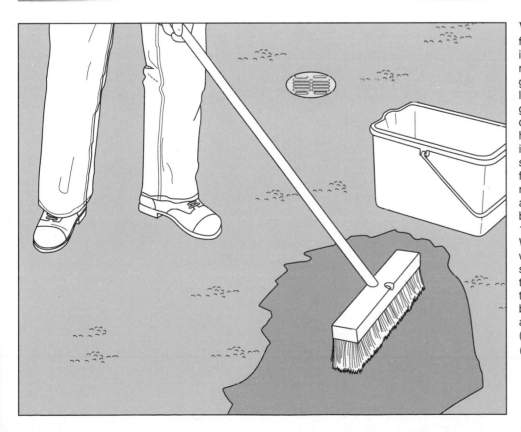

Washing off dirt and stains. Sweep the floor using a stiff-bristled push broom; if the floor is not painted, also soak it with water. Wearing rubber gloves and safety goggles, mix as many gallons of cleaner as needed in a bucket. For light dirt, mix a little household detergent per gallon of water; for tough grime, mix 1/2 cup of TSP (trisodium phosphate) and 1/2 cup of household detergent per gallon of water. Working section by section, use the push broom to scrub the solution onto the floor *(left)*; when the floor is clean, rinse it with clean water. For any remaining stain, choose an appropriate cleaning agent *(page 112)*. For example, to clean stubborn efflorescence off the floor, mix a solution of 1 part muriatic acid to 12 parts water. **Caution:** Wear a respirator and pour the acid into the water; never pour water into acid. Working on a small section at a time, wet the floor with water to keep the solution from penetrating too deeply, then scrub the solution onto it using a stiff nylon brush and rinse it with clean water. Neutralize any leftover solution with sodium bicarbonate (baking soda). If necessary, repaint the floor *(page 59)*.

REMOVING STANDING WATER

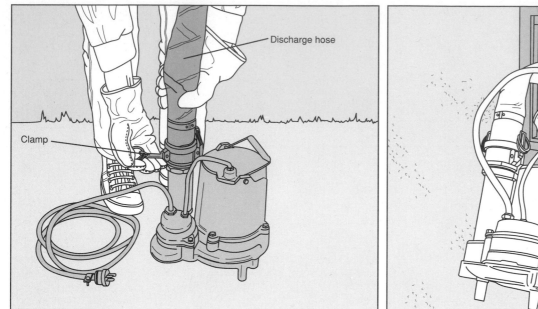

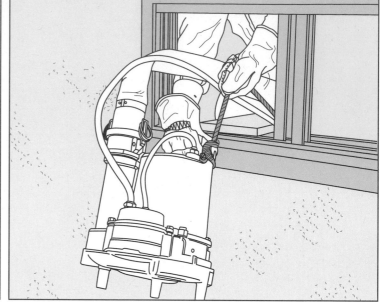

Using a submersible pump. To remove 2 inches or less of standing water, use a wet-dry vacuum *(step below, left)* or a mop. Otherwise, use a submersible pump, available at a tool rental agency; rent a discharge hose long enough to reach to an outdoor municipal storm drain. Wearing rubber gloves, set up the pump following the manufacturer's instructions, pushing the discharge hose onto the discharge pipe and clamping it *(above, left)*. Tie a rope to the handle, then lower the pump into the water through an open window *(above, right)* until it sits level on the floor. Position the discharge hose at the storm drain, then plug the pump into a dry GFCI-protected outlet and turn it on. **Caution:** Do not touch the pump or enter the basement while the pump is operating. Turn off the pump when it no longer sucks up water. Remove any remaining standing water with a wet-dry vacuum or a mop, then clean up any mud and debris *(step below, right)*.

Using a wet-dry vacuum. To remove more than 2 inches of standing water, use a submersible pump *(step above)*. Otherwise, use a mop or a wet-dry vacuum, available at a tool rental agency. Wearing rubber gloves, rubber boots and an anti-bacterial mask, set up the vacuum following the manufacturer's instructions, pushing the intake hose onto the intake fitting. Keeping the power cord and any extension cord out of the water, plug the vacuum into a dry GFCI-protected outlet and turn it on. Work the nozzle back and forth across the floor *(above)* until the standing water is removed; turn off and unplug the vacuum to empty the tank. Then, clean up any mud and debris *(step right)*.

Removing mud and debris. Wearing rubber gloves, rubber boots and an anti-bacterial mask, push the mud and debris into a pile with a push broom, then use a shovel to scoop it up and deposit it in a trash can lined with a plastic garbage bag *(above)*. Fill the bag only halfway, then knot it and take it out of the can. Continue the procedure until the mud and debris is removed. Using a solution of 1 cup household bleach per gallon of water, clean the floor *(page 57)*; if necessary, also clean the concrete *(page 17)* or masonry *(page 31)* walls. Dispose of the bags filled with mud and debris according to the regulations of your local municipality and ventilate the basement thoroughly.

TREATING A DUSTING FLOOR

Isolation joint

Floor hardener

Applying a floor hardener. To treat a dusting floor, apply a commercial concrete floor hardener containing zinc or magnesium fluosilicate or sodium silicate (water glass); buy it at a building supply center. To prepare the floor, clean it *(page 57)* and remove any stain *(page 112)*. Wearing work gloves and safety goggles, use a cold chisel and a ball-peen hammer to chip off any protuberances. Evaluate and repair any crack *(page 61)*. Wearing rubber gloves, prepare the hardener following the manufacturer's instructions. Pour a small amount of the hardener into a container, then use a paintbrush to apply a wide band of it on the floor along the edge of each wall *(above, left)* or post footing; avoid coating any isolation joint. To coat the rest of the floor, pour the hardener into a roller tray and use a long-nap roller fitted onto an extension pole. Applying firm pressure, roll the hardener in overlapping strips back and forth onto a section of the floor at a time, working it into the concrete pores. Continue the same way *(above, right)* until the floor is coated evenly. Allow the hardener to cure for the time specified by the manufacturer; follow any recommendations for additional coats and follow-up treatment.

PAINTING FLOORS AND WALLS

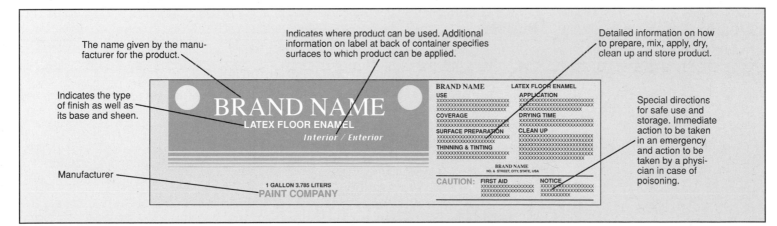

The name given by the manufacturer for the product.

Indicates where product can be used. Additional information on label at back of container specifies surfaces to which product can be applied.

Detailed information on how to prepare, mix, apply, dry, clean up and store product.

Indicates the type of finish as well as its base and sheen.

Special directions for safe use and storage. Immediate action to be taken in an emergency and action to be taken by a physician in case of poisoning.

Manufacturer

1 Choosing a paint. Choose an appropriate paint for the surface. For any painted surface, buy an identical type of paint; for an unpainted surface, buy a paint suitable for it and any sealer or primer recommended by the manufacturer. When buying a paint, read the label carefully *(above)*. Ensure that the paint is marked for use on concrete or masonry; for a floor, ensure it is labeled as a floor paint. Choose a paint of a type that can provide the performance and appearance you want: in general, a latex paint on a dry or damp surface for easy application, short drying time and easy clean-up with water; an alkyd paint on a dry surface for greater durability and easier cleaning when dry; a urethane paint on a dry surface for an extremely durable finish that resists scratching; a cementitious paint (a powder that is mixed with water or liquid latex) on a damp surface to help damp-proof it. Check the clean-up information on the paint label; buy enough of the paint solvent to clean your tools and any spills. Apply the paint *(step 2)*, following all safety precautions on the label.

PAINTING FLOORS AND WALLS (continued)

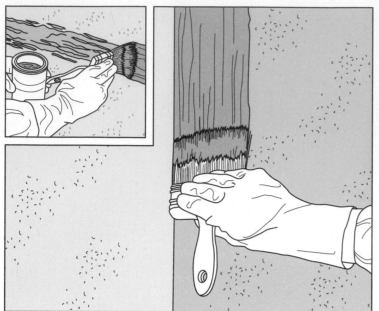

2 **Preparing and painting surfaces.** Clean the floor *(page 57)* and the concrete *(page 17)* or masonry *(page 31)* walls; remove any stain *(page 112)*. Wearing work gloves and safety goggles, use a cold chisel and a ball-peen hammer to chip off any protuberances. Scrape off any loose or peeling old paint with a putty knife. Evaluate and repair any crack in the floor *(page 61)* or a concrete *(page 18)* or masonry *(page 35)* wall. Wearing rubber gloves, apply a stain-blocking primer on any water-stained surface using a paintbrush *(inset)*; allow it to dry. Protect surfaces not to be painted with dropcloths or newspapers. Ensuring that the work area is well-ventilated, prepare the paint and any primer recommended for it following the manufacturer's instructions; apply the primer as you would the paint, then let it dry. For a cementitious paint, use a tampico fiber brush to spread it onto a section of the surface at a time and work it into the pores. For another type of paint, use a paintbrush and a long-nap roller fitted onto an extension pole. Using the paintbrush, apply a band of paint along each edge of the surface *(above, left)*; also brush it onto any depression, working the bristles into any gap or pores. Use the roller to complete the job. Starting at a corner, apply firm pressure to roll the paint in overlapping strips onto a section of the surface at a time, working it into the pores; then, roll back over it to smooth it. Continue the same way *(above, right)* until the surface is evenly coated, then paint any other surface using the same procedure. Allow the paint to dry; if necessary, apply another coat.

SEALING A JOINT AT A WALL OPENING

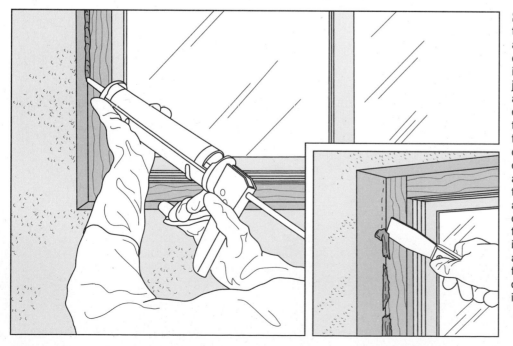

Sealing a narrow joint. Seal a joint wider than 1/4 inch with foam sealant *(page 61)*. For a narrower joint at a window, for example, buy a caulk recommended for the materials at a building supply center. Pry any old caulk out of the joint with a putty knife *(inset)*, then clean it using a stiff fiber brush and wipe it dry. If the joint is deeper than 1/2 inch, fill it to within 1/4 inch of the surface using foam backing rod, pressing it firmly into place. Wearing rubber gloves, load a caulking gun with caulk *(page 115)*. Starting at one end of the joint, hold the gun at a 45-degree angle to it. Press the tip of the caulk tube into the joint and squeeze the gun trigger, moving along the joint to eject a continuous bead of caulk into it *(left)*. Run a wet gloved finger along the caulk to press it into the joint, smoothing it into a slightly concave shape. Seal the exterior above-ground portion of the joint the same way; for any exterior below-ground portion of it, dig down using a spade *(page 121)* and apply roofing cement.

SEALING A JOINT AT A WALL OPENING (continued)

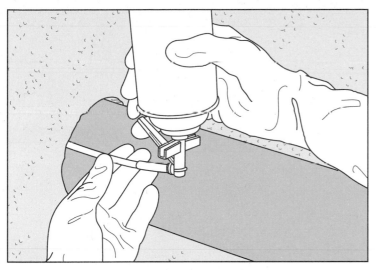

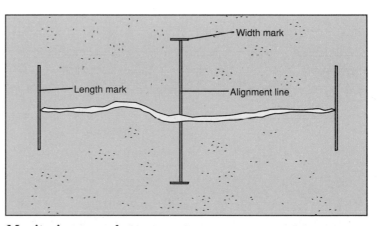

Sealing a wide joint. Seal a joint up to 1/4 inch in width with caulk *(page 60)*. For a wider joint at a dryer vent, for example, buy a foam sealant at a building supply center. Pry any old sealant out of the joint with a putty knife, then clean it using a stiff fiber brush and wipe it dry. Ensuring that the work area is well-ventilated, wear rubber gloves and safety goggles to apply the sealant. Holding the container upside down, fit the dispenser tube into the joint and depress the trigger, filling the joint to the level recommended. Allow the sealant to cure, then cut off any excess with a utility knife. Seal the exterior above-ground portion of the joint the same way; for any exterior below-ground portion of it, dig down using a spade *(page 121)* and apply roofing cement.

Pest-proofing a joint. To pest-proof a joint at a dryer vent, for example, seal it *(step left)*, then install a flange around the vent; buy sheet metal for a flange at a building supply center. Mark a circle equal to the vent diameter at the center of the metal, then mark a circle 2 inches smaller than the vent diameter concentric to the first circle. Wearing work gloves, punch a starter hole in the smaller circle and use tin snips to cut along its marked outline *(inset)*. Cut V-shaped notches between the cutout edge of the smaller circle and the marked outline of the larger circle to form tabs. Bend up the tabs with pliers, then fit the flange on the vent. Fasten the flange at each corner to the wall *(page 117)* and drive a sheet metal screw through each tab into the vent *(above)*.

EVALUATING AND MONITORING A FLOOR CRACK

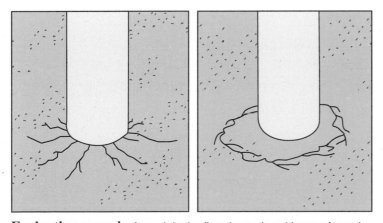

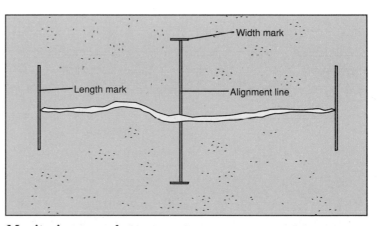

Evaluating a crack. A crack in the floor is rarely evidence of a serious structural problem; however, it must be evaluated carefully. A crack in the floor is a sign of movement, usually from foundation settlement or concrete expansion and contraction with temperature fluctuations. Closely inspect the edges and location of any crack in the floor. A crack is usually not serious if its edges are up to 1/4 inch apart and level with each other. However, a crack can be serious if its edges are more than 1/4 inch apart, slope away or toward each other, extend up a wall, or radiate from *(above, left)* or encircle *(above, right)* a post. Consult a building professional *(page 119)* for any serious or questionable crack; also for a crack that appears suddenly—after an earthquake or nearby excavation, for example. When you determine that a crack is not serious, plug it if it is leaking *(page 63)*; otherwise, monitor it *(step right)*.

Monitoring a crack. Monitor a dry, open crack in the floor to determine if it should be repaired as a stationary or moving crack. To monitor a crack in the floor, mark it using a felt-tipped pen: a length mark at each end of the crack; a width mark at the center on each side of the crack; and an alignment line between the width marks at a 90-degree angle across the crack *(above)*. Measure and record the distance between the width marks, then monitor the crack monthly over a 6- to 12-month period; brush out particles that keep it open. Consult a building professional *(page 119)* if: the distance between the width lines increases by more than 1/8 inch; points of the alignment line shift or deflect; or a crack 3 feet or longer extends in length by more than 1/4 of the distance between the length marks. Otherwise, patch the crack as a stationary crack *(page 62)* if it is stable; as a moving crack *(page 63)* if it widens and narrows.

PATCHING A STATIONARY OPEN CRACK

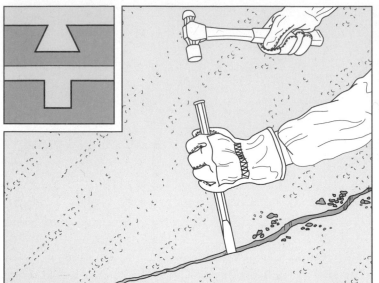

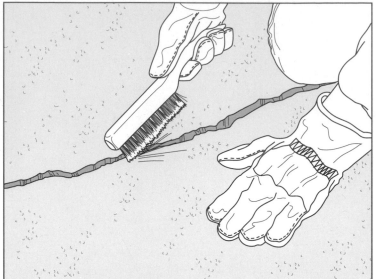

1 **Preparing the crack for patching.** Evaluate the crack to ensure that there is no structural problem *(page 61)*. To prepare the crack for patching, use a cold chisel and ball-peen hammer. Wearing work gloves and safety goggles, chisel any loose or crumbling concrete off the edges of the crack. Then, use the chisel and hammer to widen the crack to 1/4 inch and deepen it to 1/2 inch. Starting at one end of the crack, chisel in turn along each edge *(above, left)*, undercut-

ting it, if possible *(inset, top)*, or cutting it straight *(inset, bottom)*; avoid tapering the edges toward each other into a V-shaped groove. Use a stiff fiber brush to clean dirt and particles out of the crack *(above, right)*; remove any stain *(page 112)*. Buy a latex concrete patching compound at a building supply center; if recommended by the manufacturer, also a bonding agent.

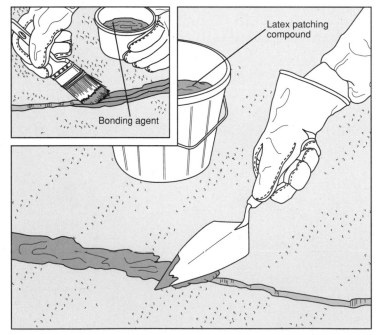

Latex patching compound

Bonding agent

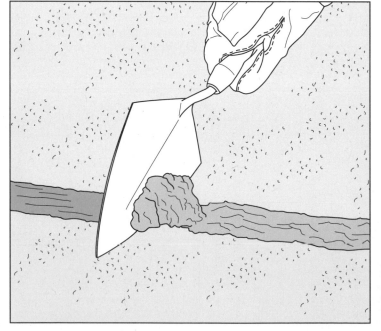

2 **Applying patching compound.** If recommended by the patching compound manufacturer, soak the crack with water. If a bonding agent is recommended by the patching compound manufacturer, wear rubber gloves and apply an even coat of it into the crack with an old paintbrush *(inset)*; allow it to set for the time specified. Prepare the patching compound following the manufacturer's instructions, mixing it to a thick consistency that does not run. Wearing work gloves, use a pointing trowel to patch a section of the crack at a time, packing the patching compound into it *(above)* and overfilling it slightly.

3 **Finishing the patch.** Working from one end to the other end of the patch, draw the edge of the pointing trowel along it, scraping off excess patching compound *(above)*. Then, draw the back of the trowel along the patch to smooth it flush with the floor; use a slight curving motion. If desired, texture the patch to match any floor texture; working from one end to the other end of it, draw the bristle tips of a whisk broom lightly over it. Allow the patching compound to cure for the time specified by the manufacturer; mist it with water when it lightens at the edges and keep plastic taped over it until it cures.

PATCHING A MOVING OPEN CRACK

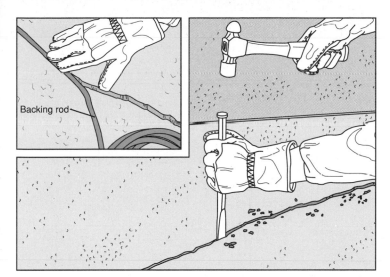

1 Preparing the crack. Evaluate the crack to ensure that there is no structural damage *(page 61)*. Wearing work gloves and safety goggles, use a cold chisel and a ball-peen hammer to chip loose or crumbling concrete off the edges of the crack, then to widen and deepen the crack to at least 1/4 inch. Cut straight along each edge *(above)*; avoid tapering the edges into a V-shaped groove. Use a stiff fiber brush to clean dirt and particles out of the crack; remove any stain *(page 112)*. Buy an elastomeric sealant for concrete at a building supply center; use a urethane type. If the crack is more than 1/2 inch deep, fill it to within 1/4 inch of the surface with foam backing rod *(inset)*. If the crack is between 1/4 and 1/2 inch deep, use waxed paper to fill it to within 1/4 inch of the surface.

2 Applying sealant. Load a caulking gun with elastomeric sealant *(page 115)*. Starting at one end of the crack, hold the caulking gun at a 45-degree angle to the floor. Push the tip of the sealant tube into the crack and squeeze the gun trigger, moving along the crack to eject a continuous bead of sealant into it *(above)*. Continue until you reach the other end of the crack. If necessary, repeat the procedure to fill the crack until it is flush with the floor surface. While the sealant is still pliable, smooth the patch using the wet blade of a putty knife. Draw the edge of the putty knife along the patch, scraping off excess sealant and smoothing it flush with the floor surface. Allow the sealant to cure for the time specified by the manufacturer, following any instructions or recommendations provided on its label.

PLUGGING A LEAKING CRACK

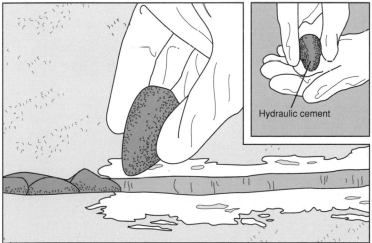

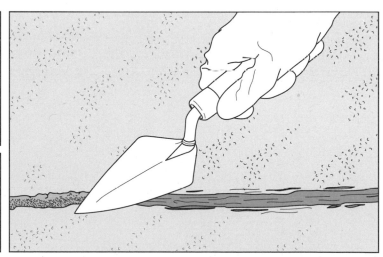

Applying hydraulic cement. Evaluate the crack to ensure that there is no structural problem *(page 61)*. Prepare the crack for patching as you would a stationary open crack *(page 62)*, widening and deepening it to at least 3/4 inch. Buy hydraulic cement at a building supply center; wearing rubber gloves, follow the manufacturer's instructions to mix a sufficient quantity of it for the job. Starting at the driest end of the crack, use your gloved hands to mold a small amount of the cement into a cone-shaped plug *(inset)*, then press it into the crack and hold it in place for a moment to ensure it sets. Continue the same way along the crack *(above, left)* to the point of heaviest leakage, leaving it unfilled; work back to it from the other end of the crack the same way. Then, press a plug of cement into the crack at the unfilled point and hold it until it sets—usually about three minutes. Working from one end to the other end of the patch, use a putty knife to scrape off excess cement and smooth it flush with the floor *(above, right)*. Troubleshoot your drainage systems *(page 78)*; if leaking recurs, suspect a drainage problem under the floor slab and consult a building professional *(page 119)*.

SEALING A WALL-FLOOR JOINT

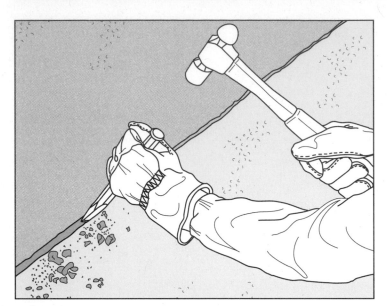

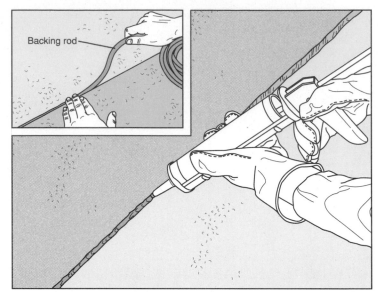

Backing rod

1 Preparing the joint. For any crack or gap more than 1/4 inch wide along the joint, consult a building professional *(page 119)*. If the joint is leaking, troubleshoot your drainage systems *(page 78)* and undertake any repair necessary; seal the joint only when it is dry. To prepare the joint for sealing, use a cold chisel and a ball-peen hammer. Wearing work gloves and safety goggles, chisel any loose or crumbling concrete off the edges of the joint *(above)*; cut straight along the edges, avoiding tapering them toward each other into a V-shaped groove. Use a stiff fiber brush to clean dirt and particles out of the joint; remove any stain *(page 112)*.

2 Sealing the joint. Buy an elastomeric sealant for concrete at a building supply center; use a urethane type. If the joint is more than 1/2 inch deep, fill it to within 1/4 inch of the surface with foam backing rod *(inset)*; if it is between 1/4 and 1/2 inch deep, use waxed paper. Load a caulking gun with the sealant *(page 115)*. Starting at one end of the joint, hold the caulking gun at a 45-degree angle to the floor and squeeze the trigger, ejecting a continuous bead of sealant *(above)*. Draw the wet edge of a putty knife along the patch, scraping off excess sealant and smoothing it flush with the floor surface. Allow the sealant to cure.

RESURFACING THE FLOOR

Slurry

1 Preparing the floor. To prepare the floor for resurfacing, clean it *(page 57)* and remove any stain *(page 112)*. Wearing work gloves and safety goggles, use a cold chisel and a ball-peen hammer to chip off any protuberances. Evaluate and repair any crack *(page 61)*. Mark the location of any control joint in the floor on the wall at the end of it. Buy enough latex concrete patching compound at a building supply center to apply a 1/8-inch layer on the floor. If a bonding agent is recommended by the patching compound manufacturer, use a commercial type or prepare a cement slurry *(page 114)* and apply it. Wet the floor with water, then use a push broom to apply a thin, even coat of the slurry onto a section of the floor at a time *(left)*, working it into any hairline cracks; avoid coating any joint between the floor and a wall or a post footing.

RESURFACING THE FLOOR (continued)

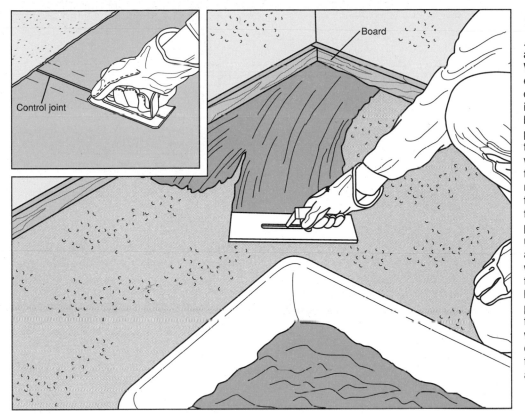

2 Applying patching compound.
Prepare the patching compound following the manufacturer's instructions and apply it while the bonding agent is damp. Wearing work gloves, use a rectangular trowel to resurface a section of the floor at a time, covering it with a 1/8-inch layer of the patching compound. To avoid covering any joint between a section of the floor and a wall or a post footing, protect it with a board. Spread the patching compound evenly and smoothly with the trowel, keeping it almost flat against the surface *(left)*. If you cover a control joint, recut it using a jointer with a cutting edge of the same size as the original joint. Position the jointer at one end of the original joint and pull it along the patching compound *(inset)* using the original joint as a guide. Continue applying the patching compound the same way until the floor is covered. If desired, texture the surface by drawing the moistened bristles of a broom lightly across it. Allow the patching compound to cure for the time specified by the manufacturer; mist it with water when it lightens and keep plastic sheeting over it until it cures. Seal any joint between the floor and a wall or a post footing with an elastomeric sealant.

GAINING ACCESS FOR BASEMENT REPAIRS

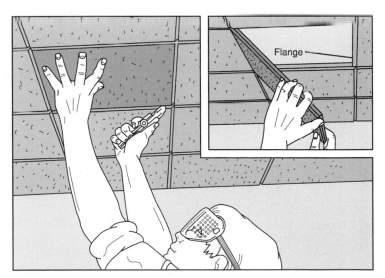

Removing a suspended ceiling panel. To remove a suspended ceiling panel, wear safety goggles and stand on a stepladder. Gently push up the panel with both hands to free it from the grid. Holding the panel by its long edges, turn it sideways and tilt it at an angle *(above)*, sliding its short edge out along the long edge of the grid. Handle the panel carefully; its edges are easily nicked. Remove as many panels as necessary to gain access for a repair. To remove a grid, unscrew its wires from the joists.

Removing a stapled ceiling tile. To remove a stapled ceiling tile, wear safety goggles and stand on a stepladder. For a tile at a wall edge, take off any trim covering it. Cut through the flange along each edge of the tile using a utility knife *(above)*, fitting the blade in turn into each joint and working along it. Then, pry out the tile *(inset)*; if it does not pull out easily, work it out with a putty knife. To remove any remaining flange, pry the staples out of it using an old screwdriver. Remove as many tiles as necessary to gain access for a repair.

GAINING ACCESS FOR BASEMENT REPAIRS (continued)

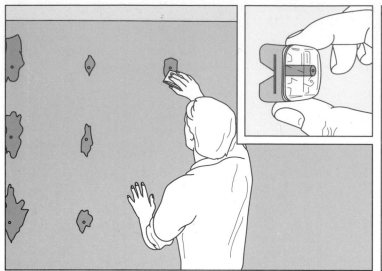

Removing a drywall panel. To remove a drywall panel from the ceiling, stand on a stepladder. Locate the studs or joists behind the panel by tapping along it and listening for a change from a hollow to a solid sound every 16 inches; or, slide a stud finder *(inset, above left)* along the panel until it signals a fastener. Sand along the stud or joist with medium sandpaper until you expose a fastener; use a utility knife to dig out the compound covering it. Continue along the stud or joist at 8-inch intervals, the usual spacing for fasteners, until you find the panel edges—indicated by joint tape. Use the same procedure on succeeding studs or joists *(above, left)* until you find the other two panel edges, then strip off the joint tape. Take off any trim covering the panel. With

a helper holding the panel, remove the fasteners; for nails, use a hammer and a nail set to drive them through the panel *(inset, above right)*. To pry out the panel, wedge a pry bar under an edge of it against a stud or joist; continue along the edge of it until a corner of it can be held securely by hand. With a firm grip on the panel, pull it away from the studs *(above, right)* or joists, jimmying it back and forth if necessary to free it. A panel at an inside corner requires careful attention: on a wall, lift out the edge farthest from the corner, then slide out the edge at the corner; on a ceiling, pull down the edge farthest from the corner, then slide out the edge at the wall. Remove as many panels as necessary to gain access for a repair.

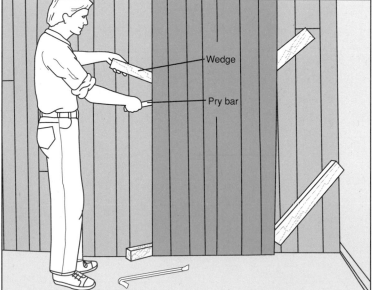

Removing a wood panel. To remove a wood panel, determine how it is fastened by rapping on it: a hollow sound signals studs or furring strips; otherwise, it is probably glued and will need to be ripped off in pieces. Take off any trim covering the panel. Inspect the grooves of the panel for nails. If the heads of the nails are small, use a hammer and a nail set to drive them through the panel *(inset)*; otherwise, use a pry bar to pull them out. Work a putty knife into the joint at the edge of the panel near a bottom corner of it, then insert a wedge behind it. Slip a pry bar behind the panel *(above, left)* and work along the edge of it to

pry it out; use the same procedure at the other bottom corner of the panel, continuing along the edges of it *(above, right)*. Watch for any nail still holding the panel; drive it through the panel or pull out the panel carefully to dislodge it. If you cannot easily pull out the panel, it may be glued in place; cut it with a handsaw and remove it in pieces, if necessary. Otherwise, stand on a stepladder and pull the panel free; if nails still hold the center of it, reach behind it with a piece of scrap wood to pry it out. Remove as many panels as necessary to gain access for a repair.

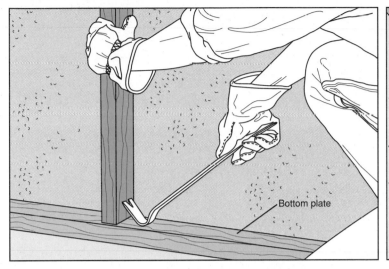

Removing a stud or furring strip. To remove a stud, grip it firmly and use a pry bar to pull out the nails holding the bottom of it to the bottom plate *(above, left)*; if necessary, fit a piece of scrap wood under the pry bar for added leverage. Stand on a stepladder to pull out the nails holding the top of the stud to the top plate or joist, then pull out the stud; if necessary, knock it with a hammer. Remove as many studs as necessary to gain access for a repair. To take off a bottom plate, work a putty knife in turn along its edge on the floor and against the wall to break any seal. If the bottom plate is nailed to the floor, work it up with a pry bar, then hammer it down to lift the nail heads; pull out the nails, then lift out the bottom plate. To remove a furring strip that is nailed, pull out the nails the same way; hold the furring strip securely against the wall to keep it from breaking. To remove a furring strip that is glued, work a putty knife into the joint between it and the wall, then insert a wedge behind it. Slip a pry bar behind the furring strip and work along it to pry it out *(above, right)*. Remove as many furring strips as necessary to gain access for a repair.

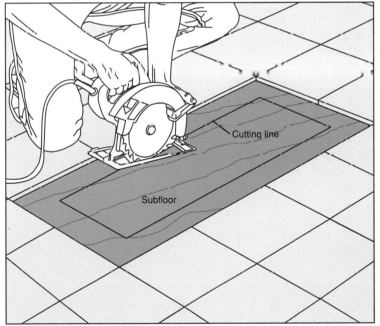

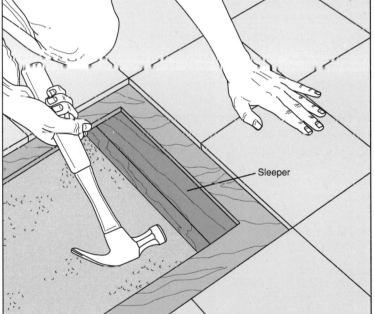

Removing a subfloor section. Remove the flooring material to expose the subfloor; use a utility knife to cut out any building paper on it. Use a carpenter's square to mark cutting lines along the edges of the subfloor section to be removed; mark at the center of sleepers using the nails in the subfloor as a guide. Pull the nails out of the subfloor section. Prepare to use a circular saw, setting its cutting depth equal to the subfloor thickness: typically 5/8 inch if it is of plywood; 3/4 inch if it is of board. Wearing safety goggles, make a plunge cut at a cutting line *(above, left)*, then continue along to the end of it; reverse the saw direction and use the same procedure to cut to the other end of it. Cut along the other cutting lines the same way, then use a pry bar to lift out the subfloor section. Use a utility knife to cut out any vapor barrier in the opening; if necessary, cut out and remove sleepers. To reinforce a cut edge of the subfloor not supported by a sleeper, cut a piece of pressure-treated wood of the same dimensions as a sleeper to fit under it. Fit the piece into the opening and use a hammer to center it under the cut edge *(above, right)*, then fasten it to the floor *(page 117)*.

CRAWLSPACES

A foundation set in the soil below the frost line usually encloses a full basement *(page 54)*; however, especially in regions where the frost line is not far below ground level, there may be only a crawlspace—an area under the first story of the house usually between 18 inches and 3 feet high. A house can have a crawlspace that is fully enclosed or open on one side to a full basement. A typical crawlspace is shown at right; the interior of the foundation walls and the structural wood that supports the house above it are its bare bones.

The floor of a crawlspace may be of soil or a slab of cast concrete placed over a vapor barrier on a gravel bed with its perimeter resting on the foundation footings. The walls of a crawlspace typically are of concrete or masonry. Electrical wiring, plumbing pipes and heating ducts may run through the crawlspace; openings in the walls for cables, pipes and ducts are sealed against water and pests. A crawlspace may house a furnace which heats only the upper stories of the house by means of ducts; or, the furnace may heat the crawlspace which then heats the upper stories of the house by means of openings in the ceiling.

Wetness, coldness and cracks are the most common problems of a crawlspace; although in most instances they are not causes for strong concern, they can be a symptom of a serious problem—or become one if the needed repairs are not undertaken. Routinely check the crawlspace of your home for cracks and wetness. To help you identify a problem and the steps to take to remedy it, use the Troubleshooting Guide in this chapter *(page 70)*; for the foundation walls, also use the Troubleshooting Guide in Concrete Foundations *(page 14)* or Masonry Foundations *(page 28)*. If you do not have access to the crawlspace under your house, refer to the information presented in this chapter on installing a trapdoor *(page 76)*.

If the crawlspace is damp or cold, install a vapor barrier on the floor if it is of soil *(page 73)*. Also check that the crawlspace ventilation is adequate; if necessary, install additional vents *(page 71)* and replace damaged vents *(page 72)*. For any wetness or dampness problem, you should also troubleshoot your drainage systems *(page 78)*. If coldness persists in the crawlspace with a vapor barrier, install insulation of the R-value recommended for use in your area: on the ceiling if the crawlspace is unheated *(page 75)*; on the walls if the crawlspace is heated *(page 74)*. If there is any risk of water pipes in the crawlspace freezing, consult a building professional for the best insulation procedure.

Refer to Tools & Techniques *(page 110)* for information on the tools needed for repairs to your crawlspace, as well as for guidance on consulting a building professional when you require expert technical assistance *(page 119)*. The crawlspaces of homes in certain regions can be vulnerable to high levels of radon gas, a consequence of radium in the soil or groundwater under the floor and around the walls; find out if you live in an area where radon gas is a problem and test for it *(page 119)*. Before undertaking a repair, familiarize yourself with the safety advice presented in the Emergency Guide *(page 8)*.

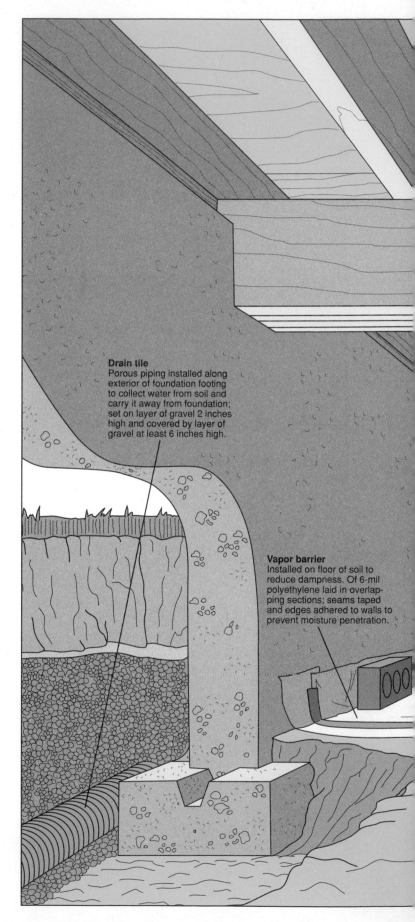

Drain tile
Porous piping installed along exterior of foundation footing to collect water from soil and carry it away from foundation; set on layer of gravel 2 inches high and covered by layer of gravel at least 6 inches high.

Vapor barrier
Installed on floor of soil to reduce dampness. Of 6-mil polyethylene laid in overlapping sections; seams taped and edges adhered to walls to prevent moisture penetration.

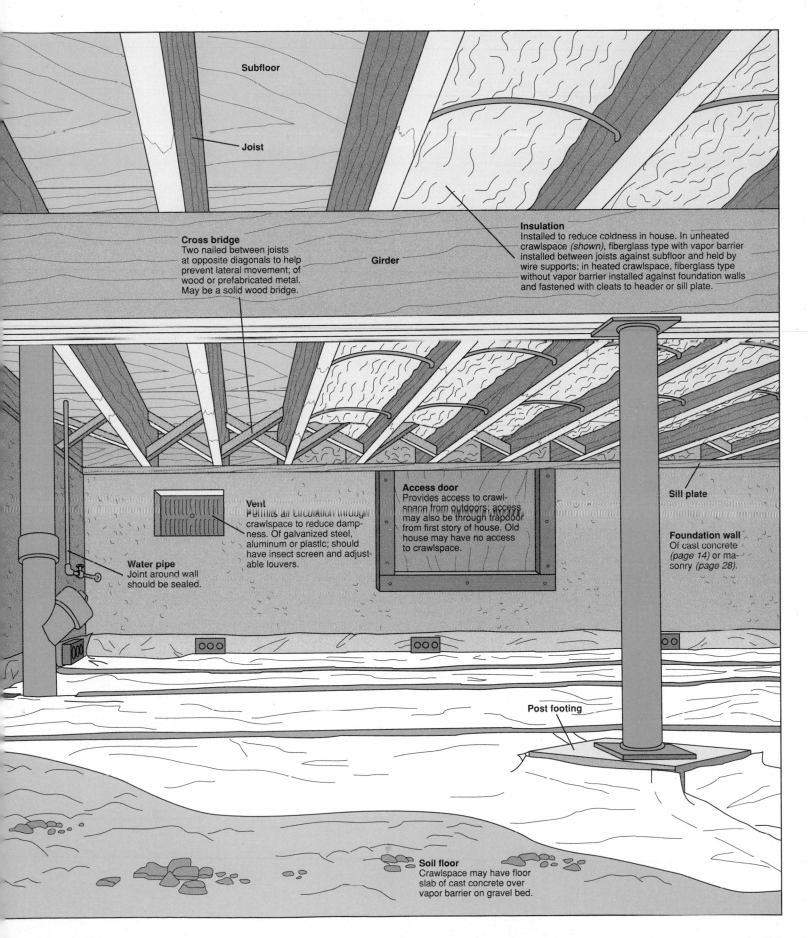

Subfloor

Joist

Cross bridge
Two nailed between joists at opposite diagonals to help prevent lateral movement; of wood or prefabricated metal. May be a solid wood bridge.

Girder

Insulation
Installed to reduce coldness in house. In unheated crawlspace *(shown)*, fiberglass type with vapor barrier installed between joists against subfloor and held by wire supports; in heated crawlspace, fiberglass type without vapor barrier installed against foundation walls and fastened with cleats to header or sill plate.

Sill plate

Access door
Provides access to crawl-space from outdoors; access may also be through trapdoor from first story of house. Old house may have no access to crawlspace.

Vent
Permits air circulation through crawlspace to reduce damp-ness. Of galvanized steel, aluminum or plastic; should have insect screen and adjust-able louvers.

Foundation wall
Of cast concrete *(page 14)* or ma-sonry *(page 28)*.

Water pipe
Joint around wall should be sealed.

Post footing

Soil floor
Crawlspace may have floor slab of cast concrete over vapor barrier on gravel bed.

TROUBLESHOOTING GUIDE

SYMPTOM	POSSIBLE CAUSE	PROCEDURE
Crawlspace flooded	Flood	Remove standing water using a submersible pump; if necessary, gain access (p. 76) ☑●
	Drainage system faulty	Troubleshoot drainage systems (p. 78)
Crawlspace wet	Leaking joint at pipe or vent	Seal joint at wall opening (p. 60) □○; if necessary, gain access (p. 76) ☑●
	Leaking crack in foundation wall	Troubleshoot concrete (p. 14) or masonry (p. 28) foundation; if necessary, gain access (p. 76) ☑●
	Leaking crack in floor slab	Troubleshoot crawlspace floor (p. 54)
	Drainage system faulty	Troubleshoot drainage systems (p. 78)
Crawlspace damp	Vent open during damp season	Close vent; if vent not adjustable type, close off vent (p. 73) □○ or replace vent (p. 72) □○
	Soil floor	Install vapor barrier (p. 73) □◔; if necessary, gain access (p. 76) ☑●
	Floor slab damp	Troubleshoot crawlspace floor (p. 54)
	Ventilation inadequate	Check crawlspace ventilation; if necessary, install additional vents (p. 71) ☑●
	Drainage system faulty	Troubleshoot drainage systems (p. 78)
Foundation wall wet, damp or cracked	Foundation wall faulty	Troubleshoot concrete (p. 14) or masonry (p. 28) foundation; if necessary, gain access (p. 76) ☑●
	Drainage system faulty	Troubleshoot drainage systems (p. 78)
Floor slab wet, damp or cracked	Floor slab faulty	Troubleshoot crawlspace floor (p. 54)
	Drainage system faulty	Troubleshoot drainage systems (p. 78)
Heated crawlspace cold	Vent open during cold season	Close vent; if vent not adjustable type, close off vent (p. 73) □○ or replace vent (p. 72) □○
	Soil floor	Install vapor barrier (p. 73) □◔; if necessary, gain access (p. 76) ☑●
	Insulation inadequate	Insulate crawlspace walls (p. 74) □●; if necessary, gain access (p. 76) ☑●
Unheated crawlspace cold	Vent open during cold season	Close vent; if vent not adjustable type, close off vent (p. 73) □○ or replace vent (p. 72) □○
	Soil floor	Install vapor barrier (p. 73) □◔; if necessary, gain access (p. 76) ☑●
	Insulation inadequate	Insulate crawlspace ceiling (p. 75) □●; if necessary, gain access (p. 76) ☑●
Vent open during cold or damp season	Improper maintenance	Close vent
	Vent not adjustable type	Close off vent (p. 73) □○ or replace vent (p. 72) □○
Vent damaged	Wear and tear	Replace vent (p. 72) □○
Foundation wall dirty or stained	Wear and tear; mildew due to excess moisture or water penetration	Clean concrete (p. 17) □○ or masonry (p. 31) □○ wall
Floor slab dirty or stained	Wear and tear; mildew due to excess moisture or water penetration	Clean crawlspace floor (p. 57) □○
Foundation wall efflorescence (white, powdery deposits)	Leaching of salts due to excess moisture	Clean concrete (p. 17) □○ or masonry (p. 31) □○ wall
Floor slab efflorescence (white, powdery deposits)	Leaching of salts due to excess moisture	Clean crawlspace floor (p. 57) □○

DEGREE OF DIFFICULTY: □ Easy ☑ Moderate ■ Complex
ESTIMATED TIME: ○ Less than 1 hour ◔ 1 to 3 hours ● Over 3 hours

VENTILATING A CRAWLSPACE

Dropcloth

1 **Checking ventilation.** Keep your crawlspace properly ventilated. In a cold climate, open the vents in seasons when the temperature averages 40 degrees Fahrenheit or more and close the vents in seasons when the temperature is cooler; if there is a furnace in the crawlspace, leave the vents open all year. In a warm climate, open the vents in dry seasons and close the vents in rainy or humid seasons. Inspect the vents regularly from the outdoors. Trim back any vegetation and remove any debris obstructing airflow. If a vent is damaged, replace it *(page 72)*. If there are no vents or dampness persists, consult a building professional *(page 119)* about the number, type and location of vents required for the crawlspace; if recommended, install vents. If the wall is of cast concrete, brick or stone, hire a building professional to make openings for vents, then install the vents *(page 72)*. If the wall is of concrete block, remove a block at the recommended location to make an opening for a vent; if there is no access to the crawlspace, install a trapdoor *(page 76)*. Starting indoors, work with good lighting and wear safety goggles, work gloves, a dust mask and a safety helmet. Using a ball-peen hammer and a plugging chisel or cold chisel, chip out the mortar around the block *(left)*, then continue outdoors to make the opening for the vent *(step 2)*.

Plugging chisel

Bull-point chisel

2 **Making an opening for a vent.** Work outdoors to continue removing the block. Wearing safety goggles and work gloves, use a ball-peen hammer and a plugging chisel or cold chisel to chip out as much mortar as possible from the joints around the block *(above, left)*. Then, try pushing the loosened block through the wall into the crawlspace; if you cannot dislodge the block, break it out. Starting a few inches from the edge of the block, use a bull-point chisel and a hand drilling hammer to break through the face of the block into the core; then, continue to chisel the block into pieces *(above, right)* small enough to remove by hand. Use a cold chisel and ball-peen hammer to chip any remaining bits of the block and mortar off the edges of the opening, then use a stiff-bristled brush to clean dust and particles out of the opening. Install a vent in the opening *(page 72)*.

REPLACING A VENT

1 **Removing a vent.** To replace a damaged vent, work outdoors. Using a putty knife, scrape any sealant off the edges of the vent *(above, left)*. Wearing safety goggles and work gloves, chip any mortar off the edges of the vent with a cold chisel and a ball-peen hammer. Insert a pry bar into the joint between the vent and the wall, then work along the joint to pry the vent out of the wall *(above, right)*. If you cannot pry out the vent, the back of it may be held in the wall opening by mortar or screws. Work indoors to remove any screws or mortar from the vent; if there is no access to the crawlspace, install a trapdoor *(page 76)*. Then, work outdoors again to pry out the vent. Use a stiff-bristled brush to clean dust and particles out of the wall opening.

Sealant

2 **Installing a vent.** Buy a vent of plastic, aluminum or galvanized steel to fit the wall opening at a building supply center; use a type equipped with an insect screen and adjustable louvers. Also buy an exterior-grade sealant such as a silicone rubber type. Working outdoors, load a caulking gun with sealant *(page 115)* and apply a bead of it along each flange of the vent. Then, fit the vent into the wall opening *(above, left)*, setting it flush with the surface. To seal the joint between the vent and the wall, apply a continuous bead of sealant along it *(above, right)*; wearing a rubber glove, run a wet finger along the sealant to smooth it and press it into the joint. If necessary for your model of vent, work indoors to screw the back of it to the sides of the wall opening.

CLOSING OFF A VENT

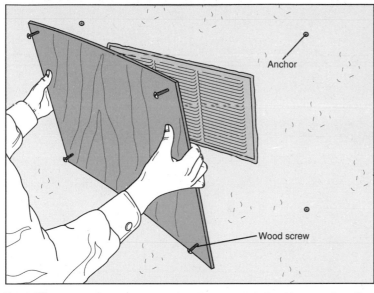

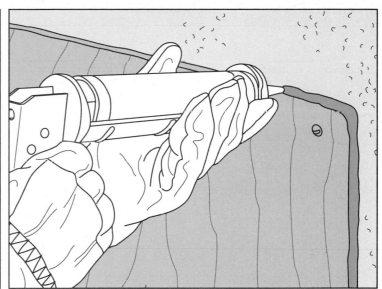

Installing a vent cover. To close off a vent with fixed louvers, install a cover on its exterior. To make the cover, cut a piece of exterior-grade plywood 5/8 inch thick at least 2 inches longer and wider than the vent; choose wood screws and anchors *(page 117)* to fasten the cover to the wall. Wearing safety goggles, use an electric drill to bore a clearance hole for a wood screw near each corner of the cover; avoid locating a hole at any mortar joint. Hold the cover in position over the vent and use the holes to mark locations for anchors on the wall. Fit the drill with a masonry bit to drill a hole for an anchor at each mark, then fit the anchors into the holes. Drive the screws partway into the holes in the cover, then reposition the cover on the wall *(above, left)* and drive the screws into the anchors. Load a caulking gun with silicone rubber sealant *(page 115)* and apply a bead of it along the joint between each edge of the cover and the wall *(above, right)*. To reopen the vent, take off the cover by scraping off the sealant and removing the screws.

INSTALLING A VAPOR BARRIER

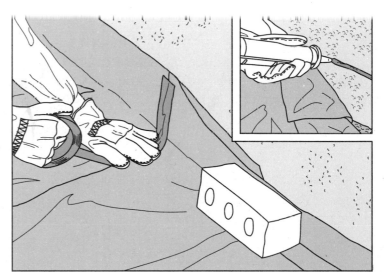

1 Installing polyethylene. Buy enough 6-mil polyethylene sheeting at a building supply center to cover the floor; if it is heavily trafficked, plan to install a double layer of sheeting. Wearing a safety helmet and soft-soled shoes, level the soil of the floor using a spade and a garden rake. Use a utility knife to cut sections of sheeting long enough to lap 6 inches up the walls; trim any section to fit at an obstruction such as a post footing. Working one section of sheeting at a time, lay it on the floor and lapped up the walls *(above)*, then weight down the ends with bricks. Continue the same way, overlapping adjacent sections of sheeting by 12 inches.

2 Adhering the polyethylene. Use duct tape to seal the seams between overlapping sections of sheeting *(above)* and the edges of the sheeting at obstructions. To adhere the sheeting to the walls, use a construction-grade adhesive. Load a caulking gun with adhesive *(page 115)* and start at one end of a wall, folding back the sheeting to apply adhesive behind it. Holding the gun at a 45-degree angle to the wall, squeeze the trigger to eject a bead of adhesive along it *(above)*. Smooth the sheeting up the wall and into the adhesive. Work along the wall to the other end of it, then work in turn along the other walls the same way. If necessary, install a second layer of sheeting *(step 1)*. Lay plywood on the sheeting for walkways.

INSULATING THE WALLS

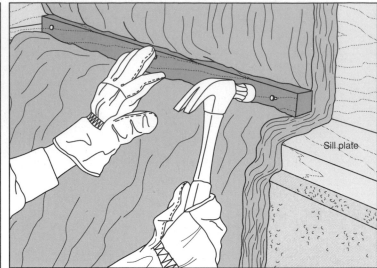

1 Insulating walls parallel to joists. If there is no access to the crawlspace, install a trapdoor *(page 76)*. For an unheated crawlspace, insulate the ceiling *(page 75)*. For a heated crawlspace, first make any repairs to the concrete *(page 14)* or masonry *(page 28)* walls, then insulate them. Buy enough fiberglass insulation to cover the walls at a building supply center; ensure it has no vapor barrier. Wearing long sleeves, work gloves, safety goggles, a dust mask, soft-soled shoes and a safety helmet, start by insulating a wall parallel to the joists. Use a utility knife to cut sections of insulation to extend from the top of the header to the bottom of the wall and lap 2 feet onto the floor; trim any section to fit at an obstruction such as a vent or pipe. To fasten each section, cut a 1-by-2 for a cleat equal in length to the section width

and drive a nail partway into it near each end and the center of it. Working one section at a time, position it against the wall and push the top of it snugly against the joint between the subfloor and the header *(above, left)*. Compressing the section as little as possible, place a cleat across it along the joint between the header and the sill plate, then drive in the nails *(above, right)*. Continue the same way along the wall to the other end, butting adjacent sections snugly. To install a section on the wall below an obstruction, nail *(page 117)* a 1-by-2 furring strip to the wall along the bottom of the obstruction and fasten the top of the section to it with a cleat. Use the same procedure to insulate the opposite wall, then insulate the walls perpendicular to the joists *(step 2)*.

2 Insulating walls perpendicular to joists. Use a utility knife to cut sections of insulation to cover the header and sill plate between each pair of joists at the top of the wall. Working along the wall, install the sections one at a time, folding it to fit against the header and lap over the top of the sill plate *(above, left)*. To insulate the wall, use a utility knife to cut sections of insulation long enough to extend from the top of the sill plate to the bottom of the wall and lap 2 feet onto the floor; trim any section to fit at an obstruction such as a vent or pipe. To fasten each section, cut a 1-by-2 for a cleat equal in length to the section width and drive a nail partway into it near each

end and the center of it. Working one section at a time, position it against the wall with the top of it against the sill plate. Compressing the section as little as possible, place a cleat across the top of it and drive in the nails. Continue the same way along the wall to the other end, butting adjacent sections snugly *(above center)*. To install a section on the wall below an obstruction, nail *(page 117)* a 1-by-2 furring strip to the wall along the bottom of the obstruction and fasten the top of the section to it with a cleat. Use the same procedure to insulate the opposite wall. When all the walls are insulated, fold out the bottom of each section to lap it onto the floor and weight it with a brick *(above, right)*.

INSULATING THE CEILING

Installing insulation between joists.

If there is no access to the crawlspace, install a trapdoor *(page 76)*. For a heated crawl-space, insulate the walls *(page 74)*. For an unheated crawlspace, first make any repairs to the structural wood *(page 100)* and insulate any cold water pipes *(page 78)*, then insulate the ceiling. If there is a risk of pipes freezing or there are unprotected ducts, consult a building professional about the best insulation procedure. Buy enough fiberglass insulation to cover the ceiling between joists at a building supply center; ensure it has a vapor barrier. Also buy wire supports to hold the insulation. Wearing long sleeves, work gloves, safety goggles, a dust mask, soft-soled shoes and a safety helmet, work across the crawlspace in turn between pairs of joists; use a utility knife to cut sections of insulation to length. To install a section, hold it with its vapor barrier facing up and fit it between the joists *(left)*; if it butts against a wall, fold the end of it to cover the header. Install a wire support every 8 inches along the section, bending each support to fit it between the joists *(inset)*. Continue the same way until the ceiling is insulated, butting adjacent sections together snugly; if necessary, fit a section at an obstruction *(step below)*.

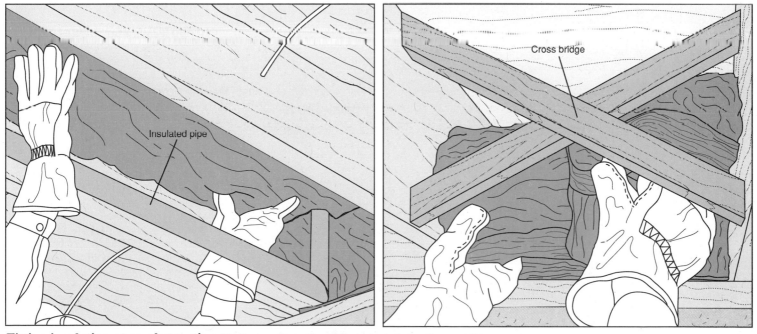

Fitting insulation at an obstruction. To fit a section of insulation at an obstruction, cut it to butt against one side of the obstruction; then, cut the next section of insulation to butt against the other side of the obstruction. For example, at a pipe, fit the sections of insulation against opposite sides of it, butting them together snugly *(above, left)*. At a pair of cross bridges, fit a section of insulation against one side by making a small slit in the center at the end of it and pressing each side of the slit into place *(above, right)*, butted against the top of the cross bridges; fit a section of insulation against the other side the same way, butting the sections together snugly. At a solid bridge, fit a section of insulation against each side of it.

INSTALLING A TRAPDOOR FOR ACCESS

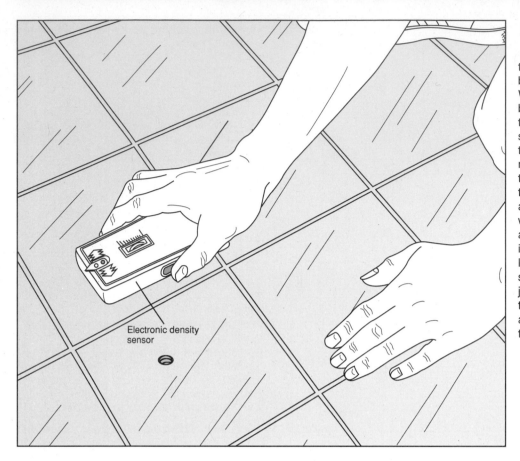

Electronic density
sensor

1 **Preparing to install a trapdoor.**
If there is no access to the crawlspace,
install a trapdoor. Choose a location for a
trapdoor in an inconspicuous area unobstructed
by pipes or ducts—inside a closet, for example.
Wearing safety goggles, use an electric drill to
bore a hole through the floor at the location,
then measure the crawlspace height. Feed a
straight, rigid wire through the hole until it butts
the crawlspace floor, mark it at floor level, then
remove it and measure the distance between
the mark and the end of it. If the distance is less
than 28 inches, consult a building professional
about gaining access to the crawlspace. Otherwise, prepare to install a trapdoor between two
adjacent joists. Following the manufacturer's
instructions, use an electronic density sensor to
locate the nearest joist on each side of the hole,
sliding it across the floor *(left)* until it signals a
joist. Mark the joist locations on the flooring,
then remove enough of the flooring to expose
a subfloor section 3 feet long and slightly wider
than the distance between the joists.

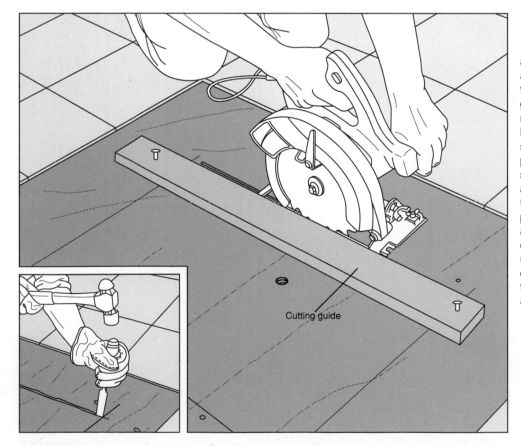

Cutting guide

2 **Cutting a trapdoor opening.** Using
a straightedge, mark a cutting outline for
a trapdoor opening on the subfloor: a line
along the center of each joist using the nails as
a guide; lines between the joists perpendicular
to them at least 2 feet apart. Wearing safety
goggles, use a pry bar to pull the nails out of the
marked subfloor section. Prepare to use a circular saw, setting the cutting depth equal to the
subfloor thickness—typically 5/8 inch if it is of
plywood; 3/4 inch if it is of board. Position the
saw a few inches from one end of a cutting line
and temporarily nail a straight-edged board to
the subfloor as a cutting guide along it. Make a
plunge cut into the line with the saw, then cut
along it *(left)* to a point a few inches short of the
other end of it. Remove the cutting guide, then
use a wood chisel and a ball-peen hammer to
complete each end of the cut *(inset)*. Cut along
the other cutting lines the same way, then use
a pry bar to lift out the subfloor section.

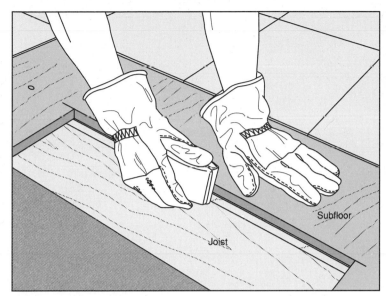

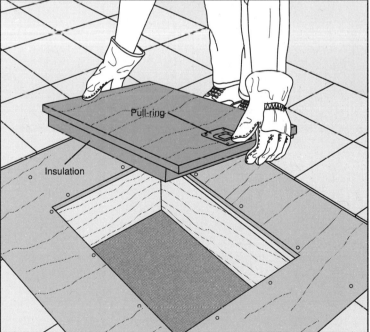

3 **Preparing the trapdoor opening.** Cut out any insulation between the joists in the subfloor opening with a utility knife. Remove any cross bridge or solid bridge between the joists; if necessary, use a mini-hacksaw to cut the nails holding it to the joists. If an electrical cable crosses the opening, consult a professional to have it relocated. Using sandpaper and a sanding block, smooth the cut subfloor edges on the sides of the opening *(above, left)*. Working from below, install a cleat under each cut edge of the subfloor between the joists. To make a cleat, measure the length of the cut edge between the joists, then use a saw to cut a piece of lumber of the same grade and dimensions as the joists to length. Wearing safety goggles and a safety helmet, fit the cleat between the joists with its narrow side facing up, pushing it against the subfloor until its top is level with the top of the joists; center it along the cut edge. To fasten the cleat, nail through the joists at each end of it with 3-inch common nails, driving a nail into the top and bottom of it *(above, right)*. Working from above, nail the cut edges of the subfloor every 6 inches to the cleats and joists under it with 2 1/2-inch ring-shank nails.

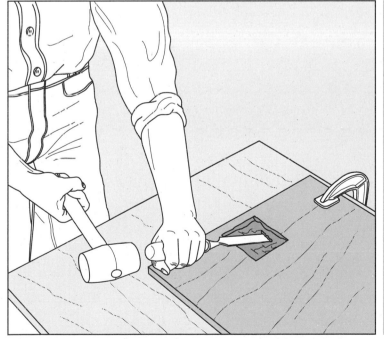

4 **Installing the trapdoor.** To make a trapdoor, measure the subfloor opening and cut a plywood sheet of the same thickness as the subfloor to size. Position a pull-ring at one end of the trapdoor and mark its outline on the surface. Wearing safety goggles, use a wood chisel and a wooden mallet to cut a mortise as deep as the thickness of the pull-ring in the outline *(above, left)*. Fit the pull-ring into the mortise and fasten it to the trapdoor with wood screws. If desired, install hinges at the end of the trapdoor opposite the pull-ring. If you cut out any insulation between the joists in the subfloor opening, cut a replacement piece of rigid foam insulation and fasten it to the bottom of the trapdoor. Fit the trapdoor into the subfloor opening *(above, right)*; if necessary, trim its edges with a plane until it lies flat. Reinstall flooring on the trapdoor and the exposed subfloor around it.

DRAINAGE SYSTEMS

The drainage systems installed in and around your house are designed to keep the foundation walls and the basement or crawlspace enclosed by them dry. A properly-working drainage system helps to prevent water accumulation along the foundation walls and under the floor slab. Typical drainage systems are shown at right. A system of gutters and downspouts carries water runoff from the roof down and away from the foundation walls to prevent soil erosion and water buildup that can damage them. Sloped ground adjacent to the foundation walls routes surface water away from rather than down them. Window wells prevent water from collecting at and leaking through windows at ground level. And in many regions, more sophisticated drainage systems are often required. An exterior drain tile system installed in gravel along the footings prevents water buildup at the perimeter of the foundation. In the same way, an interior drain tile system prevents water buildup under the floor slab. A sump pit and sump pump indoors may collect water from a drain tile system and pump it away to the outdoors.

Dampness or wetness in a basement or crawlspace is common; although in most cases it is not a cause for strong concern, it can be a symptom of a serious problem—or become one if a needed repair is not undertaken. To help you identify the cause of a dampness or wetness problem, first consult the Troubleshooting Guide in the chapter on Basement Floors And Walls *(page 54)* or Crawlspaces *(page 68)*; if your house has no basement or crawlspace, in the chapter on Slab-On-Grade Foundations *(page 44)*. Then, use the Troubleshooting Guide in this chapter on page 80 for drainage systems; on page 94 for sump pumps. If a moisture problem persists after repairs to the foundation walls and floor are made, you will need to identify the type of moisture problem *(page 81)*. If the moisture problem is due to condensation, you can take steps to reduce the level of humidity inside your home; if it is due to seepage from the exterior through a foundation wall or the floor, you will need to repair or improve the drainage systems of your home.

Repairs to drainage systems range from the simple to the complex. A minor repair such as cleaning a gutter and downspout *(page 83)* or unclogging a weep hole in an exterior wall of brick veneer *(page 84)* can be performed quickly with simple tools. However, more involved repairs such as diverting downspout runoff underground *(page 85)* or installing a window well *(page 86)* take longer to do and require the purchase of special materials. A major repair such as installing an exterior drain tile system *(page 91)* can take several days and calls for the use of many different tools and techniques. Consult Tools & Techniques *(page 110)* for information on the tools needed for repairs as well as for instructions on excavating and backfilling along the exterior of a foundation wall. Before undertaking any repair, familiarize yourself with the safety advice included in the Emergency Guide *(page 8)*. If you have any doubt about your ability to successfully complete a repair, do not hesitate to consult a building professional *(page 119)*.

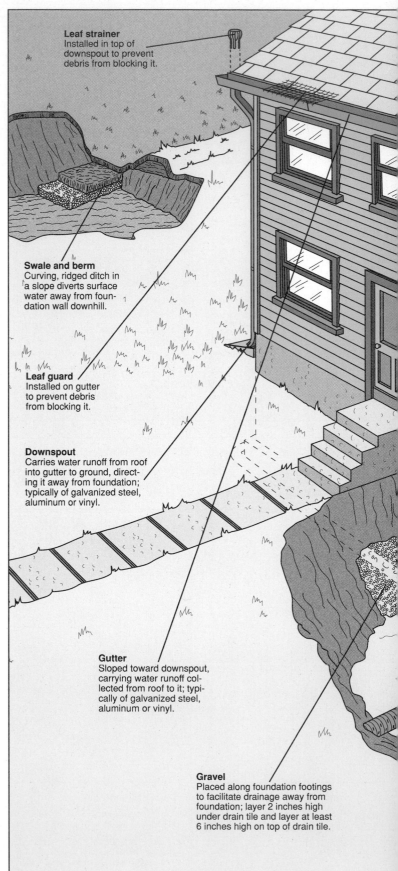

Leaf strainer
Installed in top of downspout to prevent debris from blocking it.

Swale and berm
Curving, ridged ditch in a slope diverts surface water away from foundation wall downhill.

Leaf guard
Installed on gutter to prevent debris from blocking it.

Downspout
Carries water runoff from roof into gutter to ground, directing it away from foundation; typically of galvanized steel, aluminum or vinyl.

Gutter
Sloped toward downspout, carrying water runoff collected from roof to it; typically of galvanized steel, aluminum or vinyl.

Gravel
Placed along foundation footings to facilitate drainage away from foundation; layer 2 inches high under drain tile and layer at least 6 inches high on top of drain tile.

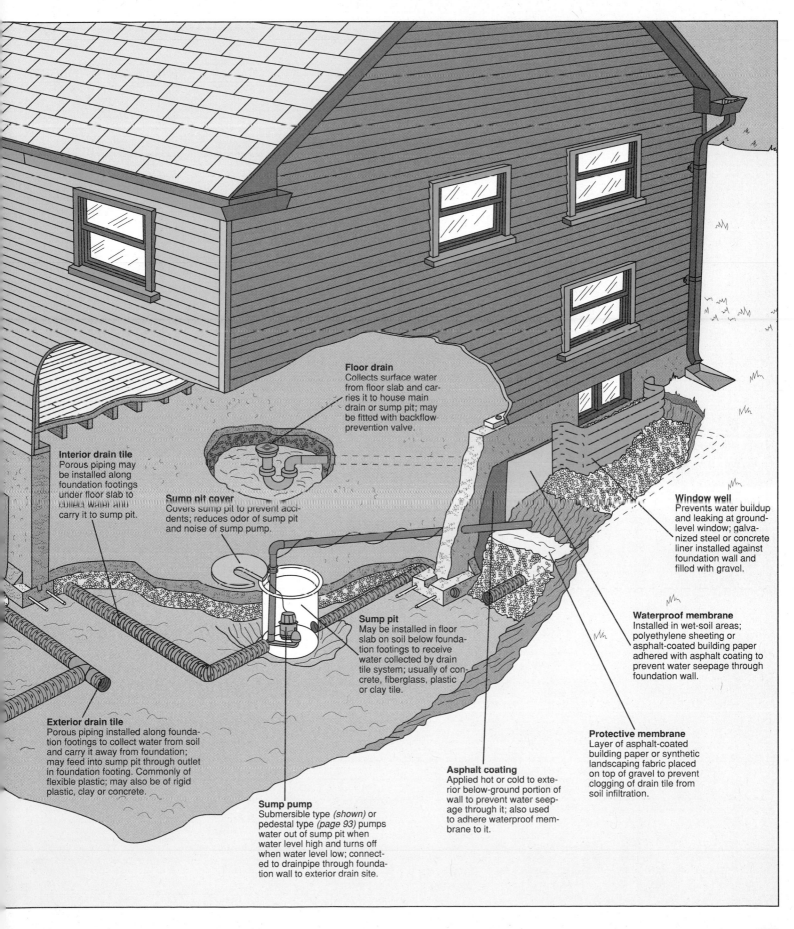

Floor drain
Collects surface water from floor slab and carries it to house main drain or sump pit; may be fitted with backflow prevention valve.

Interior drain tile
Porous piping may be installed along foundation footings under floor slab to collect water and carry it to sump pit.

Sump pit cover
Covers sump pit to prevent accidents; reduces odor of sump pit and noise of sump pump.

Window well
Prevents water buildup and leaking at ground-level window; galvanized steel or concrete liner installed against foundation wall and filled with gravel.

Sump pit
May be installed in floor slab on soil below foundation footings to receive water collected by drain tile system; usually of concrete, fiberglass, plastic or clay tile.

Waterproof membrane
Installed in wet-soil areas; polyethylene sheeting or asphalt-coated building paper adhered with asphalt coating to prevent water seepage through foundation wall.

Exterior drain tile
Porous piping installed along foundation footings to collect water from soil and carry it away from foundation; may feed into sump pit through outlet in foundation footing. Commonly of flexible plastic; may also be of rigid plastic, clay or concrete.

Protective membrane
Layer of asphalt-coated building paper or synthetic landscaping fabric placed on top of gravel to prevent clogging of drain tile from soil infiltration.

Asphalt coating
Applied hot or cold to exterior below-ground portion of wall to prevent water seepage through it; also used to adhere waterproof membrane to it.

Sump pump
Submersible type *(shown)* or pedestal type *(page 93)* pumps water out of sump pit when water level high and turns off when water level low; connected to drainpipe through foundation wall to exterior drain site.

TROUBLESHOOTING GUIDE

SYMPTOM	POSSIBLE CAUSE	PROCEDURE
Basement or crawlspace flooded	Flood	Remove standing water using a submersible pump
	Floor drain clogged	Unclog floor drain (p. 89) □○
	Floor drain backed up	Call plumber for service; install backflow-prevention valve (p. 90) □○
	Sump pump faulty	Troubleshoot sump pump (p. 94)
	Exterior drain tile clogged or damaged	Service drain tile system (p. 90) ◩●
	No exterior drain tile system	Install drain tile system (p. 91) ■●
	Interior drain tile faulty; no system	Consult a building professional
Basement or crawlspace wet	Leaking crack or joint	Troubleshoot basement floor and walls (p. 54) or crawlspace (p. 68)
	Floor drain clogged	Unclog floor drain (p. 89) □○
	Floor drain backed up	Call plumber for service; install backflow-prevention valve (p. 90) □○
	Sump pump faulty	Troubleshoot sump pump (p. 94)
	Gutter or downspout clogged; overflows onto ground at foundation	Clean gutters and downspouts (p. 83) □◗
	Downspout discharges onto ground at foundation	Divert downspout runoff at ground level (p. 84) □○ or underground (p. 85) ◩●
	Weep hole clogged (wall of brick veneer)	Unclog weep holes (p. 84) □○
	Window well clogged; retains water	Clear debris; unclog any drain as you would floor drain (p. 89) □○
	Ground at foundation sloped incorrectly	Slope ground at foundation (p. 87) □● or install shallow water-diversion system (p. 88) ◗●
	Surface water of slope runs downhill to foundation	Install swale and berm (p. 89) □●
	Exterior drain tile clogged or damaged	Service drain tile system (p. 90) ◩●
	No exterior drain tile system	Install drain tile system (p. 91) ■●
	Interior drain tile faulty; no system	Consult a building professional
Basement or crawlspace damp	Foundation wall or floor slab faulty	Troubleshoot basement floor and walls (p. 54) or crawlspace (p. 68)
	Seepage from exterior; interior condensation	Identify and control moisture (p. 81)
Foundation wall wet	Foundation wall faulty	Troubleshoot concrete (p. 14) or masonry (p. 28) foundation
	Gutter or downspout clogged; overflows onto ground at foundation	Clean gutters and downspouts (p. 83) □◗
	Downspout discharges onto ground at foundation	Divert downspout runoff at ground level (p. 84) □○ or underground (p. 85) ◩●
	Weep hole clogged (wall of brick veneer)	Unclog weep holes (p. 84) □○
	Window well clogged; retains water	Clear debris; unclog any drain as you would floor drain (p. 89) □○
	Ground at foundation sloped incorrectly	Slope ground at foundation (p. 87) □● or install shallow water-diversion system (p. 88) ◗●
	Surface water of slope runs downhill to foundation	Install swale and berm (p. 89) □●
Floor slab wet	Floor slab faulty	Troubleshoot basement or crawlspace floor (p. 54) or slab-on-grade floor slab (p. 44)
	Floor drain clogged	Unclog floor drain (p. 89) □○
	Floor drain backed up	Call plumber for service; install backflow-prevention valve (p. 90) □○
	Sump pump faulty	Troubleshoot sump pump (p. 94)
	Exterior drain tile clogged or damaged	Service drain tile system (p. 90) ◩●
	No exterior drain tile system	Install drain tile system (p. 91) ■●
	Interior drain tile faulty; no system	Consult a building professional
Foundation wall or floor slab damp	Foundation wall or floor slab faulty	Troubleshoot concrete (p. 14) or masonry (p. 28) foundation; basement or crawlspace floor (p. 54) or slab-on-grade floor slab (p. 44)
	Seepage from exterior; interior condensation	Identify and control moisture (p. 81)

DEGREE OF DIFFICULTY: □ Easy ◩ Moderate ■ Complex
ESTIMATED TIME: ○ Less than 1 hour ◗ 1 to 3 hours ● Over 3 hours

CONTROLLING INDOOR MOISTURE

Controlling humidity in the basement or crawlspace.
There can be many symptoms of a moisture problem in the basement or crawlspace: mustiness, mildew or mold, peeling paint, rusted metal, frosted or wet windows, and damp spots on the walls or floor, for example. However, although a moisture problem in the basement or crawlspace is usually easy to detect, the source can be difficult to pinpoint—and often there is more than one cause of the problem. If a moisture problem is not the result of a leaking pipe or a leaking crack or joint in a wall or the floor, it may be the result of seepage from the exterior due to a faulty drainage system or the result of condensation due to excess interior humidity—or both. To help isolate the cause of a moisture problem, test for seepage and condensation *(step below)*. If the moisture problem is seepage from the exterior through a wall or the floor, troubleshoot the drainage systems *(page 80)*. If the moisture problem is condensation due to excess interior humidity, refer to the guidelines below to help reduce it:

• Turn off any humidifier in the basement or crawlspace, including a humidifier built-in to the furnace; if the problem persists, install a dehumidifier, following the manufacturer's instructions.

• Improve ventilation in the basement or crawlspace, opening windows and vents to the outdoors; set up an exhaust fan near an open window or vent to speed air circulation. If necessary, install additional vents in the crawlspace *(page 71)*.

• Install a vapor barrier on any soil floor in the basement *(page 57)* or crawlspace *(page 73)*.

• Insulate cold-water pipes *(page 82)* and air-conditioning ducts in the basement or crawlspace.

• Seal any open joint in a wall of the basement or crawlspace at a window, vent or pipe *(page 60)*. Install weatherstripping around windows and doors.

• Ensure that any bathroom or clothes dryer in the basement is vented to the outdoors. Avoid hanging clothes indoors to dry.

• When heating the basement or crawlspace, keep the temperature as high as possible.

• If the basement has windows of only single-pane glass, install storm windows or replace the windows with windows of double- or triple-pane glass.

• Replace any wet insulation in the ceiling and walls of the basement or crawlspace.

• Repair any leaking plumbing pipe or fixture or any leaking appliance in the basement or on the first story of the house.

• Avoid curing firewood in the basement or crawlspace; cure it outdoors at least 3 feet away from any foundation wall.

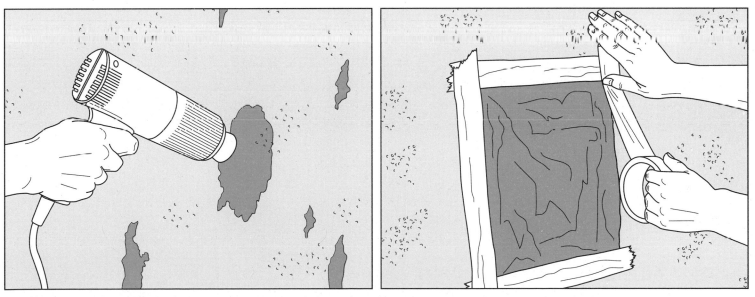

Testing for seepage and condensation. If a wall or the floor of the basement or crawlspace is damp, test the surface to determine if the cause is seepage from the exterior or condensation from excess interior humidity. Use a heat gun to thoroughly dry a section of the surface about 12 inches square *(above, left)*. Cut a piece of aluminum foil or polyethylene sheeting slightly smaller than the dried section and fasten it in place on the dried section, securing its edges to the surface with duct tape *(above, right)*; ensure all of its edges are sealed tightly to keep out air. Leave the foil or sheeting in place for 24 hours, then check it for moisture. If the exposed side of the foil or sheeting is damp, the moisture problem is condensation. Remove the foil or sheeting to check the other side of it for moisture; if the side of it against the surface is damp, the moisture problem is seepage. If the foil or sheeting is damp on both the exposed side and the side against the surface, the moisture problem is condensation and seepage.

INSULATING COLD-WATER PIPES

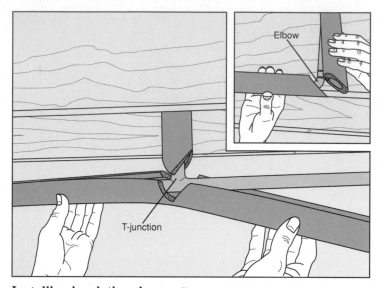

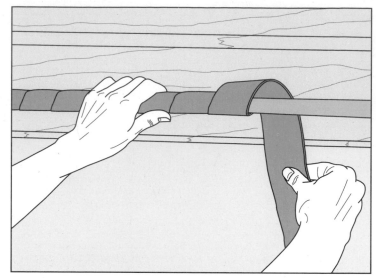

Installing insulation sleeves. Buy pre-slit foam insulation sleeves to fit the pipe at a building supply center. Starting at one end of the pipe, separate a sleeve along its slit and fit it around the pipe with its slit facing up; if necessary, cut it to length with a utility knife. Work to the other end of the pipe the same way, butting adjacent sleeves together. At a T-junction, notch one sleeve to fit around the junction and taper another sleeve to fit the notch, then install the sleeves *(above)*. At an elbow, cut a sleeve for each side of it at a 45-degree angle, then fit the sleeves around the pipe with the cut ends butted together *(inset)*. Use duct tape to seal the slits and joints of the sleeves.

Installing insulation tape. Buy adhesive-backed, aluminum-coated foam insulation tape at a building supply center. Use a cloth moistened with a solution of mild detergent and water to clean dirt and particles off the pipe, then dry it thoroughly. Starting at one end of the pipe, un- wind a lead of tape and press it firmly at a 45-degree angle onto the pipe. Wrap the tape snugly around the pipe and work to the other end of it, applying the tape in a continuous strip and overlapping the edges slightly *(above)*; unwind and rewrap any tape that buckles or gapes. Wrap the tape around T-junctions, elbows and other fittings as snugly as possible the same way.

EVALUATING SOIL TEXTURE AND DRAINAGE

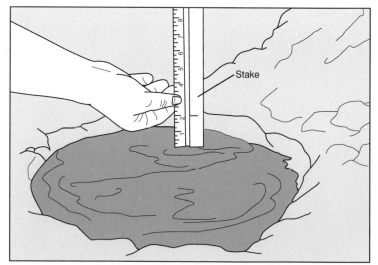

Evaluating soil texture. Use a spade to dig below the topsoil for a soil sample. Scoop up a handful of soil, then lightly moisten it and squeeze it into a ball in the palm of your hand. Release the pressure and touch the soil with your finger *(above)*. If the soil crumbles (loamy soil) or feels gritty and fails to hold together (sandy soil), it likely has good drainage capacity. If the soil remains in a tight, sticky mass that retains a fingerprint (clay soil), it may have poor drainage capacity. For clay soil or any soil with a texture you cannot assess, evaluate its drainage capacity *(step right)*.

Evaluating soil drainage capacity. Use a spade to dig a hole about 3 feet deep in the soil. Fill the hole with water twice, allowing it to empty each time. Then, drive a stake about 4 feet long into the bottom of the hole and again fill the hole with water. Mark the water level on the stake. Allow the hole to drain for one hour and measure the drop in the water level *(above)*: with a drop of 1 inch or more, the drainage capacity of the soil is good; for a drop of less than 1 inch, consult a professional about amending or replacing the soil to improve its drainage capacity.

SERVICING GUTTERS AND DOWNSPOUTS

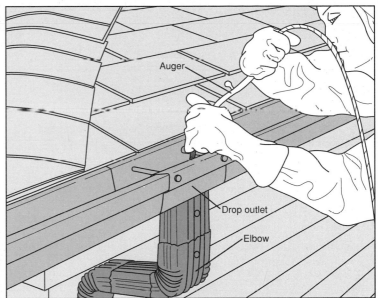

1 **Cleaning a gutter and downspout.** Work on firm, level ground to set up an extension ladder, ensuring it is long enough for you to work without standing closer than three rungs from the top of it. Wearing rubber gloves, handpick and bag any leaves or other debris along the roof edge as well as any leaf guard, open gutter and leaf strainer; reach down into an open drop outlet to pull out as much debris as possible. To flush the gutter and downspout, remove any leaf guard and leaf strainer, then use a garden hose to wash away dirt and grit, brushing it toward a downspout with a whisk broom *(above, left)*;

aim the hose into the drop outlet to flush it through the elbow and out the bottom of the downspout. If the downspout is not cleared by flushing it, unclog it using a trap-and-drain auger (plumber's snake). Push the auger coil into the drop outlet as far as possible, then lock the handle and slowly turn it clockwise *(above, right)*. When the handle moves easily, stop turning it to feed in more coil and continue until the downspout is unclogged; if necessary, also work from the bottom of it. If water leaks or continues to drain poorly out of the gutter or downspout, have it repaired. Otherwise, reinstall any leaf guard or leaf strainer you removed.

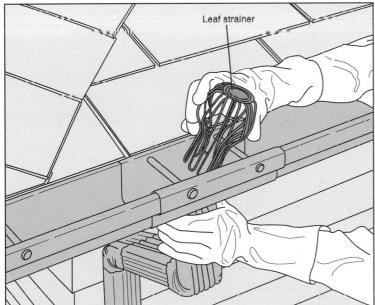

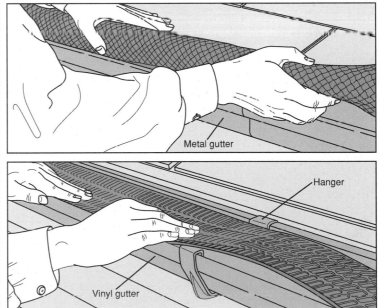

2 **Installing leaf strainers and leaf guards.** To prevent blockages in the drainage system, install a leaf strainer in each downspout and a leaf guard on each gutter; if your system is vinyl, each downspout elbow may be designed for a leaf remover. Buy leaf strainers or leaf removers and wide-mesh plastic leaf guard at a building supply center; if your system is vinyl, buy a type of leaf guard designed for it. To install a leaf strainer, wear rubber gloves and insert it into the drop outlet *(above, left)*; if necessary, adjust its tines until it fits snugly. To install a leaf remover, follow the manufacturer's instructions.

Use scissors to cut off a strip of leaf guard as long as the gutter; at a corner or if more than one strip is needed, overlap the ends by at least 1 inch. To install each strip, fit it between the roofing material and the building paper along the edge of the roof, then push it until it is aligned along the outside edge of the gutter. If the roofing material cannot be lifted, roll the leaf guard and sit it in the gutter *(above right, top)*, notching it to fit over any gutter hanger. To install a snap-on leaf guard along a vinyl gutter, press it into place under any hangers *(above right, bottom)*.

UNCLOGGING A WEEP HOLE

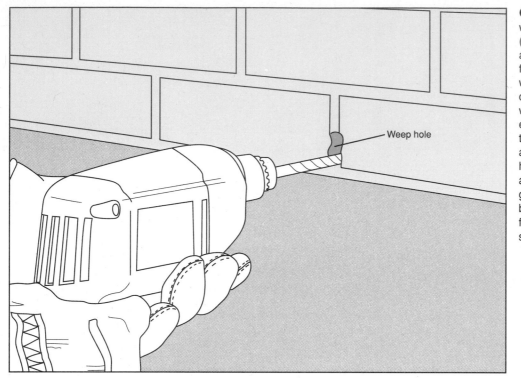

Clearing a weep hole. An exterior house wall of brick veneer usually has weep holes (open joints between bricks every 2 feet along the bottom course) to drain moisture from the wall cavity. To unclog a blocked weep hole, first try using a stiff wire. If you cannot unclog a blocked weep hole with the wire, use a cordless drill—preventing any electrical shock if there is a buildup of moisture behind the blockage. Fit the drill with a masonry bit slightly narrower than the hole and slightly longer than the width of a brick—usually 4 inches. Wearing work gloves and safety goggles, position the drill bit in the weep hole *(left)*, then angle it to follow the slope of the weep hole and drill slowly into the wall cavity behind the bricks.

DIVERTING DOWNSPOUT RUNOFF

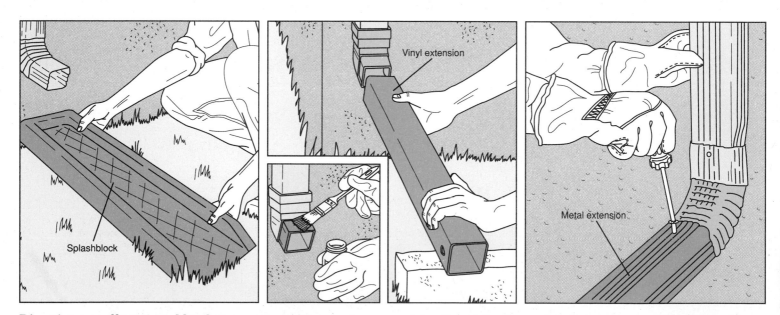

Diverting runoff at ground level. To prevent water from pooling below a downspout, divert it farther away. Choose an appropriate drain site a few feet away from the end of the downspout and evaluate the drainage capacity of the soil *(page 82)*. If the drainage capacity of the soil is poor, divert the runoff from the downspout underground *(page 85)*. Otherwise, divert the runoff from the downspout at ground level using a splashblock or an elbow extension. Buy a splashblock at least 18 inches long at a building supply center; to install it, position it on the ground directly below the downspout *(above, left)*. For an elbow extension, use a section of downspout about 3 feet long, ensuring that it matches the existing downspout; also use any connector, fastener or adhesive recommended by the manufacturer for installing it. With the vinyl downspout shown, wear rubber gloves to brush PVC solvent cement onto the outside end of the elbow *(inset)* and an inside end of the extension; then, push the cemented end of the extension onto the elbow *(above, center)*, supporting the other end of it on a block, if necessary. With the metal downspout shown, push the wider end of the extension snugly over the outside end of the elbow; then, drill a hole through the overlapped ends using a cordless drill fitted with a high-speed bit and drive a sheet metal screw into the hole *(above, right)*.

DIVERTING DOWNSPOUT RUNOFF (continued)

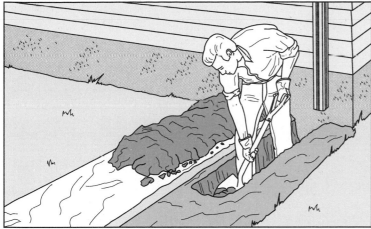

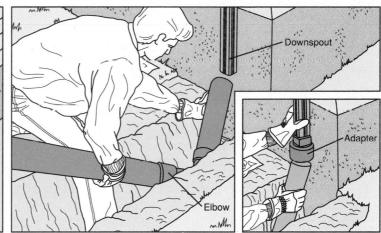

Diverting downspout runoff underground. To divert runoff from a downspout underground, connect it to a drain site such as a ditch or a storm sewer; consult your municipal authorities for an allowable drain site and a building professional about any special connection that may be needed at it. Buy enough unperforated, rigid plastic drainpipe for the job at a building supply center; also buy a 90 degree drainpipe elbow, drainpipe couplings, and any adapter available to join the drainpipe and downspout. Plan to dig a trench at least 2 feet deep and below the frost line from the downspout to the drain site. Remove any sod or vegetation *(page 120)* and lay plastic sheets on the ground to hold the soil excavated. Remove any downspout elbow, then dig the trench *(above,*

left) using a spade *(page 121)*; ensure that it slopes at least 1 inch every 8 feet to the drain site, checking it with a line level and tape measure. Place the drainpipe in the trench, cutting it only when necessary and solvent-welding a coupling at each joint *(steps below)*. Solvent-weld the elbow to the end of the drainpipe at the downspout and fit any adapter onto the bottom of the downspout. Cut a drainpipe long enough to reach from the elbow into the adapter or 1 inch over the bottom of the downspout and solvent-weld it to the elbow. Then, fit the assembled drainpipe into the adapter *(inset)* or onto the downspout *(above, right)*. Cover any open end of the drainpipe with 1/4-inch mesh. Backfill the trench *(page 122)* and put back any sod or vegetation you removed.

WORKING WITH RIGID PLASTIC DRAINPIPE

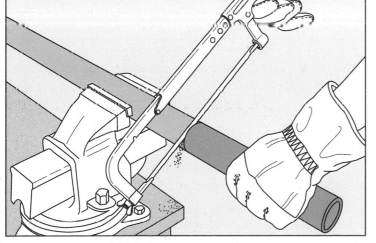

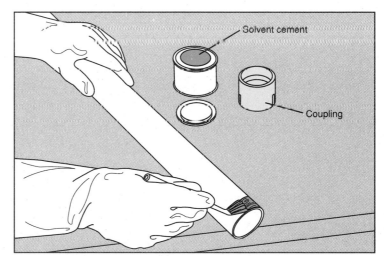

Cutting rigid plastic drainpipe. To cut a rigid plastic drainpipe, mark it to the length needed, allowing for an overlap with any coupling or other fitting of at least 1/3 its depth. Wrap a sheet of thin cardboard around the drainpipe and align an overlapped edge of it at the marked point, then mark a cutting line around the drainpipe using the edge of the cardboard as a guide. To cut a drainpipe of a small diameter, use a pipe or tubing cutter fitted with a plastic-cutting wheel following the manufacturer's instructions. To cut a drainpipe of a large diameter, clamp it securely in a vise; wearing safety goggles and work gloves, use a hacksaw fitted with a fine-toothed blade to cut it carefully along the cutting line *(above)*, turning it as necessary to complete the cut evenly. Use a file or a utility knife to remove burrs from the cut edge of the drainpipe.

Solvent-welding rigid plastic drainpipe. To solvent-weld a rigid plastic drainpipe to a coupling or other fitting, buy an appropriate solvent cement and primer at a building supply center. Ensure that the coupling fits the drainpipe snugly, overlapping by at least 1/3 its depth; also ensure that the overlapping surfaces are clean, smooth and square. Fit the coupling onto the drainpipe and mark a line along its edge around the drainpipe. Working in a well-ventilated area, use a cloth to apply the primer on the marked end of the drainpipe and the inside of the coupling; let it dry. Apply the solvent cement with an old paintbrush, heavily coating the end of the drainpipe *(above)* and lightly coating the inside of the coupling. Push the drainpipe into the coupling, twisting slightly to spread the solvent cement and extrude a bead of it along the joint. Allow the solvent cement to set.

INSTALLING A WINDOW WELL

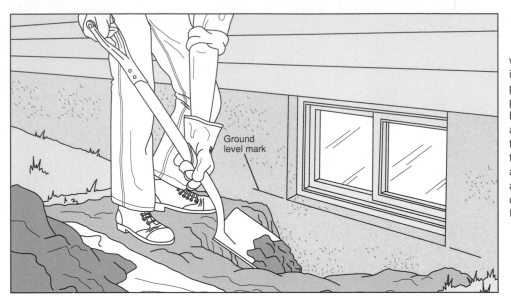

1 **Excavating the well.** To prevent a basement window at ground level from leaking, dig a hole for a well and install a well liner. Buy a galvanized window well liner 6 inches larger than the window at a building supply center; if recommended by the manufacturer, paint it with a rust-inhibiting paint. Plan to dig the hole for the well around the window 4 feet deep and large enough to hold the well liner against the foundation wall. Mark the ground level on the foundation wall on each side of the window and remove any sod or vegetation *(page 120)* adjacent to it. Lay plastic sheets on the ground or use a wheelbarrow to hold the soil excavated. Using a spade, dig the hole for the well *(left)*.

2 **Positioning the well liner.** Lower the well liner into the well below the window *(left)* and hold it in position against the foundation wall with the top edge of its flanges 4 inches higher than the ground level marks; if necessary, remove it to enlarge the well. When the well liner can be positioned correctly, note the depth of its bottom edge in the well and remove it, then use a spade to fill the well with gravel to the depth; test-fit it in the well as necessary. Add or remove gravel until the well liner stands in the well with the top edge of its flanges 4 inches above the ground level marks; if the foundation wall is of masonry, avoid aligning the fastener holes in its flanges with any mortar joint.

3 **Securing the well liner.** To secure the well liner, fasten each flange to the foundation wall using masonry nails and washers *(page 117)*. Wearing safety goggles and work gloves, fit a nail with a washer and position it in a fastener hole; keeping the flange flush against the foundation wall, use a hand drilling hammer to drive it in *(inset)*. Drive a nail fitted with a washer through the other fastener holes in the flanges of the well liner the same way. Apply a sealant *(page 115)* along the joint between each flange of the well liner and the foundation wall. Backfill *(page 122)* against the outside of the well liner *(left)* with the soil excavated, then fill the inside of it with gravel to a level 18 inches below the bottom edge of the window. Put back any sod or vegetation you removed around the outside of the well liner.

SLOPING THE GROUND AT THE FOUNDATION

1 **Measuring the slope.** The ground along a foundation wall should slope away from it by 1/2 to 1 inch every foot over at least 6 feet; for any minimum distance required between the top of the wall and ground level, consult your municipal authorities. If the ground slopes adequately or cannot be sloped adequately, install a shallow water-diversion system *(page 88)*. To measure the slope, drive a stake into the ground at the wall and 6 feet out from it. Using a line level, tie a string to the stakes level with the ground at the wall. Measure the distance between the string and the ground at the outer stake; if it is 3 inches or more, the slope is adequate. Otherwise, move the string on the outer stake 3 to 6 inches above the ground. Using the line level, move the string on the stake at the wall until it is level; its distance from the top of the wall must meet any local requirement for ground level. To use as a reference line for building up the slope, tie a string to the stake at the wall around the first string and to the outer stake at the ground *(left)*.

2 **Building up the slope.** Remove any sod or vegetation *(page 120)* adjacent to the foundation wall within 6 feet of it, then install additional stakes and reference lines at intervals along it as you did to measure the slope *(step 1)*. If you are raising the ground along the wall above the bottom of any basement window, plan to install a window well *(page 86)*. Buy enough topsoil at a garden center to raise the ground level to the height of the reference lines. Using a spade, dig into and break up the soil exposed adjacent to the wall. To build up the slope, work along the wall from it to 6 feet out from it using the spade to spread the topsoil *(left)*; mix the topsoil with the existing soil and push it toward the wall, banking it up to the level of the reference lines. Use the back of the spade to tamp the soil firmly, packing it level along the wall and sloping it evenly away from the wall. Use the back of a garden rake to smooth the soil surface. Remove the stakes and reference lines, then put back any sod or vegetation you removed.

INSTALLING A SHALLOW WATER-DIVERSION SYSTEM

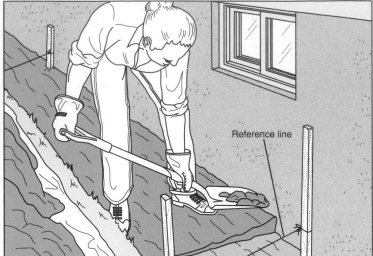

Reference line

1 **Excavating the trench.** Install a shallow water-diversion system along a foundation wall if the ground slopes adequately or cannot be sloped adequately away from it *(page 87)*. Plan to dig a trench 3 feet wide along the wall to a depth of 1 foot; wait for a dry period. To excavate along the wall, remove any sod or vegetation adjacent to it *(page 120)*. Lay plastic sheets on the ground to hold the soil excavated, then use a spade *(page 121)* to dig the trench *(above, left)*. Use the back of the spade to tamp down and smooth the bottom of the trench, leveling it as much as possible. To slope the bottom of the trench 1 inch every foot away from the wall, tie strings as reference lines to pairs of stakes. Drive pairs of stakes into the ground at the wall and out from it at the outer edge of the trench, then tie a string to each pair of stakes: 3 inches from the ground at the wall; level with the ground at the outer edge of the trench. Backfill the trench with some of the soil excavated, sloping it to the height of the reference lines *(above, right)*.

Tamper

Polyethylene sheeting

Gravel

2 **Compacting the soil.** To compact the sloped soil of the trench, use the end of a 4-by-4 about 4 to 5 feet long; if necessary, cut it to length. Wearing work gloves, work along the trench with the tamper, pounding the soil *(above)*. Backfill the trench with more soil and slope it back up to the height of the reference lines, then compact it again. Continue the same way until the compacted soil is sloped to the height of reference lines, then remove the stakes.

3 **Installing polyethylene sheeting.** Buy enough 6-mil polyethylene sheeting and cold-applied asphalt coating for the job at a building supply center; plan to cover the bottom of the trench and the wall up to ground level with sheeting, adhering it to the wall. Working along the wall from ground level to the bottom of the trench, wear safety goggles and use a wire brush to clean off dirt and particles. Wearing work gloves, use a mason's trowel to apply the asphalt coating on the wall. To install the sheeting, cut continuous sections of it to width. Starting at one end of the trench, lay a section on the bottom of the trench *(above, left)*, then smooth it up the wall, pressing it into the coating. Continue along the trench the same way, overlapping sections of the sheeting by 6 inches. Use a spade to cover the sheeting with 4 inches of gravel *(above, right)*, then cover it with landscaping fabric. Backfill the trench *(page 122)* and put back any sod or vegetation you removed.

INSTALLING A SWALE AND BERM

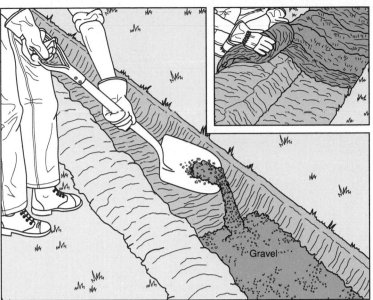

Digging a swale and berm. To divert runoff from a slope and keep it from pooling at a foundation wall, install a swale and berm—a curving, ridged ditch. Choose an appropriate route on the slope for the swale and berm, planning it to encircle and extend beyond each end of the wall; ensure that its ends slope downhill away from any neighboring property. To excavate the swale and berm, remove any sod *(page 120)* from a strip 2 1/2 feet wide along the route chosen. Using a spade *(page 121)*, dig a trench 2 foot wide and 8 inches deep for the swale, piling the excavated soil along the downhill edge of the trench for the berm *(above, left)*. Use the back of the spade to smooth and slope the sides of the berm, compacting it until it is 6 inches high. Fill the swale with 4 inches of gravel *(above, right)*, then backfill it with 2 inches of soil. Compact the soil, then put back any sod you removed, covering the berm and the swale *(inset)*; buy any additional sod needed at a garden center.

UNCLOGGING THE FLOOR DRAIN

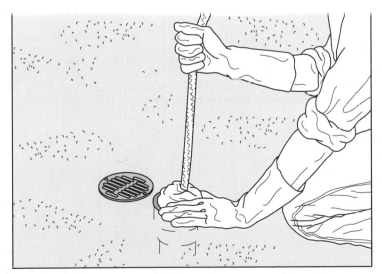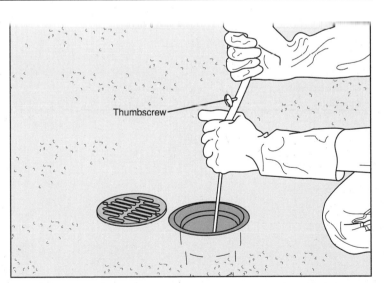

1 Using a hose. If the floor drain is clogged and drains poorly, lift off the grate and wear rubber gloves to remove any debris from the mouth of the drain; then, use a plunger to try clearing the drain. If you cannot clear the drain, insert the end of a garden hose as far as possible into it. Pack wet rags around the hose at the mouth of the drain to create a seal. Holding the hose and rags firmly in position *(above)*, have a helper turn on the water at full pressure; flush the drain until any blockage is washed down through the drainpipe, then put back the grate. If you cannot flush the drain and water begins to back up, use an auger *(step 2)*.

2 Using an auger. Clear a stubborn blockage with a trap-and-drain auger (plumber's snake), available at a building supply center. Wearing rubber gloves, unwind the auger and push the hooked end of the coil into the drainpipe until it hits the blockage and you can push it no farther; then, turn the thumbscrew to lock the handle. Slowly turn the handle clockwise; when it moves easily, stop turning it to feed in more coil. Continue the same way until you find no further obstruction, then remove the auger. Use a garden hose to run water into the drain to test it. If the water drains freely, put back the grate; otherwise, call a plumber to service the drain.

PREVENTING FLOOR-DRAIN BACKFLOW

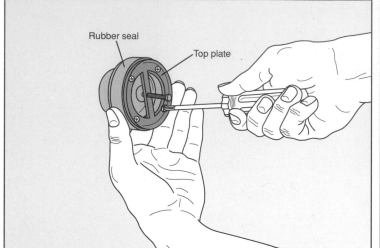

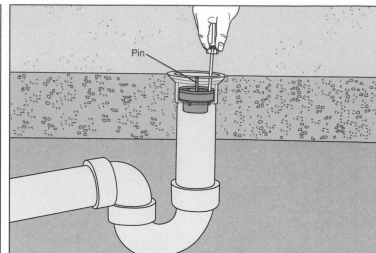

Installing a backflow-prevention valve. To prevent backflow out of the floor drain, install a backflow-prevention valve—allowing water into it but not back out of it. Check that the installation of a backflow-prevention valve is permitted by your local building code; also consult a licensed plumber to ensure that your drainpipe can withstand the pressure of any sewer backup. Buy a backflow-prevention valve suited to the diameter of the drainpipe at a building supply center and follow the manufacturer's instructions to install it. For the squeeze-in type of backflow-prevention valve shown, adjust it to fit snugly in the drainpipe without slipping down. Remove the drain grate, then tighten the screws on the top plate of the backflow-prevention valve to compress the rubber seal and increase its diameter *(above, left)*. Holding the backflow-prevention valve by its pin, insert it straight into the drainpipe; push it deep enough for the pin to sit below the mouth of the drainpipe. To lock the backflow-prevention valve in place, tighten each screw of the top plate in turn a little at a time *(above, right)*. Put back the drain grate.

SERVICING A DRAIN TILE SYSTEM

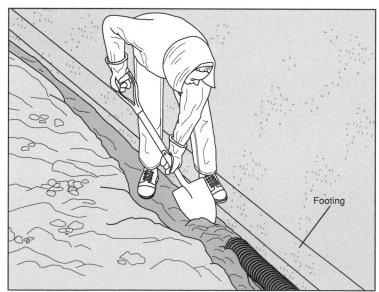

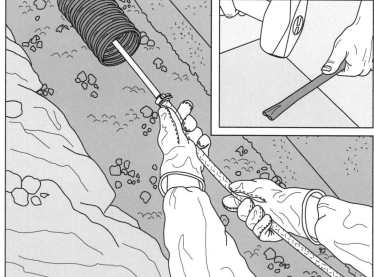

1 Inspecting the drain tile system. Check the drain tile system along a foundation wall if water continues to penetrate it after all other drainage systems are repaired. Plan to dig a trench 3 feet wide along the wall to the bottom of the footing; wait for a dry period. If a utility enters the house along the wall, it may need to be shut off; notify the utility company. Also consult your municipal authorities about the need for any building permit. To excavate along the wall, remove any sod or vegetation adjacent to it *(page 120)*; lay plastic sheets on the ground for the soil excavated. Hire a backhoe operator *(page 122)* or use a spade *(page 121)* to dig the trench, protecting it as necessary *(page 123)*; work carefully to expose the drain tile system near the footing *(above, left)*. If there is no drain tile system, install one; or, if the drain tile system is damaged extensively, replace it *(page 91)*. If a section of the drain tile system is damaged, replace it *(step 2)*. To clear a blocked section of the drain tile system, cut out or remove a section adjacent to it. Crimp one end of a copper pipe almost closed with a hand drilling hammer *(inset)* and use a hose clamp to connect the other end of it to an old garden hose; cut the hose to remove any fitting on the end of it. Fit the pipe into the blocked section and turn on the water to the hose fully, working as far into the section as necessary to clear it *(above, right)*.

SERVICING A DRAIN TILE SYSTEM (continued)

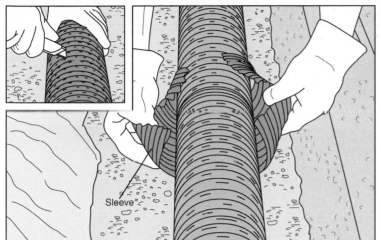

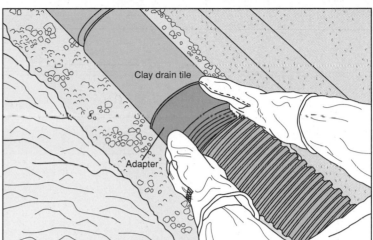

2 **Replacing a section of the drain tile system.** Replace any section of the drain tile system that is blocked and cannot be cleared or is otherwise damaged. Buy a matching replacement section for the drain tile system along with any couplings or adapters needed at a building supply center; if the system is of clay or concrete drain tile, use perforated, flexible or rigid plastic drainpipe. To install a section of flexible drainpipe, cut it to length using a utility knife *(inset)* and position it. To connect the section to other flexible drainpipe, use a coupling or a sleeve; for a sleeve, slit a short section of flexible drainpipe along its length, then fit it around the joint between the drainpipes *(above, left)*. To connect the section to clay or concrete drain tile, use an adapter; fit it onto the section, then into the drain tile *(above, right)*. Use the same procedure to install a section of rigid drainpipe, cutting it to length with a hacksaw and positioning it, then connecting it with a coupling or an adapter. After installing the section, place building paper over the joints of any clay or concrete drain tile, then cover the drain tile system with 6 to 24 inches of gravel and place landscaping fabric on it. Consider waterproofing the concrete *(page 24)* or masonry *(page 40)* foundation wall. Backfill the trench *(page 122)*, then put back any sod or vegetation you removed.

REPLACING A DRAIN TILE SYSTEM

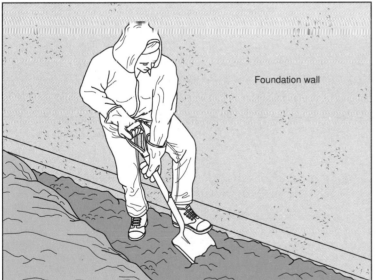

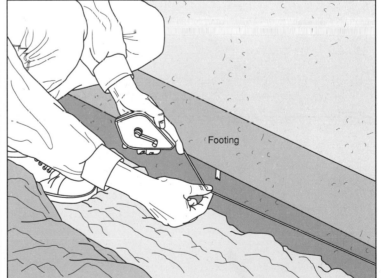

1 **Excavating and sloping the trench.** Dig a trench along each wall of the house *(above, left)* as you would to inspect a drain tile system *(page 90)*, removing any existing system; consult a building professional *(page 119)* about tunneling under any obstruction such as a driveway. If you are not replacing an existing drain tile system, also consult a building professional and your municipal authorities about having a system connected to an interior sump pit or an exterior drain site such as a storm sewer. If you are replacing an existing drain tile system, dig as deep as necessary to expose any outlet in a footing. A drain tile system should not be higher than any footing and should slope 1/2 to 1 inch every 8 feet to its low point—an outlet at a footing or an exterior drain site. To find the maximum slope possible for your drain tile system in inches per 8 feet, measure from the low point to the planned high point in feet and divide by 8, then divide the footing height in inches by the result. Mark this slope along the footings from the planned high point in each direction to the low point. Having a helper hold the end of a chalk line at the top of the footing at the planned high point, pull out 8 feet and hold the end of it down from the top of the footing by an amount equal to the slope *(above, right)*, then snap it; continue to the low point the same way.

REPLACING A DRAIN TILE SYSTEM (continued)

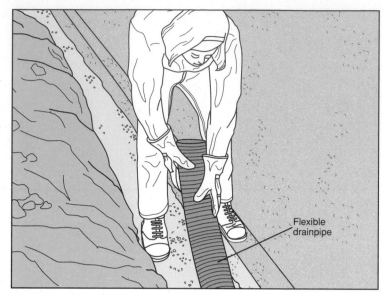

2 **Placing the drain tile system.** For a drain tile system, buy enough perforated, flexible or rigid plastic drainpipe 4 inches in diameter along with any couplings or other fittings needed at a building supply center; if the soil around the house is very fine and silty, buy a type of drainpipe wrapped in a fiber sock. Line the trench with at least 2 inches of gravel, filling and sloping it to the level of the chalk lines marked along the footings. Start at the low point of the drain tile system to place the drainpipe, working in one direction to the planned

high point and back to the low point. Place the drainpipe in the trench along the footing of each wall about 4 inches away from it *(above, left)*; set it against any outlet in a footing. Run the drainpipe in sections as long as possible to avoid joints. If necessary, cut a section of flexible drainpipe using a utility knife; cut a section of rigid drainpipe using a hacksaw. At any tunnel under an obstruction such as a driveway, feed a continuous section of drainpipe through it *(above, right)*; if necessary, connect sections of drainpipe together *(step 3)* to feed through it.

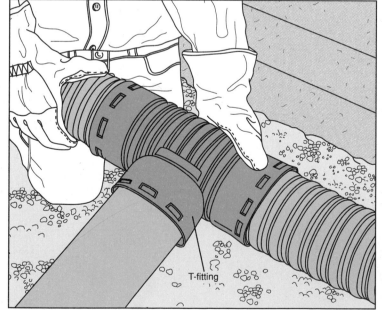

T-fitting

3 **Connecting the drain tile system and backfilling the trench.** Connect sections of drainpipe for the drain tile system using couplings. Or, if the drain tile system is of flexible drainpipe, connect sections using sleeves; for a sleeve, slit a short section of flexible drainpipe along its length, then open it and fit it around the joint between the sections. To connect sections of drainpipe to a drainpipe to an exterior drain site, use a T-fitting or other type of fitting suited to the drainpipes; if necessary, cut the sections to the length needed. If the drain tile system is of flexible drainpipe, push each section into the fitting *(above, left)* until its contours lock with the tabs. After connecting

the sections of drainpipe, cover the drain tile system with 6 to 24 inches of gravel *(above, right)* and place landscaping fabric on it; for any section of the system run through a tunnel under an obstruction such as a driveway, have a building professional cover it with gravel and place landscaping fabric on it, then backfill it. Consider waterproofing any concrete *(page 24)* or masonry *(page 40)* foundation wall. Evaluate the soil near the trench *(page 82)*; if its drainage capacity is poor, replace the soil excavated with soil of a higher drainage capacity. Backfill the trench *(page 122)*, then put back any sod or vegetation you removed.

SUMP PUMPS

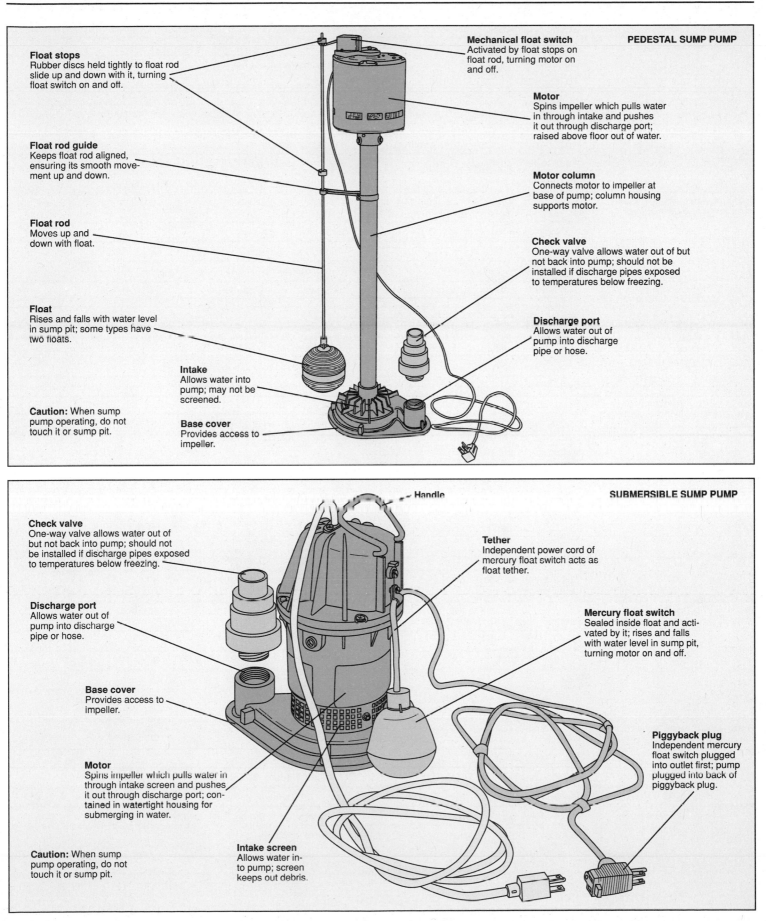

PEDESTAL SUMP PUMP

Float stops
Rubber discs held tightly to float rod slide up and down with it, turning float switch on and off.

Float rod guide
Keeps float rod aligned, ensuring its smooth movement up and down.

Float rod
Moves up and down with float.

Float
Rises and falls with water level in sump pit; some types have two floats.

Caution: When sump pump operating, do not touch it or sump pit.

Mechanical float switch
Activated by float stops on float rod, turning motor on and off.

Motor
Spins impeller which pulls water in through intake and pushes it out through discharge port; raised above floor out of water.

Motor column
Connects motor to impeller at base of pump; column housing supports motor.

Check valve
One-way valve allows water out of but not back into pump; should not be installed if discharge pipes exposed to temperatures below freezing.

Discharge port
Allows water out of pump into discharge pipe or hose.

Intake
Allows water into pump; may not be screened.

Base cover
Provides access to impeller.

SUBMERSIBLE SUMP PUMP

Handle

Check valve
One-way valve allows water out of but not back into pump; should not be installed if discharge pipes exposed to temperatures below freezing.

Discharge port
Allows water out of pump into discharge pipe or hose.

Base cover
Provides access to impeller.

Motor
Spins impeller which pulls water in through intake screen and pushes it out through discharge port; contained in watertight housing for submerging in water.

Caution: When sump pump operating, do not touch it or sump pit.

Intake screen
Allows water into pump; screen keeps out debris.

Tether
Independent power cord of mercury float switch acts as float tether.

Mercury float switch
Sealed inside float and activated by it; rises and falls with water level in sump pit, turning motor on and off.

Piggyback plug
Independent mercury float switch plugged into outlet first; pump plugged into back of piggyback plug.

TROUBLESHOOTING GUIDE (SUMP PUMPS)

SYMPTOM	POSSIBLE CAUSE	PROCEDURE
Sump pump does not turn on	Water level of sump pit too low	Allow water level of sump pit to rise
	Sump pump or piggyback float switch unplugged from outlet	Plug sump pump and any piggyback float switch into outlet
	No power to circuit or outlet faulty	Restore power to circuit; have outlet serviced
	Sump pump positioned incorrectly in sump pit; float obstructed by wall of sump pit	Reposition sump pump in sump pit; ensure float not obstructed
	Float switch adjusted incorrectly	Adjust float switch (p. 97) □○
	Float switch faulty	Test and replace float switch (p. 98) □◗
	Motor faulty	Take sump pump for professional service
Sump pump turns on; water level of sump pit too low	Sump pump positioned incorrectly in sump pit; float obstructed by wall of sump pit	Reposition sump pump in sump pit; ensure float not obstructed
	Float switch adjusted incorrectly	Adjust float switch (p. 97) □○
	Float switch faulty	Test and replace float switch (p. 98) □◗
	Float assembly faulty	Take sump pump for professional service
Sump pump turns on; no water pumped out of sump pit	Water level of sump pit too low	Allow water level of sump pit to rise
	Sump pump dirty	Clean sump pump (p. 96) □◗
	Float switch adjusted incorrectly	Adjust float switch (p. 97) □○
	Float switch faulty	Test and replace float switch (p. 98) □○
	Check valve faulty or missing	Service check valve (p. 99) ◳◗
	Float assembly faulty	Take sump pump for professional service
Sump pump turns on; water pumped out of sump pit only slowly	Sump pump dirty	Clean sump pump (p. 96) □◗
	Check valve faulty or missing	Service check valve (p. 99) ◳◗
	Sump pump capacity inadequate; sump pit too small	Call for professional evaluation
Sump pump does not turn off	Water level of sump pit too high	Allow water level of sump pit to drop
	Sump pump positioned incorrectly in sump pit; float obstructed by wall of sump pit	Reposition sump pump in sump pit; ensure float not obstructed
	Sump pump dirty	Clean sump pump (p. 96) □◗
	Float switch adjusted incorrectly	Adjust float switch (p. 97) □○
	Float switch faulty	Test and replace float switch (p. 98) □◗
	Sump pump capacity inadequate; sump pit too small	Call for professional evaluation
Sump pump turns off; water level of sump pit too high	Sump pump positioned incorrectly in sump pit; float obstructed by wall of sump pit	Reposition sump pump in sump pit; ensure float not obstructed
	Float switch adjusted incorrectly	Adjust float switch (p. 97) □○
	Float switch faulty	Test and replace float switch (p. 98) □◗
	Float assembly faulty	Take sump pump for professional service
	Sump pump capacity inadequate; sump pit too small	Call for professional evaluation
Sump pump turns on and off; noisy	Sump pump positioned incorrectly in sump pit	Reposition sump pump in sump pit
	Sump pump dirty	Clean sump pump (p. 96) □◗
	Motor faulty	Take sump pump for professional service
Sump pump turns on and off; overheats	Sump pump dirty	Clean sump pump (p. 96) □◗
	Motor faulty	Take sump pump for professional service
	Sump pump capacity inadequate; sump pit too small	Call for professional evaluation
Sump pit emits odor	Water stagnating; sump pump dirty	Clean sump pump (p. 96) □◗

DEGREE OF DIFFICULTY: □ Easy ◳ Moderate ■ Complex
ESTIMATED TIME: ○ Less than 1 hour ◗ 1 to 3 hours ● Over 3 hours

REMOVING AND REINSTALLING THE SUMP PUMP

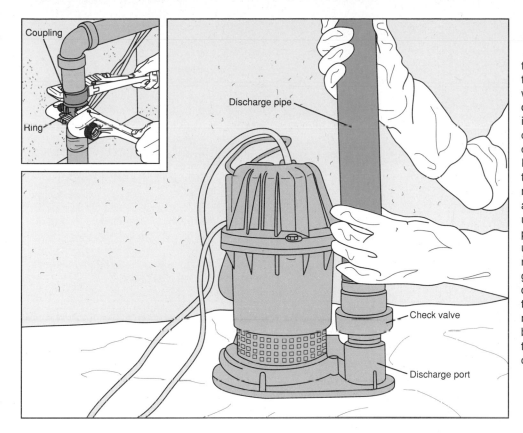

1 Removing the sump pump. Unplug the pump and any piggyback float switch; if the floor is wet, first shut off power to the circuit *(page 10)*. Free the power cord from the discharge pipe, removing any tape and unwinding it. Disconnect the pump from the main discharge pipe following the owner's manual instructions. If there is a flexible discharge hose connected to the pump, unscrew any hose clamp connecting it to the main discharge pipe. If there is a rigid discharge pipe connected to the pump, loosen the union connecting it to the main discharge pipe; if there is no union, have a plumber disconnect the pump and install a union. To loosen the union shown, hold the coupling steady with a pipe wrench and turn the ring using another pipe wrench *(inset)*. Thread the ring off the coupling by hand. Wearing rubber gloves, lift the sump pit cover and slide it off the discharge pipe or hose connected to the pump, then lift the pump out of the sump pit. Disconnect the discharge pipe or hose from the pump by unscrewing the check valve connecting it to the discharge port *(left)*. Empty any water out of the pump.

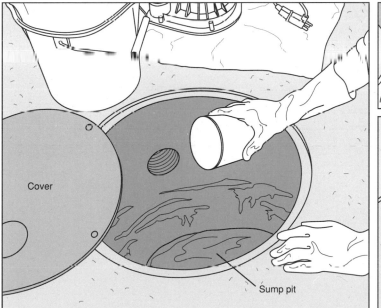

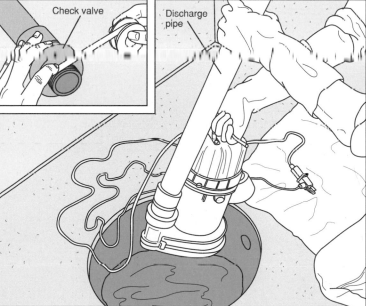

2 Reinstalling and testing the sump pump. Before reinstalling the pump, clean the sump pit. Wearing rubber gloves, use a container to scoop water and debris out of the sump pit *(above, left)*; also clean debris out of any drainpipe opening in the pit wall. Remove any gravel from the sump pit, then wash it and reinstall it. To reinstall the pump, reconnect any discharge pipe or hose you removed; for a pipe, wrap pipe tape around the threads of the check valve *(inset)*, then screw it onto the discharge port. Lower the pump into the sump pit *(above, right)*, standing it firmly on the bottom with its float assembly clear of the pit wall. Reinstall the sump pit cover, then reconnect the discharge pipe or hose to the main discharge pipe. Coil the power cord around the discharge pipe and tape it in place. Plug in any piggyback float switch and the pump; if necessary, restore power to the circuit. Test the pump following the owner's manual instructions. Wearing safety goggles, lift the sump pit cover and use a garden hose to fill the sump pit with water, noting the water level at which the pump turns on; remove the hose and allow the pump to operate, noting the water level at which it turns off. Repeat the procedure several times. If the pump does not turn on and off at the water levels recommended in the owner's manual, adjust the float level *(page 97)*; otherwise, reinstall the sump pit cover.

CLEANING THE SUMP PUMP

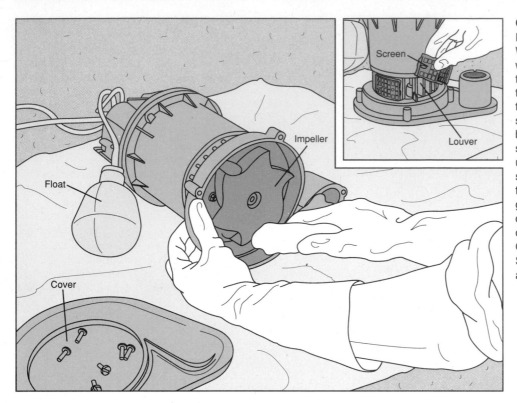

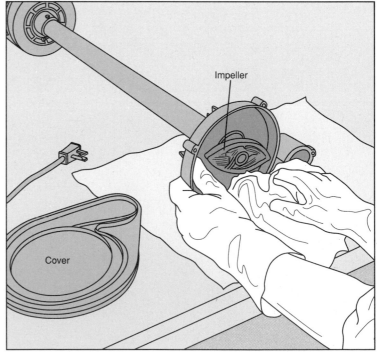

Cleaning a submersible sump pump.
Remove the pump from the sump pit *(page 95)*. Wearing rubber gloves, use a damp cloth to wipe dirt and debris off the float assembly and the pump housing. To disassemble and clean the pump, follow the owner's manual instructions. For the model shown, unscrew the intake screen *(inset)* and wipe off the intake louvers behind it, then wash the intake screen and reinstall it. Carefully lay the pump on its side and unscrew the base cover, then wipe off the inside of the base and the impeller *(left)*. Check the operation of the impeller; spin it, then try to gently wiggle it from side to side. If the impeller does not spin freely, is loose and wiggles, or is otherwise damaged, take the pump for service. Otherwise, wash the base cover and reinstall it. Service the check valve *(page 99)*, then reinstall and test the pump *(page 95)*.

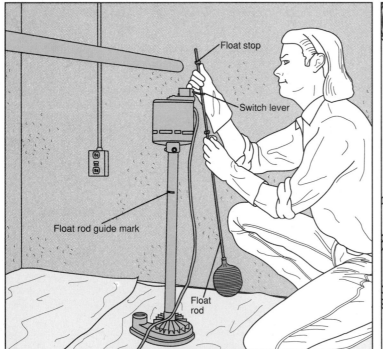

Cleaning a pedestal sump pump. Remove the pump from the sump pit *(page 95)*. Wearing rubber gloves, use a damp cloth to wipe dirt and debris off the float assembly, the pump housing and the intake ports. To disassemble and clean the pump, follow the owner's manual instructions. For the model shown, remove the float assembly, marking the position of each part for reassembly. Mark the position of the float rod guide on the motor shaft, then unscrew it. Mark the position of the upper float stop on the float rod, then slide it off *(above, left)*. Slide the float rod through the hole in the switch lever and set it aside; if it is bent or otherwise damaged, buy an exact replacement from the manufacturer. Carefully lay the pump on its side and unscrew the base cover, then wipe off the inside of the base and the impeller *(above, right)*. Check the operation of the impeller; spin it, then try to gently wiggle it from side to side. If the impeller does not spin freely, is loose and wiggles, or is otherwise damaged, take the pump for service. Otherwise, wash the base cover and reinstall it. Reinstall the float rod, float stop and float rod guide using the position marks to align them properly. Service the check valve *(page 99)*, then reinstall and test the pump *(page 95)*.

ADJUSTING THE FLOAT SWITCH

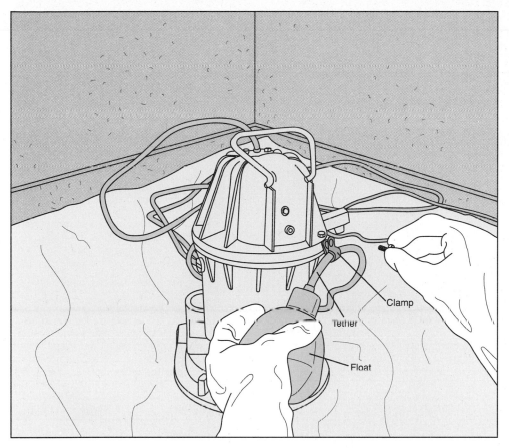

Adjusting a mercury float switch. Unplug the pump and the piggyback float switch; if the floor is wet, first shut off power to the circuit *(page 10)*. To adjust the float switch, wear rubber gloves and follow the owner's manual instructions. For the model shown, remove the pump from the sump pit *(page 95)* and unscrew the clamp holding the switch tether to the pump housing. Lift off the tether and the clamp *(left)*, then spread the prongs of the clamp to slide it along the tether, adjusting the switch; in general, adjust the switch to start the pump when water in the sump pit is 10 inches below floor level. If the pump starts when water in the sump pit is less than 10 inches below floor level, slide the clamp toward the float to shorten the tether; if the pump starts when water in the sump pit is more than 10 inches below floor level, slide the clamp away from the float to lengthen the tether. Reinstall and test the pump *(page 95)*.

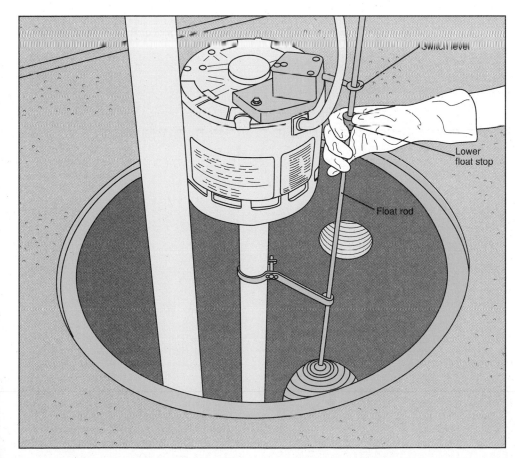

Adjusting a mechanical float switch. Unplug the pump. If the floor is wet, first shut off power to the circuit *(page 10)*. If necessary, remove the pump from the sump pit *(page 95)*; otherwise, lift off the sump pit cover. To adjust the float switch, wear rubber gloves and follow the owner's manual instructions. For the model shown, hold the float rod firmly and slide the appropriate float stop up or down it *(left)*. In general, position the lower float stop on the float rod so it presses up against the bottom of the float switch lever and turns on the pump when the water level in the sump pit rises to 10 inches below floor level; position the upper float stop on the float rod so it presses down against the top of the float switch lever and turns off the pump when the water level in the sump pit falls below the intake ports. Reinstall the pump or the sump pit cover, then test the pump *(page 95)*.

REPLACING THE FLOAT SWITCH

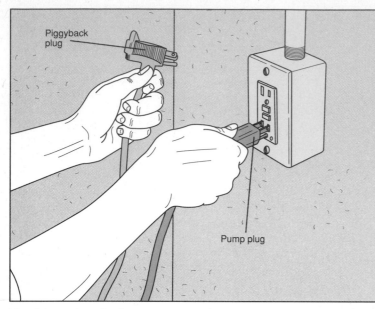

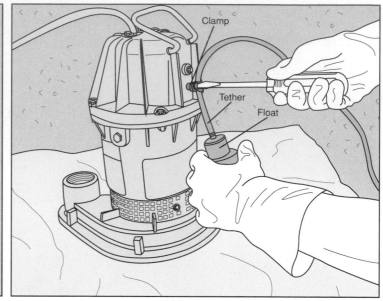

Testing and replacing a mercury float switch. Unplug the pump and the piggyback float switch; if the floor is wet, first shut off power to the circuit *(page 10)*. To test the outlet, restore power to the circuit, then plug a working lamp in turn into each receptacle and turn it on; if the lamp does not light, the outlet is faulty and must be repaired. Otherwise, remove the pump from the sump pit *(page 95)* to test the motor. Momentarily plug in the pump—but not the piggyback float switch *(above, left)*. If the motor does not start, take the pump for service. If the motor starts, immediately unplug the pump and replace the float switch following the owner's manual instructions. For the model shown, measure and record the length of the tether between the clamp and the float, then unscrew the clamp *(above, right)* and spread its prongs to free the tether. Buy a replacement float switch from the manufacturer, ensuring its float, tether and plug match those of the old switch; dispose of the old switch according to local environmental regulations. To install the new float switch, fit the clamp onto its tether at the same point the clamp was fitted onto the tether of the old switch; then, screw the clamp onto the pump housing. Reinstall and test the pump *(page 95)*.

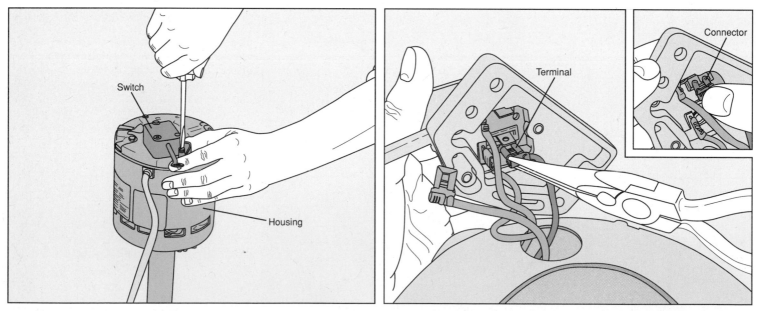

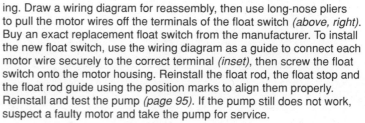

Testing and replacing a mechanical float switch. Unplug the pump; if the floor is wet, first shut off power to the circuit *(page 10)*. To test the outlet, restore power to the circuit, then plug a working lamp in turn into each receptacle and turn it on; if the lamp does not light, the outlet is faulty and must be repaired. Otherwise, remove the pump from the sump pit *(page 95)* and replace the float switch following the owner's manual instructions. For the model of pedestal pump shown, remove the float assembly as you would to clean the pump *(page 96)*, then unscrew the float switch *(above, left)* and lift it off the motor hous- ing. Draw a wiring diagram for reassembly, then use long-nose pliers to pull the motor wires off the terminals of the float switch *(above, right)*. Buy an exact replacement float switch from the manufacturer. To install the new float switch, use the wiring diagram as a guide to connect each motor wire securely to the correct terminal *(inset)*, then screw the float switch onto the motor housing. Reinstall the float rod, the float stop and the float rod guide using the position marks to align them properly. Reinstall and test the pump *(page 95)*. If the pump still does not work, suspect a faulty motor and take the pump for service.

SERVICING THE CHECK VALVE

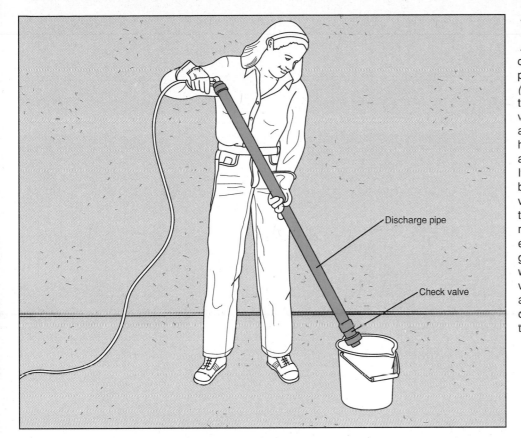

1 **Testing the check valve.** Remove the pump from the sump pit *(page 95)*. If there is no check valve on the end of the discharge pipe or hose you disconnected from the pump, install a check valve and discharge pipe *(step 2)* or hose *(step 3)* if recommended by the manufacturer; otherwise, test the check valve to ensure that it is unblocked and operating properly. Holding the discharge pipe or hose with the check valve over a bucket, use a garden hose to trickle water through it *(left)*. If water passes through the check valve into the bucket, remove any blockage keeping the check valve open and test it again; if water still passes through, the check valve is faulty. If water does not pass through the check valve into the bucket, invert the discharge pipe or hose and use the garden hose to trickle water through it again; if water does not pass through this time, the check valve is faulty. If the check valve is faulty, install a new check valve and discharge pipe *(step 2)* or hose *(step 3)*; otherwise, reinstall and test the pump *(page 95)*.

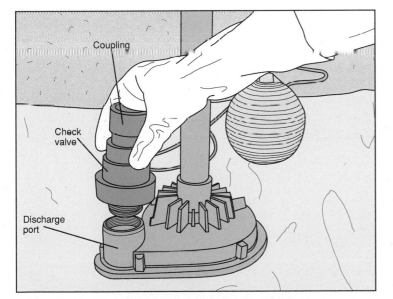

2 **Installing a check valve and discharge pipe.** To install a check valve and discharge pipe, buy a plastic check valve to fit the discharge port of the pump; also buy a discharge pipe to connect the pump to the main discharge pipe and a coupling to attach each end of it. Solvent-weld *(page 85)* a coupling to the discharge side of the check valve, then wrap pipe tape around the threads on the other side of it and screw it onto the discharge port *(above)*. Solvent-weld one end of the discharge pipe to the coupling on the check valve and the other end of it to the other coupling. Reinstall and test the pump *(page 95)*, connecting the discharge pipe to the main discharge pipe.

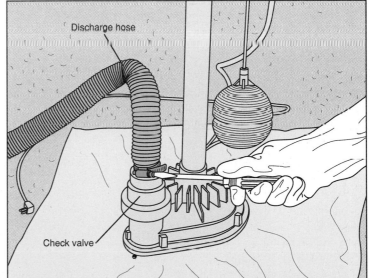

3 **Installing a check valve and discharge hose.** To install a check valve and discharge hose, buy a plastic check valve to fit the discharge port of the pump; also buy a discharge hose to connect the pump to the main discharge pipe and a hose clamp to attach each end of it. Wrap pipe tape around the threads of the check valve and screw it onto the discharge port. Connect one end of the discharge hose to the discharge side of the check valve with a hose clamp, using a screwdriver to tighten it *(above)*. Reinstall and test the pump *(page 95)*, connecting the other end of the discharge hose to the main discharge pipe with a hose clamp the same way.

STRUCTURAL WOOD

The structural wood in your basement or crawlspace works with the foundation walls and the floor to safely support the house above it. The basic structural wood members found in the basement or crawlspace of a house with conventional platform framing are shown at right; the specific size and spacing of the members may vary according to local building code. Sill plates set on top of the foundation walls and post-supported girders that span the distance between the walls support joists and headers laid on top of them. The joists and headers, in turn, support a subfloor that provides a base for the house flooring and walls. In new houses, members such as girders and posts may be of metal rather than of wood; for repairs, consult a building professional.

Although wood is a common and durable building material, wood members can weaken with age or as a result of foundation movement or settlement, resulting in cracks or sags; and wood is always vulnerable to rot and insect damage. Inspect the structural wood in the basement or crawlspace of your home regularly, paying particular attention to the members that are in contact with the foundation walls, such as sill plates, headers and girders, and with the floor, such as posts. Have a helper walk across the flooring above while you look for loose joints and moving components, as well as damage to the wood. To help you identify a problem and the steps you should take to remedy it, use the Troubleshooting Guide *(page 102)*.

If you find wood that is soft and spongy, pitted or crumbling, suspect rot or insect damage *(page 102)*. For any insect damage or for extensive rot damage to a wood member, consult a building professional. In most instances, minor rot damage to a sill plate, header, girder or post can be repaired. If you repair a rot problem, also troubleshoot your drainage systems *(page 78)* to solve the dampness or wetness problem that is causing the rot. Before starting a structural wood repair, consult your local building inspection office to ensure that the repair is made in compliance with the current building code.

Familiarize yourself with the safety advice presented in the Emergency Guide *(page 8)*. If the basement in your home is finished, refer to the chapter entitled Basement Floors And Walls *(page 54)* for procedures on gaining access to the structural wood above the ceiling. Consult Tools & Techniques *(page 110)* for information on the tools needed for repairs; a repair such as bracing a girder with scabs *(page 105)*, replacing a post *(page 106)* or supporting a girder with a permanent jack *(page 108)* requires you to rent and use a telescoping jack *(page 105)*. The basement or crawlspace of homes in certain regions can be vulnerable to high levels of radon gas, a consequence of radium in the soil or groundwater under the floor and around the walls; find out if you live in an area where radon gas is a problem and test for it *(page 119)*. If you have any doubt about your ability to successfully complete a repair, do not hesitate to consult a building professional *(page 119)*.

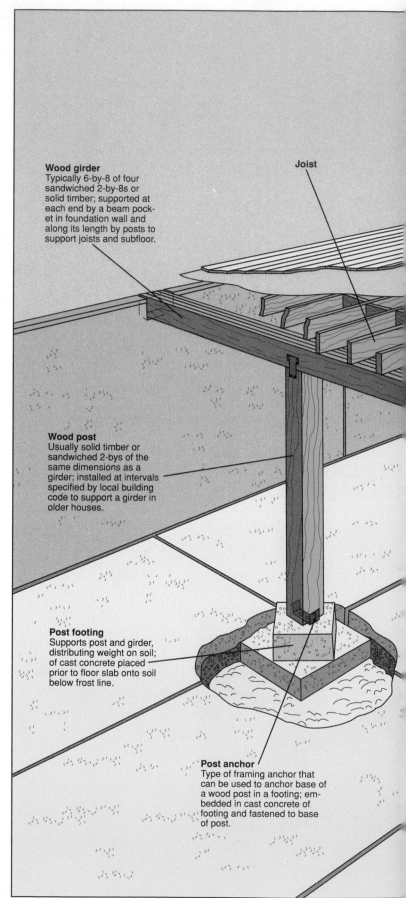

Wood girder
Typically 6-by-8 of four sandwiched 2-by-8s or solid timber; supported at each end by a beam pocket in foundation wall and along its length by posts to support joists and subfloor.

Joist

Wood post
Usually solid timber or sandwiched 2-bys of the same dimensions as a girder; installed at intervals specified by local building code to support a girder in older houses.

Post footing
Supports post and girder, distributing weight on soil; of cast concrete placed prior to floor slab onto soil below frost line.

Post anchor
Type of framing anchor that can be used to anchor base of a wood post in a footing; embedded in cast concrete of footing and fastened to base of post.

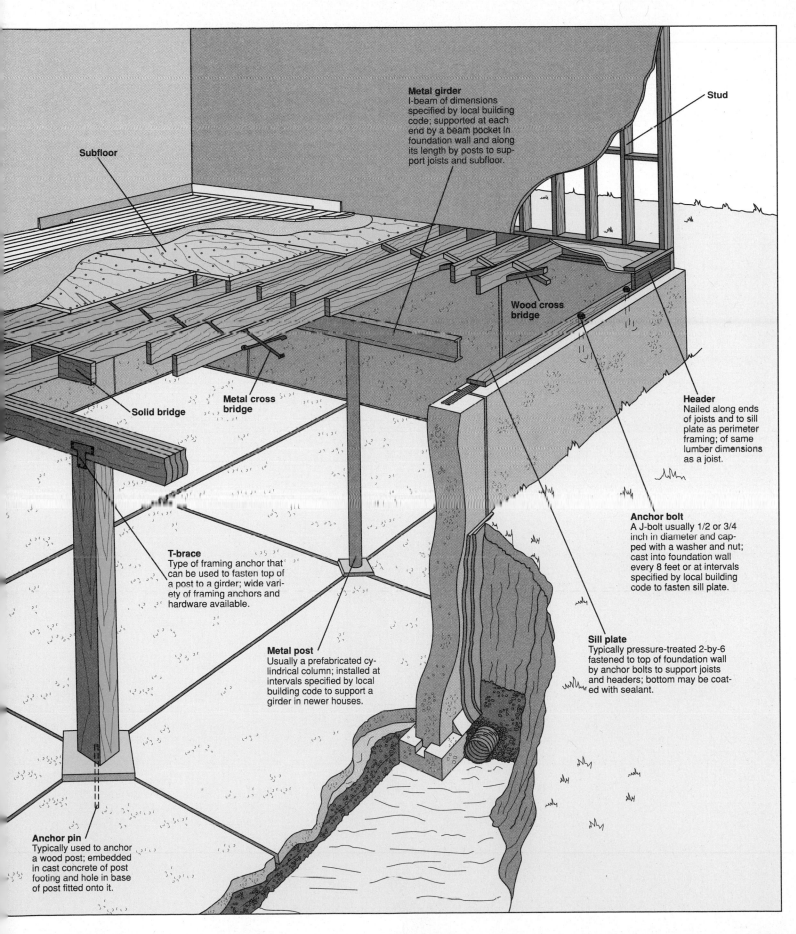

Metal girder
I-beam of dimensions specified by local building code; supported at each end by a beam pocket in foundation wall and along its length by posts to support joists and subfloor.

Stud

Subfloor

Wood cross bridge

Header
Nailed along ends of joists and to sill plate as perimeter framing; of same lumber dimensions as a joist.

Metal cross bridge

Solid bridge

Anchor bolt
A J-bolt usually 1/2 or 3/4 inch in diameter and capped with a washer and nut; cast into foundation wall every 8 feet or at intervals specified by local building code to fasten sill plate.

T-brace
Type of framing anchor that can be used to fasten top of a post to a girder; wide variety of framing anchors and hardware available.

Metal post
Usually a prefabricated cylindrical column; installed at intervals specified by local building code to support a girder in newer houses.

Sill plate
Typically pressure-treated 2-by-6 fastened to top of foundation wall by anchor bolts to support joists and headers; bottom may be coated with sealant.

Anchor pin
Typically used to anchor a wood post; embedded in cast concrete of post footing and hole in base of post fitted onto it.

TROUBLESHOOTING GUIDE

SYMPTOM	POSSIBLE CAUSE	PROCEDURE
Girder crooked, twisted or sagging	Girder damaged	Brace girder with scabs (p. 105) ◨◐▲ or support girder with permanent jack (p. 108) ◼◐▲
	Post supporting girder damaged	Replace post (p. 106) ◨◐▲
	Post footing or foundation wall damaged	Consult a building professional
Girder split or cracked; or, wood spongy, pitted or crumbling	Rot or insect damage	Inspect wood for rot and insect damage (step below) □○; patch minor wood rot (p. 103) □○ and troubleshoot drainage systems (p. 78)
	Wood shrinkage; foundation settlement	Brace girder with scabs (p. 105) ◨◐▲ or support girder with permanent jack (p. 108) ◼◐▲
Post crooked, twisted or leaning	Post damaged	Replace post (p. 106) ◨◐▲
	Post footing damaged	Consult a building professional
Post split or cracked; or, wood spongy, pitted or crumbling	Rot or insect damage	Inspect wood for rot and insect damage (step below) □○; patch minor wood rot (p. 103) □○ and troubleshoot drainage systems (p. 78)
	Wood shrinkage; foundation settlement	Replace post (p. 106) ◨◐▲
Header split or cracked; or, wood spongy, pitted or crumbling	Rot or insect damage	Inspect wood for rot and insect damage (step below) □○; patch minor wood rot (p. 103) □○ and troubleshoot drainage systems (p. 78)
	Wood shrinkage; foundation settlement	Reinforce header section (p. 103) □○
Sill plate split or cracked; or, wood spongy, pitted or crumbling	Rot or insect damage	Inspect wood for rot and insect damage (step below) □○; patch minor wood rot (p. 103) □○ and troubleshoot drainage systems (p. 78)
	Wood shrinkage; foundation settlement	Replace sill plate section (p. 104) ◨◐▲

DEGREE OF DIFFICULTY: □ Easy ◨ Moderate ◼ Complex
ESTIMATED TIME: ○ Less than 1 hour ◐ 1 to 3 hours ● Over 3 hours

▲ Special tool required

INSPECTING WOOD FOR ROT AND INSECT DAMAGE

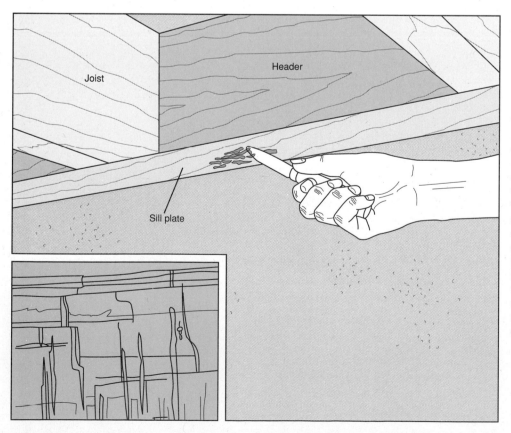

Joist

Header

Sill plate

Identifying wood damage. To check for rot and insect damage, closely inspect any structural wood in the basement or crawlspace; wood near plumbing fixtures or in contact with a foundation wall or floor slab is especially vulnerable. Include in your check the subfloor, the joists, the headers, the sill plates, the outside end of joists, the bottom of posts and the base of staircase stringers. If the wood is pitted or powdery, riddled with tiny holes or tunnels, or supporting long, gray tubes, suspect insect damage and consult a pest control professional. Spongy wood fibers and gray or dark discoloration are telltale signs of rot; look for wood that is damp, split or cracking across the grain (inset). Wood suffering from rot may also exhibit no visible signs of a problem. To test for rot, press the point of a knife or an awl as deeply as possible into the wood (left). If the wood is soft and gives way, crumbling instead of splintering, it is weakened by rot. For a small area of surface rot, repair it (page 103). For extensive rot damage, consult a building professional.

PATCHING MINOR WOOD ROT

Repairing damaged wood. To patch a small area of surface rot, use a wood chisel. Wearing work gloves and safety goggles, scrape out all of the soft, rotted wood down to firm, healthy wood *(above, left)*. Buy epoxy patching compound at a building supply center and prepare it following the manufacturer's instructions. Use a putty knife to pack patching compound into the depression in the wood, overfilling it slightly *(above, right)*; then, draw the edge of the putty knife along the patch to scrape off excess patching compound and level the patch flush with the surrounding surface. Allow the patching compound to cure for the time specified by the manufacturer.

REINFORCING A HEADER SECTION

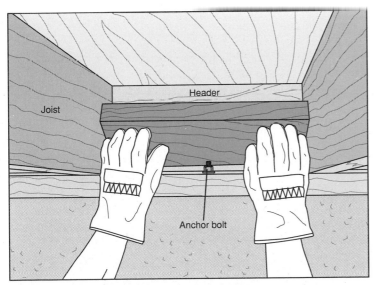

1 Installing blocking. If the header is damaged extensively, consult a building professional. For minor damage to a small section of the header, reinforce the section between two joists with blocking. To make blocking, measure the length of the header section between the joists, then wear work gloves and a dust mask to cut a piece of pressure-treated lumber of the same dimensions as the joists to length; apply wood preservative to the cut edges. Wearing safety goggles and a safety helmet, fit the blocking between the joists, angling it behind any anchor bolt in the sill plate *(above)*; then, push the blocking flush against the header section.

2 Fastening the blocking. Fasten the blocking to the header section behind it and to the joist at each end of it using 2 1/2-inch common nails. To fasten the blocking to the header section behind it, drive a nail through the top and the bottom of the blocking into the header section a few inches from each end of it. To fasten the blocking to the joist at each end of it, nail at an angle through the top and the bottom of the blocking into the side of the joist *(above, left)*; if there is access to the end of a joist on the side of it opposite the blocking, also drive a nail through the top and bottom of the joist into the end of the blocking *(above, right)*.

REPLACING A SILL PLATE SECTION

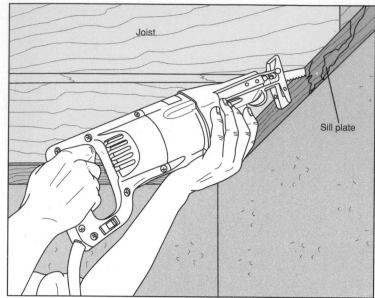

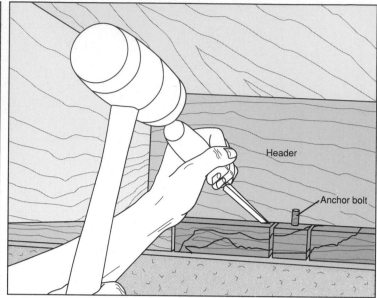

1 **Removing the damaged section.** If the sill plate is damaged extensively, consult a building professional. For minor damage to a small section of the sill plate, replace the damaged section. Wearing safety goggles and a safety helmet, use a pry bar to pull out any nails holding the damaged section to the header or any joists it supports; also remove the nut and washer from any anchor bolt protruding from the top of it. If the damaged section supports a joist, use a telescoping jack to raise the end of the joist 1/16 inch as you would a girder *(page 105)*; to raise the end of more than one joist, set up a

jack under at least every second joist and use a 4-by-4 longer than the distance between them as a brace on the 2-by-8 pad, temporarily nailing the top plate of the jack to the pad and the pad to the brace. Use a reciprocating saw to cut down at a 90-degree angle through each end of the damaged section *(above, left)*; also cut down the same way on each side of any anchor bolt protruding from the top of it. Then, use a wood chisel and a mallet to chip out the damaged section *(above, right)*, working under the header and any joist supported by it.

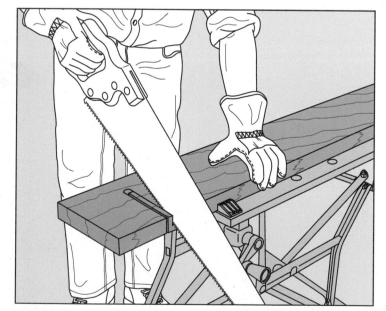

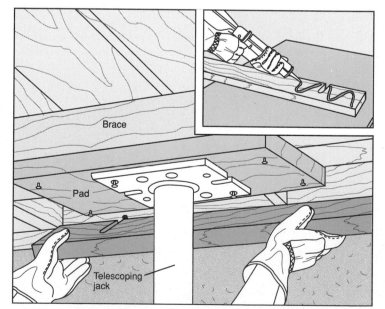

2 **Preparing the replacement section.** Measure the length of the opening in the sill plate, then wear work gloves to cut a piece of pressure-treated lumber of the same dimensions as the sill plate to size. Measure the position of any anchor bolt in the sill plate opening and mark it on the replacement section. Use an electric drill to bore a hole for the anchor bolt at the marked point, then use a saw to cut a notch for it; cut straight to each side of the hole from the edge to be fitted under the header *(above)*. Apply wood preservative to the cut edges of the replacement section.

3 **Installing the replacement section.** Use a caulking gun to apply a bead of urethane caulk along the bottom of the replacement section *(inset)*. Wearing safety goggles and a safety helmet, fit the replacement section into position under the header and any joist, aligning any notch in it with the anchor bolt *(above)*; if necessary, use a hand drilling hammer to tap it. Remove any telescoping jack. Fit any anchor bolt protruding from the replacement section with a washer and install a nut on it. Use 3-inch box nails to nail at an angle through the header into the replacement section; nail through any joist supported by the replacement section into it the same way.

USING A TELESCOPING JACK

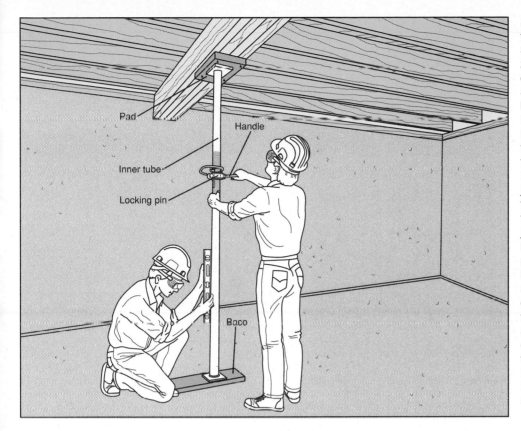

Supporting or raising a girder. Rent a telescoping jack at a tool rental agency. Using 3-inch box nails, temporarily nail a 2-by-8 pad 2 feet long to the bottom of the girder at the center of the damaged section of it. Then, place a 2-by-8 base 2 feet long on the floor directly below the pad. To set up the jack, work with a helper and wear safety goggles and a safety helmet. Assemble the jack following the manufacturer's instructions supplied with it. Measure the distance between the base and the pad. Detach the locking pin from the inner tube of the jack and extend the inner tube until the length of the jack is slightly less than the measured distance; then, reattach the locking pin to lock the jack. Lift the jack to an upright position and fit it between the base and the pad, centering the top plate under the pad and the bottom plate on the base. With a helper using a carpenter's level, align the jack so it is plumb; then, turn the handle of the screw jack assembly counterclockwise to raise the jack until its top plate presses firmly against the pad *(left)*, supporting the girder without raising it. If you are repairing the girder, continue extending the jack to raise the girder until it is level, raising it no more than 1/8 inch per day. If a crack develops while raising the girder, consult a building professional.

BRACING A GIRDER WITH SCABS

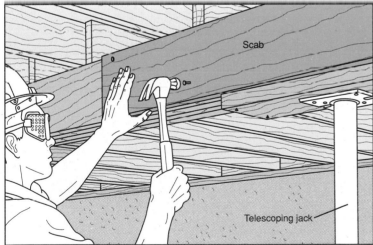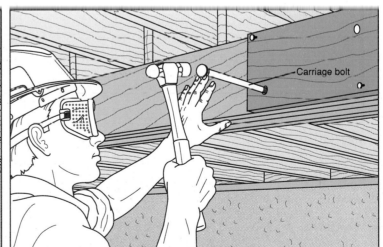

Installing scabs. If the girder is damaged extensively or sags along its entire length, consult a building professional. If the damage to the girder is localized and the sag is slight, reinforce the girder by installing a scab on each side of the damaged section. Use a telescoping jack to raise the girder until it is level *(step above)*; raise it no more than 1/8 inch per day and 1/2 inch per week. To make each scab, use a saw to cut a piece of lumber of the same grade and dimensions as a joist 6 feet longer than the damaged section. Wearing safety goggles and a safety helmet, position a scab on one side of the girder, centering it on the damaged section; temporarily nail it to the girder with 3-inch common nails, driving a nail every 12 to 16 inches along it, alternating between the top and the bottom edge *(above, left)*. Position the other scab on the other side of the girder and temporarily nail it in place the same way. Then, bore holes for carriage bolts through the scabs and the girder; plan to use carriage bolts that are 10 inches long. Fit an electric drill with an auger bit of the same diameter as a carriage bolt, then bore a hole every 12 to 16 inches through the scabs and the girder, alternating between the top and the bottom about 2 inches from any edge. Use a ball-peen hammer to tap a carriage bolt into each hole *(above, right)*, then install a washer and a nut on the threaded end of each carriage bolt, tightening the nuts with a wrench. Remove the telescoping jack.

REPLACING A POST

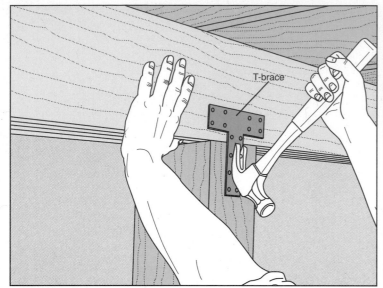

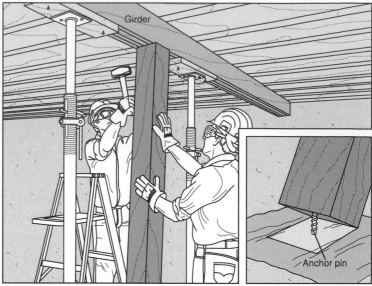

Anchor pin

1 **Removing the post.** To replace a post, install a telescoping jack within 2 feet of it under the girder on each side of it *(page 105)*. Wearing safety goggles and a safety helmet, work with a helper to remove the post. If the base of the post is held by a post anchor, have your helper steady the post while you remove the fasteners from the post anchor; if the base of the post rests directly on the footing, trace its outline on the footing. Then, remove the fasteners and any framing anchor holding the top of the post to the girder; to remove the T-brace shown, pull out the nails *(above, left)*. With your helper steadying the post, use a hand drilling hammer to knock the top of it from under the

girder *(above, right)*. Then, pull away the post; if the base of it sits on an anchor pin embedded in the footing, lift it off *(inset)*. Check that the girder is level using a carpenter's level; if necessary, extend the jacks until it is level, raising it no more than 1/8 inch per day and 1/2 inch per week. Each time you extend the jacks, have a helper check the nearby walls on the stories above the girder for cracks. If a crack develops while raising the girder, consult a building professional. Otherwise, continue extending the jacks the same way, raising the girder until the joists supported by it are level.

Footing

2 **Preparing the replacement post.** To make a replacement post, measure the vertical distance between the bottom of the girder and the footing *(above, left)* or the post anchor where the old post stood. Then, use a handsaw to cut lumber of the same grade and dimensions as the old post to length *(above, right)*. Or, cut lumber of the same grade and dimensions as the joists to length, cutting as many pieces as necessary to make a post of the same thickness as

the girder. To make a post of four 2-by-8s, for example, use 3-inch common nails; fasten one 2-by-8 to another 2-by-8 by driving a nail every 12 to 16 inches along it, alternating between the top and the bottom edges of it, then fasten a 2-by-8 to each side of the fastened 2-by-8s the same way. If the footing for the post has a post anchor or an anchor pin, install the replacement post *(step 4)*; otherwise, first install an anchor pin in the footing *(step 3)*.

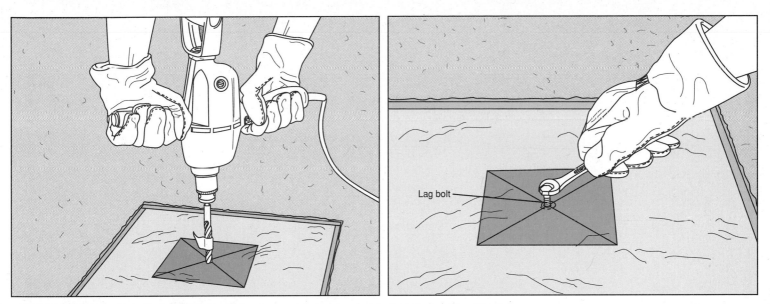

3 **Installing an anchor pin.** For a makeshift anchor pin, use a 2 inch lag bolt and a 1 inch shield of the same diameter as it. To determine the location for the anchor pin, use the outline of the old post traced on the footing *(step 1)*, marking lines between the corners diagonally opposite to each other. Wearing safety goggles and a dust mask, use a hammer drill fitted with a percussion-type masonry bit to drill a hole for the shield in the footing at the intersection of the marked lines between the corners; drill the hole equal in diameter to the shield and equal in depth to its length *(above, left)*, wrapping masking tape around the bit to mark the drilling depth. Tap the shield into the hole with a ball-peen hammer, then fit the lag bolt into the shield and use a wrench to turn it *(above, right)* until it protrudes 1 inch out of the footing. Cut the head off the lag bolt using a hacksaw.

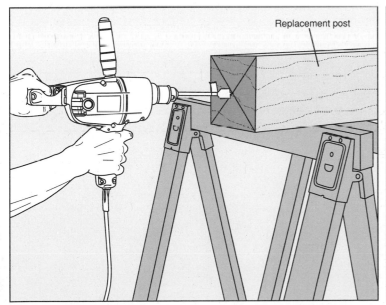

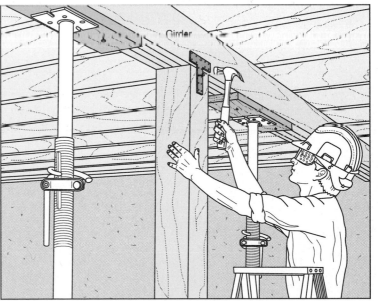

4 **Installing the replacement post.** If there is an anchor pin in the footing, bore a hole for it in the base of the replacement post. Fit an electric drill with a bit of the same diameter as the anchor pin and wrap masking tape around it to mark a drilling depth equal to the amount the anchor pin protrudes out of the footing. To determine the location for the hole in the base of the post, mark lines on it between the corners diagonally opposite to each other. Then, bore a hole of the marked depth into the base of the post at the intersection of the marked lines between the corners *(above, left)*. To install the post, work with a helper to stand it upright, fitting the base of it onto the anchor pin

or any post anchor; then, slide the top of the post into position under the girder. If the post fits tightly, use a hand drilling hammer to tap it into place; if it fits loosely, use a hammer to drive a shim on opposite sides of it between it and the girder. Use a carpenter's level to check that the post is plumb; if necessary, reposition it. When the post is plumb, fasten the top of it to the girder using framing anchors; for example, nail a T-brace to the post and the girder on opposite sides of the girder *(above, right)*. If the base of the post is installed in a post anchor, also fasten the post anchor to the post. Remove the telescoping jacks.

SUPPORTING A GIRDER WITH A PERMANENT JACK

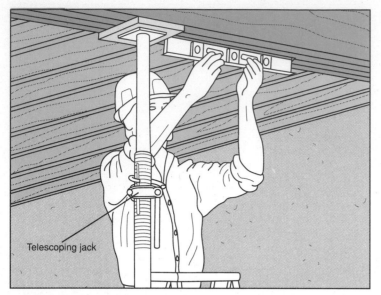

Telescoping jack

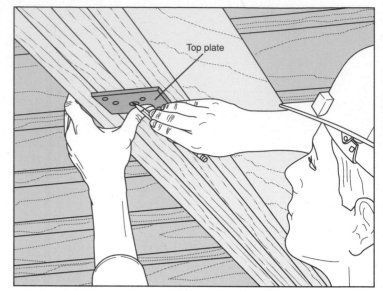

Top plate

1 **Preparing to support the girder.** If the damage to the girder is localized and the sag is slight, reinforce the girder by installing a scab on each side of the damaged section *(page 105)*. If the girder is damaged extensively or sags along its entire length, consult a building professional; if recommended, support it by installing a permanent jack under it at a specified location on any specified footing. Set up a telescoping jack *(page 105)* under the girder a few feet from the point to be supported with a permanent jack and raise the girder until it is level *(above)*; raise it no more than 1/8 inch per day and 1/2 inch per week.

2 **Marking the location for a permanent jack.** Buy a permanent jack to use as a post for supporting the girder at a building supply center. Hold the top plate of the jack against the bottom of the girder at the point to be supported and mark its center point on the girder *(above)*. Drive a nail partway into the marked point, then hang a plumb bob from the nail. If you are installing the jack on the floor, install the base plate *(step 4)*; if you are installing a footing to support the jack, mark the location for a footing of the size specified on the floor using the point below the plumb bob as a center point.

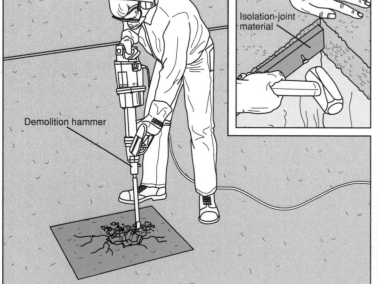

Demolition hammer

Isolation-joint material

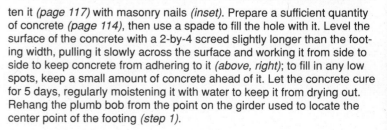

Screed

3 **Installing a footing.** Rent a demolition hammer at a tool rental agency and use it to break up the concrete at the footing location. Wearing ear protection, safety goggles, a dust mask and work gloves, chip holes 6 to 8 inches apart in the concrete within the footing marks, cracking it into pieces *(above, left)*. Use a spade to remove the concrete pieces and the gravel or soil below them, digging to the depth specified. To prepare the hole for concrete, install 1/2-inch isolation-joint material along the floor edge on each side of it; buy the isolation-joint material at a building supply center, cut it to size and fas-

ten it *(page 117)* with masonry nails *(inset)*. Prepare a sufficient quantity of concrete *(page 114)*, then use a spade to fill the hole with it. Level the surface of the concrete with a 2-by-4 screed slightly longer than the footing width, pulling it slowly across the surface and working it from side to side to keep concrete from adhering to it *(above, right)*; to fill in any low spots, keep a small amount of concrete ahead of it. Let the concrete cure for 5 days, regularly moistening it with water to keep it from drying out. Rehang the plumb bob from the point on the girder used to locate the center point of the footing *(step 1)*.

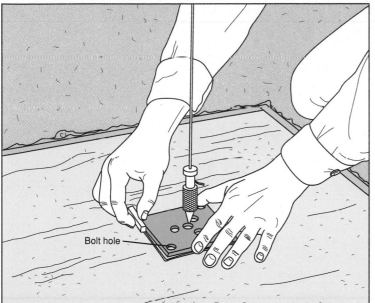

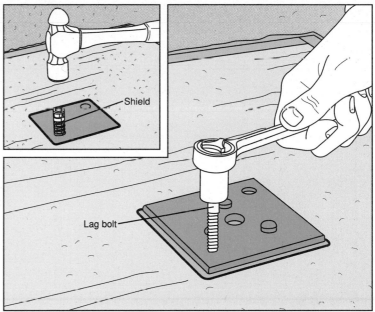

4 **Installing the jack base plate.** To install the base plate for a permanent jack, use lag bolts and shields; if necessary, rent a 1/2-inch hammer drill and a percussion-type masonry bit at a tool rental agency to drill holes for the shields in the floor or footing. To position the base plate, center it on the floor or footing under the plumb bob and mark its outline and bolt-hole positions on the surface *(above, left)*, then remove it. Wearing safety goggles and a dust mask, use the ham-mer drill to drill a hole at each bolt-hole mark equal in diameter to a shield and equal in depth to its length. Tap a shield into each hole with a ball-peen hammer *(inset)*, then reposition the plate over the lag shields. Check that the base plate is level using a carpenter's level; if necessary, insert a steel shim under an edge to level it. Then, install the lag bolts, fitting each one in turn into a shield and driving it with a socket wrench *(above, right)* until its head is tight against the base plate.

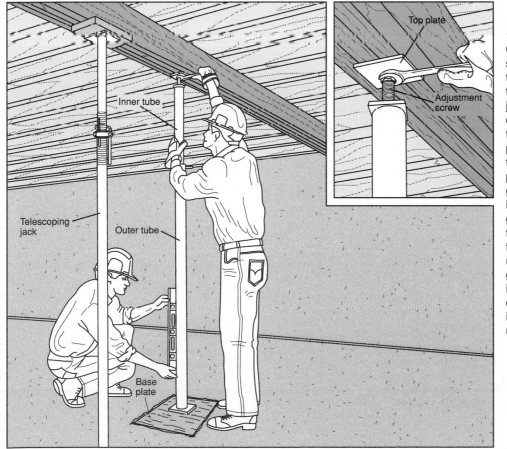

5 **Installing a permanent jack.** Install the jack on the base plate following the manufacturer's directions for your model. On the model shown, install the adjustment screw and the top plate on the end of the inner tube, then fit the bottom of the outer tube onto the base plate. With a helper supporting the jack, raise the inner tube to within 2 to 3 inches of the bottom of the girder; insert the pin through the holes to lock it. With the helper using a carpenter's level, align the jack so it is plumb; then, turn the adjustment screw *(inset)* to raise the top plate until it fits snugly against the bottom of the girder *(left)*, supporting the girder without raising it. Use the carpenter's square to check that the girder is level by holding it against the bottom of the girder between the permanent jack and the telescoping jack. If the girder is not level, continue extending the permanent jack to raise the girder until it is level, raising it no more than 1/8 inch per day and 1/2 inch per week. If a crack develops while raising the girder, consult a building professional. When the girder is level, remove the telescoping jack.

TOOLS & TECHNIQUES

This section introduces basic tools and techniques used in repairing basements and foundations, such as mixing concrete or mortar *(page 114)*, applying sealant *(page 115)*, fastening to concrete or masonry *(page 117)* and digging *(page 121)*. Charts on cleaning agents, concrete and mortar mixes, and fasteners are designed for easy reference. Instructions on working with heavy materials *(page 113)*, working with electricity *(page 115)*, and working with ladders *(page 125)* are included for your safety.

Most repairs can be handled with the basic kit of tools and supplies shown below and on page 111. You can buy most tools and supplies at a building supply center. Special equipment such as a demolition hammer or a telescoping jack can be obtained at a tool rental agency. Materials such as bentonite sheets or granules and elastomeric urethane caulk may be available only at a construction material supplier; parts for drainage systems may be available only through a specialized dealer or the manufacturer.

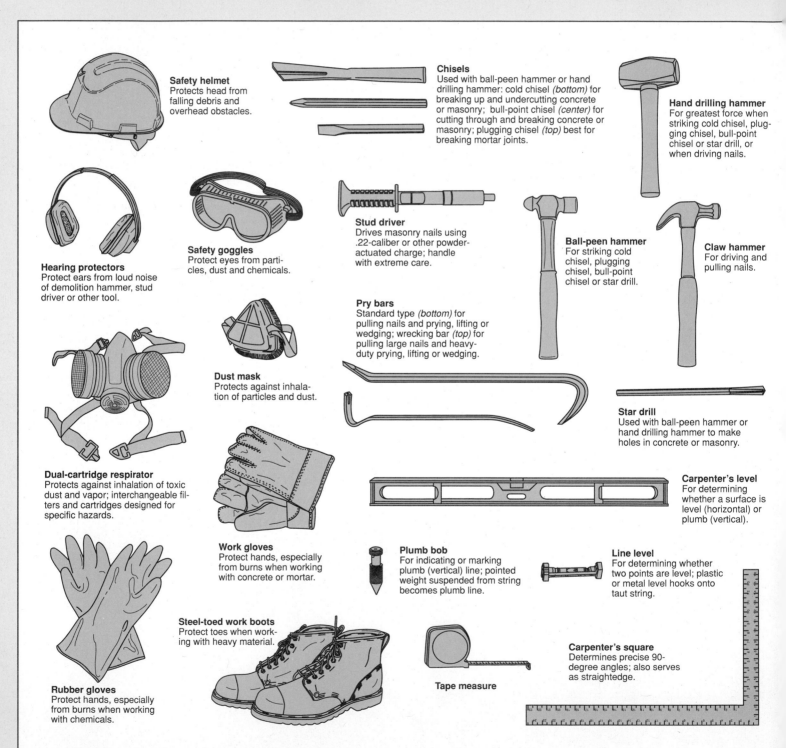

Safety helmet
Protects head from falling debris and overhead obstacles.

Chisels
Used with ball-peen hammer or hand drilling hammer: cold chisel *(bottom)* for breaking up and undercutting concrete or masonry; bull-point chisel *(center)* for cutting through and breaking concrete or masonry; plugging chisel *(top)* best for breaking mortar joints.

Hand drilling hammer
For greatest force when striking cold chisel, plugging chisel, bull-point chisel or star drill, or when driving nails.

Hearing protectors
Protect ears from loud noise of demolition hammer, stud driver or other tool.

Safety goggles
Protect eyes from particles, dust and chemicals.

Stud driver
Drives masonry nails using .22-caliber or other powder-actuated charge; handle with extreme care.

Ball-peen hammer
For striking cold chisel, plugging chisel, bull-point chisel or star drill.

Claw hammer
For driving and pulling nails.

Pry bars
Standard type *(bottom)* for pulling nails and prying, lifting or wedging; wrecking bar *(top)* for pulling large nails and heavy-duty prying, lifting or wedging.

Dust mask
Protects against inhalation of particles and dust.

Star drill
Used with ball-peen hammer or hand drilling hammer to make holes in concrete or masonry.

Dual-cartridge respirator
Protects against inhalation of toxic dust and vapor; interchangeable filters and cartridges designed for specific hazards.

Carpenter's level
For determining whether a surface is level (horizontal) or plumb (vertical).

Work gloves
Protect hands, especially from burns when working with concrete or mortar.

Plumb bob
For indicating or marking plumb (vertical) line; pointed weight suspended from string becomes plumb line.

Line level
For determining whether two points are level; plastic or metal level hooks onto taut string.

Steel-toed work boots
Protect toes when working with heavy material.

Carpenter's square
Determines precise 90-degree angles; also serves as straightedge.

Tape measure

Rubber gloves
Protect hands, especially from burns when working with chemicals.

For the best results, always use the right tool for the job—and be sure to use the tool correctly. When you are shopping for new tools, purchase the highest-quality ones you can afford. Take the time to care for your tools properly. Avoid laying tools on the ground unprotected. Clean off metal tools immediately and remove any rust *(page 113)*; lubricate tools according to the manufacturer's instructions and have any tool sharpened by a professional. Store tools safely away, well out of the reach of children.

Read and follow the safety information in the Emergency Guide *(page 8)*. Always wear the proper clothing and protective gear for the job. Set up a temporary barrier to keep others away from the work area, especially if a trench has been dug; ensure that any excavation is protected from caving in *(page 123)*. Get expert technical help when you need it; if you are ever in doubt about your ability to undertake or complete a repair, do not hesitate to consult a building professional *(page 119)*.

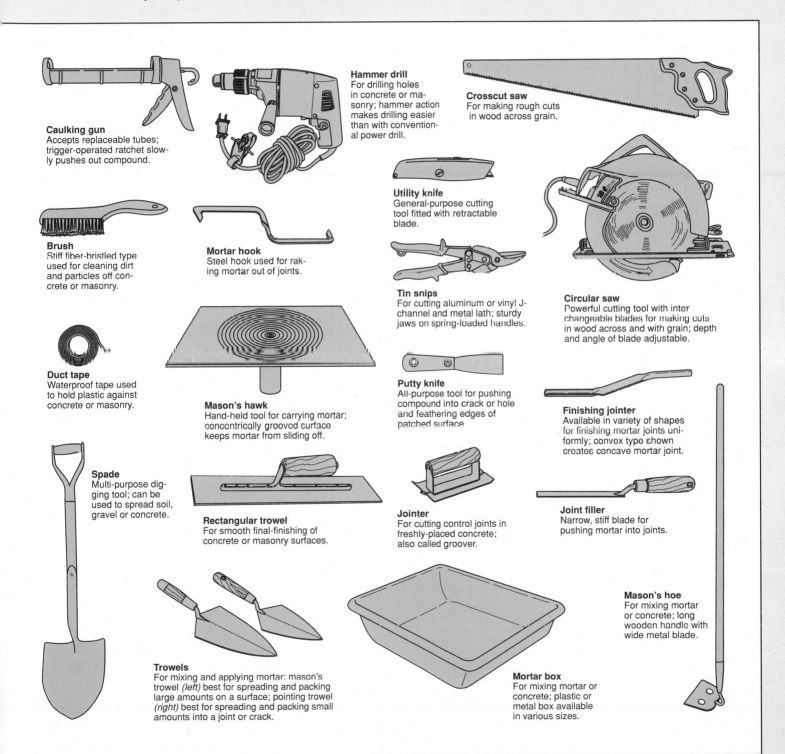

Caulking gun
Accepts replaceable tubes; trigger-operated ratchet slowly pushes out compound.

Hammer drill
For drilling holes in concrete or masonry; hammer action makes drilling easier than with conventional power drill.

Crosscut saw
For making rough cuts in wood across grain.

Brush
Stiff fiber-bristled type used for cleaning dirt and particles off concrete or masonry.

Mortar hook
Steel hook used for raking mortar out of joints.

Utility knife
General-purpose cutting tool fitted with retractable blade.

Tin snips
For cutting aluminum or vinyl J-channel and metal lath; sturdy jaws on spring-loaded handles.

Circular saw
Powerful cutting tool with interchangeable blades for making cuts in wood across and with grain; depth and angle of blade adjustable.

Duct tape
Waterproof tape used to hold plastic against concrete or masonry.

Mason's hawk
Hand-held tool for carrying mortar; concentrically grooved surface keeps mortar from sliding off.

Putty knife
All-purpose tool for pushing compound into crack or hole and feathering edges of patched surface.

Finishing jointer
Available in variety of shapes for finishing mortar joints uniformly; convex type shown creates concave mortar joint.

Spade
Multi-purpose digging tool; can be used to spread soil, gravel or concrete.

Rectangular trowel
For smooth final-finishing of concrete or masonry surfaces.

Jointer
For cutting control joints in freshly-placed concrete; also called groover.

Joint filler
Narrow, stiff blade for pushing mortar into joints.

Trowels
For mixing and applying mortar: mason's trowel *(left)* best for spreading and packing large amounts on a surface; pointing trowel *(right)* best for spreading and packing small amounts into a joint or crack.

Mortar box
For mixing mortar or concrete; plastic or metal box available in various sizes.

Mason's hoe
For mixing mortar or concrete; long wooden handle with wide metal blade.

CLEANING CONCRETE AND MASONRY

STAIN	CLEANING AGENT AND METHOD
Asphalt or tar	Apply ice until asphalt or tar brittle, then scrape off with putty knife
	Using reagent of mineral spirits, apply poultice *(step below, right)*
Caulking compound	Scrape off with putty knife
	Using reagent of denatured alcohol, apply poultice *(step below, right)*
Efflorescence	Brush off or scrub off with water
	Scrub off with solution of 1 cup TSP and 1 cup household detergent per gallon of water
	Scrub off with solution of 1 part muriatic acid to 12 parts water. **Caution:** Add acid to water; never add water to acid
Grease or oil	Scrape off with putty knife or blot up with absorbent cloth or cat litter
	Scrub off with scouring powder and water or solution of 1 cup TSP and 1 cup household detergent per gallon of water
	Using reagent of mineral spirits, apply poultice *(step below, right)*
Mildew	Scrub off with solution of 1 cup TSP and 1 cup household detergent per 1 quart of household bleach and 3 quarts of water
Moss	Apply commercial herbicide following manufacturer's instructions
Paint	Scrape off with putty knife
	Using reagent of commercial paint remover, apply poultice *(step below, right)* and remove after 30 minutes
Rust	Scrub off with solution of 1 part oxalic acid to 10 parts water. **Caution:** Add acid to water; never add water to acid
	Using reagent of 1 part sodium or ammonium citrate, 7 parts lime-free glycerine and 6 parts warm water, apply poultice *(step below, right)*

Removing stains. Use the chart at left to choose an appropriate cleaning agent and method for the stain; for any commercial product, follow the manufacturer's instructions, heeding to the letter all safety recommendations. Always start with the mildest cleaning agent and method, listed first in the chart; continue to the strongest as necessary. Before applying a cleaning agent to a surface, protect the surfaces adjacent to it with dropcloths, then remove any climbing plant from it *(step below, left)* and soak it with water. Test a cleaning agent such as a poultice *(step below, right)* on an inconspicuous spot of the surface; wait several days to judge its effectiveness. Scrub using a stiff fiber brush—not a wire brush; dislodged particles of it can rust. Rinse off any cleaning agent thoroughly with water; if necessary, use a little scouring powder, household detergent or TSP (trisodium phosphate) to remove any residue, then rinse again. Store or dispose of leftover cleaning agents safely.

Removing a climbing plant. To remove a climbing plant, use an ammonium sulfate paste or a herbicide; buy it at a garden center and follow the manufacturer's instructions to apply it. Cut the plant stems about 6 inches from ground level using pruning shears, then wear rubber gloves and goggles to apply the paste or herbicide to the cut stems with an old paintbrush *(above)*. When the plant withers, remove it; wherever plant growth remains, repaint it with the paste or herbicide. When the plant stems stop growing, use a spade to dig up the roots.

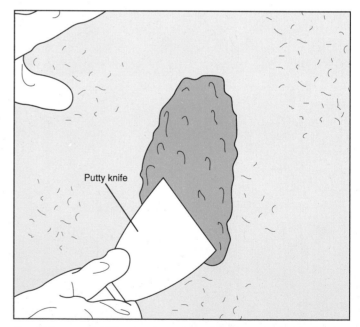

Putty knife

Applying a poultice. Work in a temperature of 60 to 80 degrees Fahrenheit and wear rubber gloves to prepare a poultice, mixing it to a stiff paste; refer to the chart above for the appropriate reagent and use an inert material such as talcum powder, diatomaceous soil, fuller's earth or bentonite. Soak the stain with water, then coat it heavily with the poultice using a putty knife *(above)* and tape plastic sheeting over it with duct tape. After 24 hours, remove the plastic sheeting and scrape off the poultice, then rinse the surface with water.

CLEANING HAND TOOLS

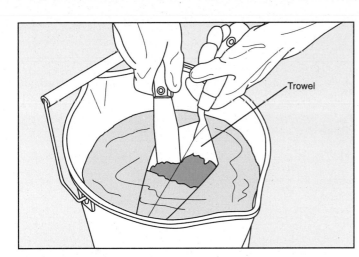

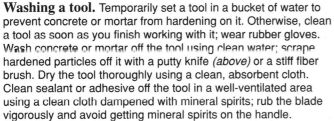

Washing a tool. Temporarily set a tool in a bucket of water to prevent concrete or mortar from hardening on it. Otherwise, clean a tool as soon as you finish working with it; wear rubber gloves. Wash concrete or mortar off the tool using clean water; scrape hardened particles off it with a putty knife *(above)* or a stiff fiber brush. Dry the tool thoroughly using a clean, absorbent cloth. Clean sealant or adhesive off the tool in a well-ventilated area using a clean cloth dampened with mineral spirits; rub the blade vigorously and avoid getting mineral spirits on the handle.

Removing rust from a tool. Clean rust off a tool as soon as you notice it. Wearing rubber gloves, dip the tool in clean water, then scrub the rust off it with steel wool *(inset)*; rub until the metal is shiny. Dry the tool thoroughly using a clean, absorbent cloth. To help protect the tool from rusting, use another clean cloth to coat the metal with a small amount of light machine oil *(above)*; work carefully to avoid getting any machine oil on the handle.

WORKING SAFELY WITH HEAVY MATERIALS

Lifting and moving heavy material. Repairs to a basement or foundation can call for the use of heavy materials that must be handled carefully. Wear work gloves to protect your hands and steel-toed work boots to protect your feet; be sure to take periodic breaks. Always lift heavy materials with a straight back *(above, left)*, relying on the muscles in your legs for strength. Use a wheelbarrow to transport heavy materials; a heavy-duty type with a

pneumatic (air-filled) tire is easiest to use. To move a heavy bag of cement, for example, set the wheelbarrow on its side and roll the bag of cement into it; be careful not to twist your back. Use both hands to push the wheelbarrow upright, squatting to grip it securely by the sides *(above, right)*, then standing up without bending your back; work with a helper, if necessary. **Caution:** To avoid back injury, do not try to stand the wheelbarrow upright using the handles.

PREPARING CONCRETE AND MORTAR

MIX	INGREDIENTS	REMARKS
Bonding slurry	Portland cement	Mix with water to runny, creamy consistency; apply with stiff fiber brush before it sets (dries white) just before main coat
Mortar (type M)	Packaged mortar mix	Mix with water to thick, buttery consistency that holds shape; apply with trowel up to 2 hours after mixing, retempering once by adding water, if necessary
	1 part portland cement, 1/4 part hydrated lime and 3 parts sand	
	1 part portland cement, 1 part type II masonry cement and 6 parts sand	
Concrete	Packaged concrete mix	Mix with water to thick consistency that slides without crumbling; place useing wheelbarrow or spade up to 1 1/2 hours after mixing
	1 part portland cement, 2 1/2 parts wet sand and aggregate: 1 1/2 parts 3/8-inch gravel; 2 parts of 1/2 inch gravel; or 2 1/2 parts 3/4-inch gravel	
Concrete patching mix	Latex concrete patching compound (may require no water)	Mix with water to thick, buttery consistency that holds shape; apply with trowel up to 1 hour after mixing
	1 part portland cement and 2 1/2 parts fine sand	

Choosing the right recipe. Use the chart above to choose the right recipe for the job; for more information on preparing mortar, see page 32. Buy the ingredients listed for your recipe by volume at a building supply center. For concrete, calculate the volume you need in cubic feet: surface area multiplied by depth; in general, 1 cubic foot requires 1/3 of a typical 94-pound bag of portland cement. If you are using a commercial packaged mix or latex concrete patching compound, follow the manufacturer's instructions; otherwise, mix the ingredients *(step below)* in the correct proportions to achieve the consistency indicated in the chart.

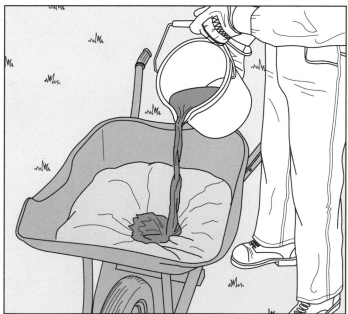

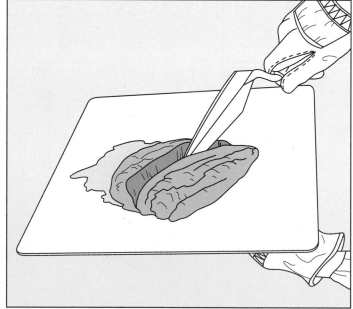

Mixing the ingredients. Mix the ingredients for your recipe in a clean wheelbarrow, mortar box or bucket; fill it no more than 3/4 full. Wearing work gloves, measure the correct proportion of each dry ingredient by volume in a graduated container; for a large volume, use full or partial spadefuls. Use a pointing or mason's trowel, a mason's hoe, or a spade to mix the dry ingredients together, then form a well in the center of them and add clean water a little at a time *(above, left)*. Lift and turn the ingredients to mix them thoroughly, adding water until the consistency indicated in the chart is achieved. To test a mix of concrete or mortar, use a trowel to place a small mound of it on a mason's hawk or a piece of plywood and slice it in half along its length *(above, right)*; it should hold its shape and separate firmly without crumbling or collapsing. If the mound collapses, add dry ingredients in the correct proportions; if it crumbles or is too stiff to flow slightly, add water a little at a time.

APPLYING CAULK, SEALANT AND ADHESIVE

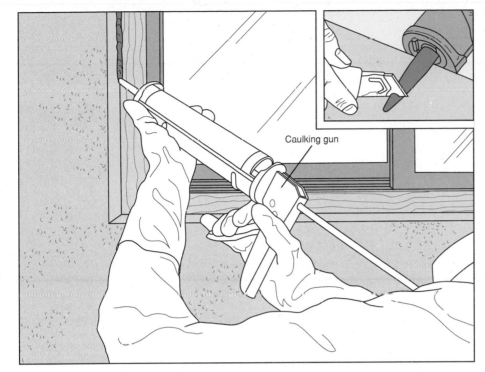

Caulking gun

Using a caulking gun. Buy a cartridge of caulk, sealant or adhesive at a building supply center and follow the manufacturer's instructions to apply it. Ensure that use of the product is recommended for your job and materials; for an opening that may expand or contract, choose an elastomeric sealant—a urethane type, for example. To prepare the surfaces, scrape dirt and particles off them with a putty knife, clean them using a solution of mild household detergent and water, and let them dry; apply any primer recommended and let it dry. For an opening deeper than 1/2 inch, fill it to within 1/4 inch of the surface with foam backing rod. Load the cartridge into a caulking gun, then cut off its tip at a 45-degree angle with a utility knife (inset); make the opening in it slightly narrower than any opening you are filling. Use an awl or a long nail to puncture the cartridge seal. Holding the caulking gun at a 45-degree angle to the surfaces, squeeze the trigger to eject a continuous bead of the product (left). If necessary, run a wet rubber-gloved finger or putty knife along the product to press it into place, smoothing and shaping it.

WORKING SAFELY WITH ELECTRICITY

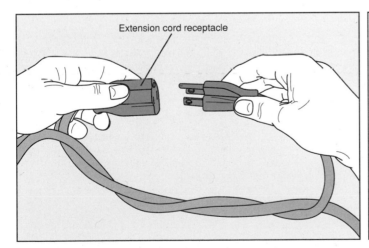

Extension cord receptacle

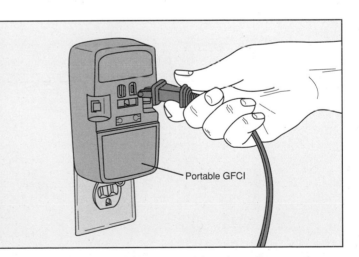

Portable GFCI

Plugging in safely. Use only a power tool that is grounded or double-insulated; check it to ensure that it is UL- (Underwriters Laboratories) or CSA- (Canadian Standards Association) approved. Use only a heavy-duty, three-prong extension cord rated for outdoor use; never use a standard household extension cord and avoid working with a series of extension cords. Inspect the power cord of the tool and the extension cord before plugging in; have a damaged power cord repaired and replace any damaged extension cord. Otherwise, loop the power cord and the extension cord together loosely (above, left) to prevent them from disconnecting. Plug the extension cord only into an outlet protected by a GFCI (ground-fault circuit interrupter)—a requirement of the U.S. National Electrical Code for any new outlet installed outdoors, in a garage or basement, or within 6 feet of an area subject to moisture. If an outlet does not have a built-in GFCI, use an extension cord with a built-in GFCI or install a portable GFCI, plugging it into the outlet following the manufacturer's instructions, then plugging into it (above, right).

DRILLING

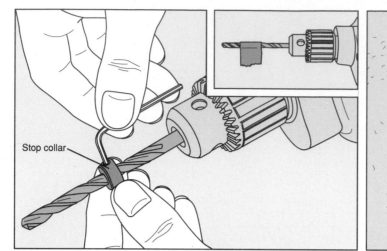

Using a drill. Always use a drill fitted with an appropriate bit for the job; to drill into concrete or masonry, use a hammer drill fitted with a masonry bit. Install the bit in the chuck of the drill and set the speed of the drill following the manufacturer's instructions. To drill to a specified depth, use a stop collar; slide it into position on the bit and tighten it *(above, left)*. Or, wrap a strip of masking tape around the bit to create a short flag *(inset)* that can be seen when the drill is running. Wearing safety goggles and respiratory protec-

tion, plug in the drill; with a cordless type, ensure that the battery pack is charged and loaded correctly. Position the bit against the surface to be drilled at a 90-degree angle to it; hold the drill with both hands without blocking an air vent. Slowly depress the trigger switch *(above, right)*, gradually increasing pressure after the hole is started. Stop drilling periodically to blow particles out of the hole; withdraw the bit before releasing the trigger switch and allow the motor and the bit to cool before continuing.

CUTTING

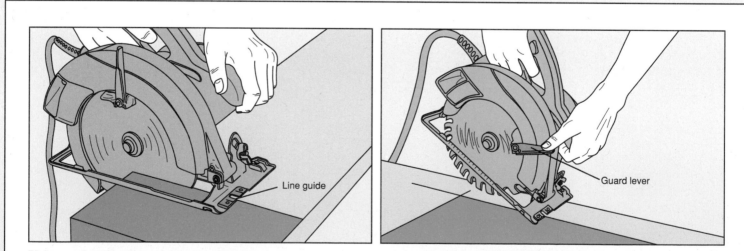

Using a circular saw. Install an appropriate blade on the saw, then adjust the cutting depth and angle following the manufacturer's instructions. Wearing safety goggles, plug in the saw and position it. For a standard cut, rest the toe of the baseplate on the surface at one end of the cutting line without the blade touching it. Standing to one side of the saw, depress and hold the trigger switch; when the blade is turning at full speed, guide the saw along the cutting line, watching the line guide position *(above, left)*; let the blade cut at its own speed. At the end of the cutting line, release the trigger switch, then let the blade stop turning before set-

ting the saw down. For a plunge cut, hold the saw by the top handle and retract the lower blade guard manually. Resting the toe of the baseplate on the surface near one end of the cutting line, align the blade and line guide with the cutting line. Pivot the saw to raise the blade off the surface *(above, right)*, then depress and hold the trigger switch; when the blade is turning at full speed, lower it straight into the cutting line. When the baseplate rests flat on the surface, release the lower blade guard and guide the saw along the cutting line. At the end of the cutting line, release the trigger switch and let the blade stop turning, then lift the saw and set it down.

CUTTING (continued)

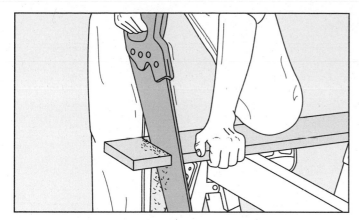

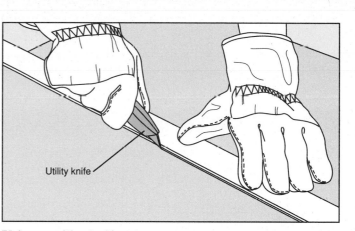

Utility knife

Using a handsaw. Hold the saw perpendicular to the surface and butt the blade against one end of the cutting line. With your thumb resting against the blade to guide it, draw the saw up several times to notch the edge. Lower the saw to a 45-degree angle, align your arm and shoulder with the blade, and start the cut with short strokes, push down firmly and pull up lightly. Gradually lengthen the strokes *(above)*, fully extending your arm on the downstroke and drawing it back on the upstroke. To finish the cut, hold the saw almost perpendicular and use short strokes; if necessary, brace any unsupported edge with your free hand.

Using a utility knife. Use a utility knife to score or cut a variety of thin materials; wear work gloves. To score or cut along a straight line, align the tip of the blade with the cutting line at one end of it, then position a metal straightedge along it. With your fingers out of the way, hold the straightedge steady and draw the utility knife along it, keeping the blade butted against it *(above)*. To score lightly, hold the knife at a low angle to the surface and apply light pressure; to cut deeply, hold the knife at a high angle to the surface and apply moderate pressure. If necessary, repeat the procedure, pressing the blade deeper.

FASTENING TO CONCRETE AND MASONRY

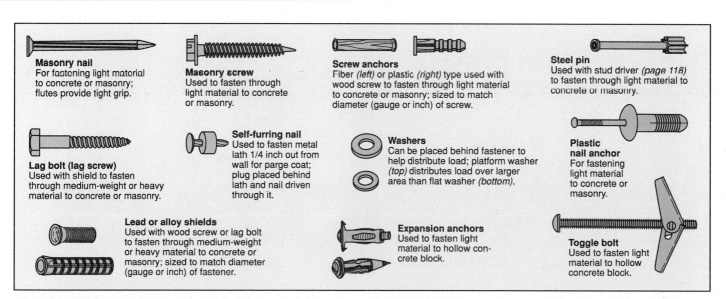

Masonry nail
For fastening light material to concrete or masonry; flutes provide tight grip.

Masonry screw
Used to fasten through light material to concrete or masonry.

Screw anchors
Fiber *(left)* or plastic *(right)* type used with wood screw to fasten through light material to concrete or masonry; sized to match diameter (gauge or inch) of screw.

Steel pin
Used with stud driver *(page 118)* to fasten through light material to concrete or masonry.

Lag bolt (lag screw)
Used with shield to fasten through medium-weight or heavy material to concrete or masonry.

Self-furring nail
Used to fasten metal lath 1/4 inch out from wall for parge coat; plug placed behind lath and nail driven through it.

Washers
Can be placed behind fastener to help distribute load; platform washer *(top)* distributes load over larger area than flat washer *(bottom)*.

Plastic nail anchor
For fastening light material to concrete or masonry.

Lead or alloy shields
Used with wood screw or lag bolt to fasten through medium-weight or heavy material to concrete or masonry; sized to match diameter (gauge or inch) of fastener.

Expansion anchors
Used to fasten light material to hollow concrete block.

Toggle bolt
Used to fasten light material to hollow concrete block.

Choosing a fastener. Common fasteners for concrete and masonry are shown above; use a type suited to your job. A fastener must be able to hold the weight placed on it; follow the guidelines listed on its package or ask for sales assistance at a building supply center or hardware store. In general, fasten a light material to concrete or masonry with a masonry screw 1 to 1 1/2 inches longer than the thickness of the material or a masonry nail 3/4 to 1 inch longer than the thickness of the material. With masonry, position the fastener at a masonry unit rather than a mortar joint for maximum holding power. Drill any hole for a shield or fastener perpendicular to the surface. Check the shield or fastener or its package for the bit size (gauge or inch) needed; or, start with a small bit and work up to a bit of the correct size.

FASTENING TO CONCRETE AND MASONRY (continued)

Using a hand drilling hammer. To drive a masonry nail, wear safety goggles and use a hand drilling hammer. Grip the hammer near the base of the handle; for greater control, grip it closer to the head. Set the face of the head squarely on the nail head, then pull the hammer straight back and swing it forward in a smooth arc *(above)*, striking the nail head sharply.

Using a stud driver. To fasten a stud, a furring strip or other material to concrete or masonry, use a stud driver—a gunpowder-actuated tool that fires a steel pin. **Caution:** Before using a stud driver, carefully read the manufacturer's instructions; when using it, wear safety goggles, hearing protection and work gloves to protect against flying particles. To use the stud driver, load a steel pin into it. Position the stud driver against the surface of the material perpendicular to it, then strike the firing pin sharply with a ball-peen hammer *(above)*, actuating a charge that fires the steel pin through the material into the concrete or masonry.

CONTROLLING PESTS

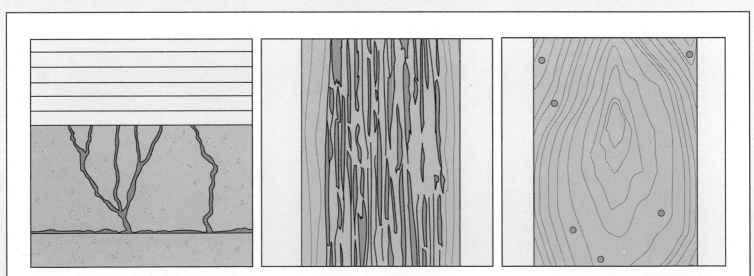

Controlling vermin and insects. To help keep pests out of your basement or crawlspace, repair any crack in the foundation wall or floor slab and seal any opening—at a window, along sill plate, or around a vent or a pipe *(page 60)*, for example. Take measures to control moisture in the basement or crawlspace *(page 81)*. Although many pests are bothersome but not harmful to the structural wood of the house, some pests can attack the structural wood of the house. Check periodically for signs of termites, carpenter ants and powderpost beetles, in particular. Subterranean termites build mud-like tubes *(above, left)* from their underground nest up a foundation wall to burrow into and eat wood—usually along the grain. Carpenter ants also form channels in wood along the grain *(above, center)* when burrowing for nests; they leave piles of chewed wood resembling sawdust. Powderpost beetles bore into wood and lay eggs; the larvae feed on the wood and exit as adults, leaving small round holes *(above, right)*. If you see any of these signs, or see or hear any vermin or insects in the house, consult a pest control professional; consult a building professional about repairs to the structural wood of the house.

TESTING FOR RADON

Using a radon detector. Radon gas, produced by uranium decay, is colorless and odorless; it can seep into a house through cracks or pores in the foundation walls and floor, a sump pit or other openings. Prolonged exposure to radon gas increases the risk of lung cancer. To test for the presence of radon gas, buy a radon gas detection kit at a building supply center. To perform short-term screening with an activated charcoal monitor, follow the manufacturer's instructions to set it up; in general, place it at the lowest level of your house about 20 inches from the floor *(left)*, keeping it away from any heat source or draft. Record any information requested on the log sheet provided with the kit. After the test period, seal the kit in its storage packet and send it to the manufacturer for analysis; ensure that the lab is listed by the Environmental Protection Agency (EPA). If no radon gas is detected by short-term screening, consider testing over a year with an alpha-track detector, following the manufacturer's instructions to install and monitor it. If radon gas is detected by any type of test, consult the EPA Radon Office at your state or your local public health department for measures to take.

Activated charcoal monitor

HIRING A BUILDING PROFESSIONAL

Many foundation, basement and crawlspace problems result from causes hidden from view behind walls or under the floor and may require expensive or large-scale repairs. When a problem is too complex to assess or a job is too big to undertake, consult a trustworthy professional.

To select a **contractor** for repairs, ask friends and neighbors for their recommendations. Take the time to solicit estimates from 4 or 5 contractors; however, do not assume that the lowest estimate provides the best value. Ask to visit the offices of the contractors and select several references yourself, pulling at random from their client files. Also ask to visit the work site of a current client, allowing you to evaluate the equipment, the work crew and the quality of work-in-progress; contact the client a month later for his comments. Check the names of contractors with your local consumer affairs office; ask if there are any complaints registered against them. Most contractors will agree to repair any defective materials or workmanship, but the best guarantee is a contractor with a long history of good work in your community.

Have a contractor explain the repairs to be done in simple language. Your contract should specify the materials to be used and give a schedule for the work, including any site clean-up. Also, make sure that a contractor carries adequate general-liability insurance—as well as workman's compensation for the work crew. Do not pay more than 20 percent of the total price in advance; make a final payment of at least 20 percent only when you are satisfied with the completed job. If appropriate in your state, a contractor should be prepared to supply waivers of lien from anyone who is involved with the job.

Call your local **building inspector** if you are unsure about any repair recommendations you receive, as well as for advice on local building code requirements; ask about the need for any building permit. If you acquire a building permit, determine when the building inspector will come to the site to evaluate the materials and workmanship. Do not cover up work performed under a building permit until you have approval of the building inspector; otherwise, you may be required to uncover it for his evaluation and approval.

Consult a **structural** or **foundation engineer** for any problem with the structure of your house: a serious crack in the foundation or uneven settlement of the foundation, for example. An engineer can assess the structural integrity of the house and calculate the forces acting on it that may be the cause of a problem. Once an engineer has indicated the repairs required, you may be able to carry out the job yourself or by hiring a contractor. An engineer also can determine if an excavation will undermine the stability of the house and assess the safety of the excavation itself.

If you are considering a major renovation of your basement or the mechanical systems of your basement require upgrading or replacing, an **architect** may be able to provide you with the plans or designs you need. For specific repairs to basement systems, you can call on the services of various professional tradespeople. To frame and finish the walls, floor and ceiling of an unfinished basement or to repair any damage to a finished basement, hire a **carpenter** or a **remodeling contractor**. Repairs to the water-supply, sump-pump or waste systems of the house require a licensed **plumber**; for work to the electrical system of the house, you should hire a licensed **electrician**.

REMOVING AND REPLANTING SOD AND VEGETATION

Removing and putting back sod. Water the sod the day before removing it, then cut it out in strips 3 feet long and 1 foot wide using a lawn edger. Wearing work gloves, use the edger to out-line a strip, cutting straight down about 2 inches deep along each edge of it *(inset)*. Push the edger about 1 inch into a cut edge, then work the blade horizontally as far as possible under the strip, loosening it; continue along each edge of the strip the same way *(above, left)*. When the strip is loose, lift one end of it and slowly roll it up tightly *(above, right)*, being careful not to tear it. Work the same way to remove the rest of the sod. To prevent the rolled sod from drying, cover it with wet burlap and water it periodically. Before putting back the rolled sod, sprinkle bone meal on the soil. Put back the rolled sod one strip at a time. Position a strip and slowly unroll it, gently and evenly pressing it into the soil. Continue the same way until all the rolled sod is put back, butting adjacent edges together as closely as possible. Fill the gaps between strips with topsoil, then water the sod thoroughly; repeat the watering daily for 2 to 3 weeks until the sod is well rooted.

Removing and putting back a shrub. Call a professional to remove a tree. Water a shrub the night before removing it, then dig it out using a square spade. Wearing work gloves, outline the root ball of the shrub by scratching a circle in the soil around the spread of its branches no more than 1 foot from its trunk. Position the spade on the outline at a 30-degree angle toward the trunk and push down firmly *(above, left)*, cutting the roots cleanly in one stroke. Continue along the outline the same way, then scrape a layer of soil 4 inches deep off the top of the root ball. Use the spade to dig around the root ball to a depth of 18 inches, then work horizontally under it to loosen it. To wrap the root ball, use burlap covered with topsoil and wet peat moss. Hold the shrub by its trunk and lever it out with the spade, then set it on the burlap. Wrap the burlap around the root ball *(above, right)* and tie it with twine. Shade the shrub and water it regularly to keep it from drying. To put back the shrub, dig a hole large enough for the wrapped root ball; tamp the bottom of it gently and sprinkle bone meal on it. Position the shrub with its root ball centered in the hole, then backfill halfway around it with soil. Tamp the soil gently, then water it thoroughly. Cut the twine and unwrap the root ball, spreading the burlap in the hole. Add soil and tamp gently until the hole is filled, covering the burlap. Soak the root ball with water; water it frequently over the next few weeks.

DIGGING WITH A SPADE

Long-handled spade

Digging a hole or shallow trench. Notify the utility company of any utility near the site; you may need to have it shut off or its line marked. Remove any sod or vegetation *(page 120)* from the site and lay plastic sheets on the ground to hold the soil excavated. For the digging, use a spade; for a deep hole, use a long-handled type. Wearing work gloves and work boots, hold the spade a little in front of you, positioning its blade at a 30-degree angle toward the direction you are working; stand on ground that is level with the soil you are digging. Gripping the handle of the spade with both hands, press down firmly on the blade with your foot *(above, left)*, pushing it as deep into the soil as possible; lean forward slightly for maximum leverage. Take your foot off the blade of the spade and step back slightly, pushing down on the handle to lever up the soil. Flex your knees and bend forward to lift out the soil with spade *(above, center)*, keeping one hand near the top of the handle and sliding the other hand down to the bottom of it. Straighten up and pivot on one foot to pitch the soil off the blade of the spade *(above, right)*, twisting the handle slightly to help it slide off. Continue the same way, working slowly and rhythmically—without overloading the spade.

Digging a deep trench. Notify the utility company of any utility near the site; you may need to have it shut off or its line marked. Consider hiring a backhoe operator *(page 122)*; otherwise, plan a safe excavation *(page 123)*. Remove any sod or vegetation *(page 120)* from the site, then lay plastic sheets on the ground at least 4 feet from it to hold the soil excavated. For the digging, use a spade; for deep digging, use a long-handled type. Wearing work gloves and work boots, dig progressively deeper from one edge to the other edge along the site. As the trench deepens, have a helper slope the soil excavated, making a pile at the edge of the trench for him to pitch *(above)*; wear safety goggles and a safety helmet, if necessary.

Sledgehammer

Breaking compacted soil and rocks. Wearing safety goggles and work gloves, break hard, dry soil with a pick-ax. For a large rock, consult a professional. Otherwise, dig around the rock and lever it out of the way using a long pry bar. Or, dig a deep hole out of the way nearby and roll the rock into it. Alternatively, break the rock into pieces with a sledgehammer. Standing on firm ground back from the rock, spread your legs slightly for balance and grip the sledgehammer with one hand at each end of the handle. Lift the sledgehammer and raise the head above your shoulders, then flex your knees slightly and swing forward using your full weight, sliding your hand away from the head to meet your other hand as the head hits the rock *(above)*.

HIRING A BACKHOE OPERATOR

Excavating with a backhoe. Plan a safe excavation *(page 123)*, having any utility near the site shut off or marked. Consult your municipal authorities about any building permit needed for the excavation. Get estimates for the excavation from a number of backhoe operators and ensure that the backhoe operator you choose is insured against damage and injury; to cut costs, ask how to prepare the site. Remove any sod or vegetation *(page 120)* from the site and have plastic sheeting on hand to hold the soil excavated; work with the backhoe operator to have it positioned correctly. Watch the excavation as it progresses *(left)* to ensure that it is done safely—and without damage to the foundation or any drain tile system, for example.

BACKFILLING AN EXCAVATION

1 **Putting back the soil.** Before backfilling, evaluate the soil near the excavation *(page 82)*; if its drainage capacity is poor, consider replacing the soil excavated. Cover any layer of gravel at the bottom of the excavation with asphalt-coated building paper or synthetic landscaping fabric to keep soil from infiltrating it. To backfill a large excavation, consider hiring a backhoe operator. Otherwise, backfill the excavation with 12 inches of soil at a time using a spade, compacting each layer of it *(step 2)*. Work from one edge to the other edge along a trench to backfill it, breaking up any clumps of soil with the spade. For a slope-walled trench, load a wheelbarrow with soil and wheel it down into the trench to dump it, then level the soil with the back of the spade *(left)*. For a straight-walled trench, remove any shield from it and stand a safe distance from its edges to pitch soil into it with the spade.

BACKFILLING AN EXCAVATION (continued)

2 **Compacting the soil.** For a small excavation, compact the soil by pounding it with the bottom of a 4-by-4 about 4 to 5 feet long. Otherwise, rent a power tamper at a tool rental agency; ask for a demonstration. To compact the soil of a slope-walled trench, work with a helper to carry the tamper into it; for a straight-walled trench, protect it with a shield *(page 124)*, then work with a helper to lower the tamper into it using a rope. Work from one edge to the other edge along the trench to compact the soil; if it is dry and powdery, moisten it first using a garden hose. Wearing safety goggles, work gloves and steel-toed work boots, grip the tamper firmly and turn it on. Walk slowly forward with the tamper, guiding it to control its jumping action *(left)*. If you are working at a foundation wall, ensure that the last layer of soil slopes correctly away from it *(page 87)*. Put back any sod or vegetation you removed.

PLANNING A SAFE EXCAVATION

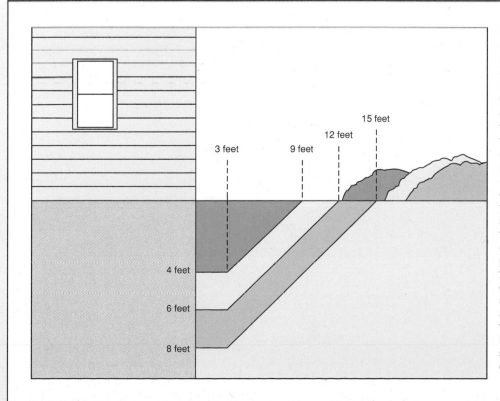

Protecting an excavation. For a large excavation, consult a building professional *(page 119)*. To plan for a trench to the footing of a foundation wall, estimate the depth by subtracting the above-ground height of the wall outdoors from its height indoors. For a depth up to 3 feet, dig a straight-walled trench; otherwise, dig a slope-walled trench wider at the top than at the bottom *(left)*. To estimate the ground-level width of a trench 3 feet wide at the bottom, multiply the depth in feet by 1.5 and add 3; start digging at this distance from the foundation wall to slope the wall of the trench safely. Determine a safe site for the soil excavated at least 4 feet from any edge of the trench. If there is not enough space to safely slope the trench and pile the soil excavated, dig a straight-walled trench 3 feet deep, then protect it before digging deeper using a shield *(page 124)* or a shoring system—available at a tool rental agency. Keep tools and equipment away from the edges of the trench. Set up barriers and light the trench at night. Watch for danger signs: a wall fissure, falling soil or a sinking edge, for example.

USING AN EXCAVATION SHIELD

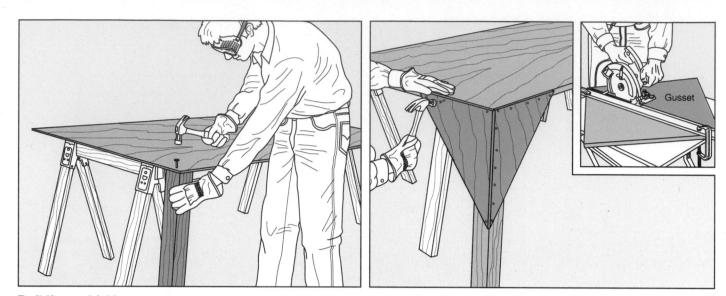

Building a shield. To protect a straight-walled trench from a cave-in, build as many shields as necessary. For each shield, use two sheets of thick 4-by-8 plywood and four equal lengths of 2-by-4 a few inches shorter than the width of the trench. Lay one sheet of plywood on sawhorses and fasten the 2-by-4s to it as braces. Wearing safety goggles, position the end of each brace in turn at a corner of the plywood and nail through the plywood into it *(above, left)*. Use the other sheet of plywood to make gussets, cutting four square pieces with sides equal to 2/3 the length of a brace, then cutting each piece in half across diagonally opposite corners *(inset)*. Fasten a gusset in turn to each side of the braces, aligning it with the edges of the brace and plywood, then driving a nail every few inches along it into them *(above, right)*.

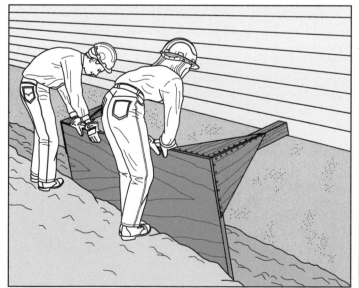

Installing and working with a shield. While you are working in a straight-walled trench, use a shield; install a shield at the site in the trench you are working and move it along with you or install shields side by side along the trench. To install a shield, work with a helper. Rest the shield lengthwise on the ground at the edge of the trench with the braces facing it. Gripping the shield firmly by the top, lift it and carry it forward, then slowly lower it straight down into the trench *(above, left)*; adjust it until it rests flush against the wall of the trench with its braces a few inches from the foundation wall. If the top of the shield is below ground level, start 6 inches from the top of it to slope the soil as you would to protect an entire excavation *(page 123)*. If necessary, use a ladder to get into and out of a section of the trench protected by a shield; set its rails against the top of the shield and brace its feet against the foundation wall. To move a shield along the trench, work with a helper to lift and carry it *(above, right)*, being careful not to disturb the wall of the trench. To remove a shield, work with a helper to pull it straight up and carry it back from the edge of the trench.

WORKING SAFELY ON A LADDER

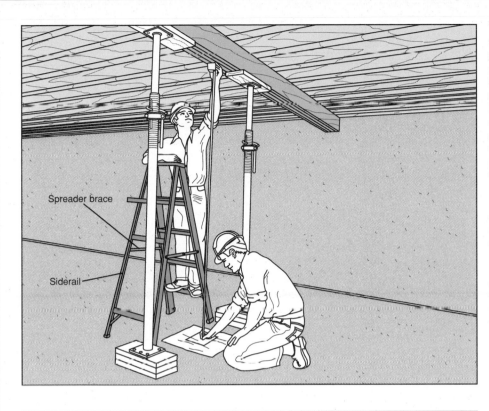

Using a stepladder. To work up to 10 feet from ground level, use a stepladder at least 2 feet longer than the height at which you need to stand. Do not use the stepladder if it is damaged; check for a worn foot, loose step or bent spreader brace. Read the safety instruction label on the stepladder—usually on a siderail. Indoors, if the stepladder feet slip, place a non-slip rubber mat under them. Outdoors, if the ground is soft or uneven, place boards under the stepladder feet; dig the soil with a spade to level the boards. Pull down the bucket tray and set tools and materials on it before climbing the stepladder; or, carry tools in a tool belt. Climb the stepladder facing it, using both hands to grasp the steps rather than the siderails. Lean into the stepladder while working from it, keeping your hips between the siderails; do not stand higher than the third step from the top *(left)*. Never overreach or straddle the space between the stepladder and the work surface; instead, climb down from the stepladder and reposition it.

Spreader brace

Siderail

Using an extension ladder. To work more than 10 feet from the ground, such as at a gutter, use an extension ladder that can extend 3 feet above the roof edge. Do not use the ladder if it is damaged; check for a worn shoe, loose rung or bent rung lock. Read the safety instruction label on the ladder—usually on a rail. Set the unextended ladder on the ground perpendicular to the wall, its fly section on the bottom and its feet out from the wall 1/4 of the height to which it will be raised. With a helper bracing the bottom of the ladder, raise the top of it above your head. Walk under the ladder toward the bottom of it, moving your hands along the rails to push it upright. Bracing the bottom of the ladder with your foot, pull on the rope to release and raise the fly section *(left)*; when it is extended to the height desired, ease pressure on the rope to lock it. Carefully rest the ladder against the gutter. If the ground is soft or uneven, place a board under the feet of the ladder; level uneven soil with a spade. To stabilize the ladder, drive a stake into the ground between it and the wall, then tie each rail to the stake. Carrying tools in a tool belt, climb the ladder; use both hands to grasp the rungs and keep your hips between the rails. To work from the ladder, never overreach or straddle the space between it and the work surface; instead, climb down from it and reposition it.

Fly section

INDEX

Page references in *italics* indicate an illustration of the subject mentioned. Page references in **bold** indicate a Troubleshooting Guide for the subject mentioned.

ACKNOWLEDGMENTS

The editors wish to thank the following:
Dinu Boumbaru, Heritage Montreal, Montreal, Que.; Teresa Bowsman, Wayne Home Equipment, Fort Wayne, Ind.; Gary Branson, Richfield, Minn.; Brice-Fielding Associates, Scarborough, Ont.; Daniel J. Bruton, James Clem Corporation, Chicago, Ill.; James E. Burson, The Plank Company, Houston, Tex.; Alan Carson, Carson, Dunlop & Associates Ltd., Toronto, Ont.; William P. Chessick Jr., Colbertson Restoration Ltd., Westchester, Pa.; H.M. ("Chuck") Clark, Clark Home Inspections Inc., Falls Church, Va.; Paul Clemons; Alvah O. Conley, U.S. Department of Labor, Occupational Safety and Health Administration, Chicago, Ill.; Charlie Cook, Liberty Pumps, Bergen, N.Y.; James Craig, WaterStop Services Reg'd., Montreal, Que.; Paige Davis, Witten Automatic Vent Co. Inc., Gastonia, N.C.; Direct Equipment Ltd., Oakville, Ont.; Dow Chemical Canada Inc.; Robert Dunlop, Carson, Dunlop & Associates Ltd., Toronto, Ont.; Robert Fortier, Astro Jet Service Reg'd., Verdun, Que.; Dr. Thomas G. Glass, Jr., San Antonio, Tex.; Goulds Pumps Inc., Seneca Falls, N.Y.; Gerry Halton, Robert Hunt Corporation, Montreal, Que.; Jean-Louis Houle, Argus Construction Inc., Montreal, Que.; Chuck Hughes, Speed Shore Corp., Houston, Tex.; Christopher Kamenfek, A.K. Draft Seal Ltd., Vancouver, B.C.; Steven Kosmatka, Portland Cement Association, Skokie, Ill.; Robert P. Krehl, Retro Technologies Inc., Waunakee, Wis.; Lafarge Canada Inc.; Jean Paul Legault, Montreal Pump Services Ltd., Montreal, Que.; Leigh Metal Products, London, Ont.; Dr. Ralph Leonard, Bowman Gray Medical School, Winston-Salem, N.C.; Elliot Levine, Levine Brothers Plumbing, Montreal, Que.; Location d'Outillage ERA Inc., Montreal, Que.; Julia Loktev, Montreal, Que.; Macklanburg-Duncan, Oklahoma City, Okla.; Mark Medicoff, The Foundation Doctor Inc., Montreal, Que.; John Meiorin, Bricklayer's Masons Independent Union of Canada (Local 1), Toronto, Ont.; Menard Pump Services, Laval, Que.; Clive W. Mills, Armtec Construction Products, Guelph, Ont.; Robert Parsons, Black Hills Bentonite Co., Casper, Wyo.; Herb Pattison, Wayne Home Equipment, Fort Wayne, Ind.; Rosario Pecoraro, Aldo Pecoraro Enterprises Inc., Montreal, Que.; Michael J. Plank, Speed Shore Corp., Houston, Tex.; Russell Pryde, Polyquip of Canada Ltd., Montreal, Que.; Michel Ravary, Ravary Builders Supply Co., Ltd., St. Leonard, Que.; Gary Roberts, Sta-Rite Consumer Markets Group, Waterford, Wis.; Joseph Romeo, Joseph Romeo Building & Renovations Inc., Montreal, Que.; André Roy, Location Outremont, Montreal, Que.; Bruno Sabels, Radon Environmental Monitoring, Northbrook, Ill.; Dr. Earl Schwartz, Bowman Gray Medical School, Winston-Salem, N.C.; Peter Sciamanna, Centre Do-It D'Agostino, Montreal, Que.; Sealant, Waterproofing & Restoration Institute, Kansas City, Mo.; Bill Simpson, James Clem Corporation, Chicago, Ill.; Martin Simpson, James Clem Corporation, Chicago, Ill.; Spall-Bowman Ltd., Guelph, Ont.; Robert Stanley, Fish & Stanley Architects, Montreal, Que.; Sump & Sewage Pump Manufacturers Association, Chicago, Ill.; Jonathan Wheatley, Abracadabra Design, Montreal, Que.; Kenneth Wiggers, Ph.D., American Radon Services Ltd., Ames, Iowa.

The following persons also assisted in the preparation of this book:
Linda Burnett, Megan Durnford, Dominique Gagné, Robert Galarneau, Graphor Consultation, Shirley Grynspan, Jennifer Meltzer, Kelly Mulcair and Solange Pelland.

Time-Life Books Inc. offers a wide range of fine recordings, including a *Big Bands* series. For subscription information, call 1-800-621-7026, or write TIME-LIFE MUSIC, Time & Life Building, Chicago, Illinois 60611.